Green Finance and Investment



# Clean Energy Finance and Investment Roadmap of Thailand

OECD
BETTER POLICIES FOR BETTER LIVES

**Please cite this publication as:**
OECD (2024), *Clean Energy Finance and Investment Roadmap of Thailand*, Green Finance and Investment, OECD Publishing, Paris, https://doi.org/10.1787/d0cd6ffc-en.

ISBN 978-92-64-66430-2 (print)
ISBN 978-92-64-97578-1 (PDF)
ISBN 978-92-64-74860-6 (HTML)
ISBN 978-92-64-50118-8 (epub)

Green Finance and Investment
ISSN 2409-0336 (print)
ISSN 2409-0344 (online)

**Photo credits:** Cover © Nakornthai/shutterstock.com.

Corrigenda to OECD publications may be found on line at: www.oecd.org/about/publishing/corrigenda.htm.

# Preface

In recent years, Thailand has scaled up its ambition to reduce greenhouse gas (GHG) emissions. The country updated its Nationally Determined Contribution in 2022, committing to reduce GHG emissions by 30% by 2030 from 2005 levels, while continuing its efforts to meet the long-term goal of carbon neutrality by 2050 and net-zero GHG emissions by 2065. To achieve these objectives, Thailand's Long-Term Low Emissions Development Strategy (LT-LEDS) aims to increase new power generation capacity from renewables, as reaching carbon neutrality would require increasing the share of renewable electricity from 13% of total electricity generation in 2022 to 68% by 2040 and 74% by 2050.

Achieving these targets will require a rapid acceleration of finance and investment in renewable power and energy efficiency: it is estimated that a total investment of approximately THB 779 billion (USD 22 billion) in new renewable power is required between 2022 and 2037, while investment in energy efficiency improvements in industrial, commercial, residential and agricultural sectors would need to reach THB 974 billion (USD 28 billion) over the same period. Scarce public finance, both domestic and international, will need to be used more effectively to leverage private finance and de-risk investments in clean energy.

This Clean Energy Finance and Investment Roadmap of Thailand ("the Roadmap") provides tailored recommendations for the Government of Thailand to help unlock finance and investment in clean energy. The recommendations are based on extensive stakeholder consultations, new modelling and analysis, as well as emerging international practices tailored to Thailand's national circumstances. The Roadmap was developed as part of the OECD Clean Energy Finance and Investment Mobilisation (CEFIM) Programme, which aims to accelerate finance and investments in selected emerging economies in clean energy, including renewable power, energy efficiency and decarbonisation of industry.

The Roadmap focuses on two clean energy sectors identified and selected in consultation with the Department of Alternative Energy Development and Efficiency (DEDE) of the Ministry of Energy of Thailand: small-scale renewable power and energy efficiency in the building sector, with a focus on cooling. In addition to mitigating GHG emissions, the deployment of small-scale renewables systems in Thailand could increase energy security, deliver energy cost savings, provide green jobs for local businesses and improve access to clean power in rural communities and off-grid islands. To support the Government of Thailand in promoting and de-risking small-scale renewable power investment, the Roadmap provides recommendations on financial support; policy, regulation and governance; and capacity building.

Incentivising finance and investment in energy efficiency in buildings and cooling appliances is another key action area for Thailand. As one of the largest consumers of electricity in the country – representing on average approximately 25% of the total electricity consumed in Thailand in 2019 – and as temperatures continue to rise, the building sector has a high demand for energy-intensive cooling appliances. As cooling made up for over half of the Thai commercial building sector's electricity consumption and 20% of its GHG emissions, improving the energy efficiency of cooling applications is a critical priority to reach Thailand's 30% energy intensity reduction target by 2037 (compared to 2010 levels), under its draft Energy Efficiency Plan (EEP).

The recommendations presented in this report can serve as a roadmap to help Thailand strengthen conditions to unlock the much-needed finance and investment to achieve its clean energy transition. Going forward, the OECD can support the Government of Thailand in implementing the Roadmap's recommendations, including through tailored analysis, capacity building and knowledge sharing activities, to boost investments in renewables and energy efficiency.

Mathias Cormann
Secretary-General, OECD

# Foreword

The Clean Energy Finance and Investment Roadmap of Thailand ("the Roadmap") is one of the key outputs of the Organisation for Economic Co-operation and Development (OECD)'s Clean Energy Finance and Investment Mobilisation (CEFIM) programme. Launched in 2019, the CEFIM programme aims to support governments in selected emerging economies in South and Southeast Asia, Latin America and Africa[1] to unlock finance and investment in clean energy, including renewable power and energy efficiency as well as industry decarbonisation.

The Roadmap was developed in close co-operation and collaboration with the Department of Alternative Energy Development and Efficiency (DEDE) of the Ministry of Energy of Thailand. The Roadmap was developed by the OECD CEFIM programme, with funding from the Government of Denmark. In addition, the Roadmap contributes to Phase 2 of the OECD Thailand Country Programme in 2023-2025.

The Roadmap presents a clear action plan that identifies and addresses bottlenecks constraining finance and investment in Thailand's clean energy sector. In close consultation with DEDE, two sectors – renewable power, with a special attention to small-scale systems, and energy efficiency in large-scale public and commercial buildings, with a focus on cooling applications – were identified as priorities in the near-term to accelerate the clean energy transition in Thailand and selected accordingly as the two focus areas for this Roadmap. The Roadmap aims to support the Government of Thailand in implementing its energy plans. Conscious of the opportunities that clean energy transition offers to realise its long-term goals of carbon neutrality by 2050 and net-zero greenhouse gas (GHG) emissions by 2065, Thailand prioritised the accelerated deployment of renewable power and energy efficiency to ensure a sustainable, affordable and resilient energy system while supporting the country's broader economic development and environmental objectives. The Roadmap also aims to support the development of sustainable finance in Thailand, by providing recommendations to help the financial sector offer sustainable investment products and advance the implementation of Thailand's sustainable finance initiatives.

The Roadmap is structured as follows:

- a Roadmap Action Plan for the Government of Thailand to consider to mobilise finance and investment for small-scale renewable power and energy efficient buildings and cooling appliances
- an overview of key trends, policies and market developments for renewable energy and energy efficiency in Thailand (Chapter 1)
- an estimation of the finance and investment needed to reach Thailand's clean energy plans as well as estimates of the related economic benefits (Chapter 2)
- analysis of challenges, market barriers, opportunities and solutions to mobilise finance and investment for small-scale renewable power (Chapter 3) and energy efficiency in buildings and cooling applications (Chapter 4)
- supporting Annexes: Process of developing the Roadmap and key stakeholders involved (Annex A); case studies (Annex B); methodology for modelling Thailand's clean energy finance and investment needs (Annex C) and building Energy Code standards (Annex D).

The modelling work conducted to estimate the clean energy investment and financing needs to meet Thailand's National Energy Plan has been conducted by the Thai consultancy firm The Creagy, which has supported the OECD throughout the preparation of this Roadmap since September 2022.[2] Further details on the methodology applied for the modelling work can be found in Annex C. These models can be updated to reflect the targets of the forthcoming National Energy Plan. The Creagy delivered a training to DEDE staff in 2023 on how to update the models in the future.

The development of the Roadmap builds on strong government ownership and stakeholder engagement. The process for preparing the Roadmap included two in-person stakeholder consultation workshops held in Bangkok, Thailand on 28 April and 24 November 2023, to consult Thai and international public and private stakeholders (see Annex A for the full list) and discuss barriers and possible solutions for unlocking finance and investment in small-scale renewable power and energy efficiency in buildings and cooling systems in Thailand.[3] Thanks to the fruitful discussions during these workshops, the OECD CEFIM Programme gathered valuable inputs and feedback to identify key financing solutions, discuss preliminary Roadmap findings and reach consensus on the Roadmap's actions and recommendations. In addition to engagement and feedback received through the two workshops, the Roadmap has benefited from desktop research and analysis, case studies and bilateral interviews with relevant Thai, regional and international experts. The process of developing this Roadmap is described in detail in Annex A. In the future, the aim is to implement some of the key recommendations form the Roadmap through implementation support activities in Thailand in close co-ordination with the Government of Thailand, to create an impactful collaboration across relevant domestic and international stakeholders.

This report is an output of the OECD Environment Policy Committee (EPOC) and its Working Party on Finance and Investment for Environmental Goals (WPFIEG). This report was produced by the OECD Environment Directorate, directed by Jo Tyndall. The Roadmap was drafted by Valentina Bellesi (OECD), with valuable inputs from Kannikar Srithunyalucksana (The Creagy) and Deger Saygin (OECD), under the supervision of Geraldine Ang, Team Lead of the OECD CEFIM Programme, as well as Yuval Laster, Head of the Finance, Investment and Global Relations Division and Mathilde Mesnard, Deputy Director in the OECD Environment Directorate. The authors are grateful for the valuable support from The Creagy to develop this Roadmap, including Boonrod Yaowapruek, Kannikar Srithunyalucksana and Preechaya Rassadanukul. Lylah Davies (OECD) and Aksornchan Chaianong (consultant) contributed to the background research. The authors would like to thank Dominique Haleva for her administrative support and editorial assistance as well as Ria Sandilands and Beth Del Bourgo for communications support.

The authors are extremely grateful for the excellent collaboration with DEDE to develop the Roadmap, especially to Prasert Sinsukprasert, previous Director General of DEDE and current Permanent Secretary of the Ministry of Energy, Wattanapong Kurovat, current Director General of DEDE, and Apiradee Thummamanomai, Director of Strategy and Planning Division (DEDE). Other DEDE staff involved in the development and review of the Roadmap include: Sutthasini Glawgitigul, Siriphat Khwunpetch, Patcharee Sattayarangsan, Praphaphan Pankaew and Phatiphorn Srinorin (Strategy and Planning Division); Charuwan Phipatana-phuttapanta (Solar Energy Development Division), Yaowateera Achawangkul, Juthamas Kijjanuluck and Jirawadee Nitsunkit (Energy Research Division); Nuttanon Jivapaisarnpong and Suthanee Wachasit (Energy Efficiency Promotion Division); Lapastsatorn Jiengwareewong and Ratchaphak Tantisanghirun (Energy Regulation and Conservation Division).

The authors are extremely grateful for the precious inputs and feedback received from the following OECD experts: Joseph Cordonnier, Lylah Davies, Benjamin Denis, Sofie Errendal, Ariola Mbistrova, Takayoshi Kato, Chizuru Kobayashi, Tiyarat Niamkohphet-Cader, Jolien Noels, Cornelia Schenk, Klas Wetterberg and Yuki Yasarani, as well as experts from the International Energy Agency (IEA), Natalie Kauf and Clara Camarasa.

In addition, the Roadmap benefited from the review and written feedback and inputs from the following Thai and international experts: Surapong Praepattharaprasit (Energy Policy and Planning office (EPPO) of the Ministry of Energy of Thailand), Tanach Fuangaromya (Ministry of Finance of Thailand), Phirat Inphanich (Office of the Permanent Secretary of the Ministry of Energy of Thailand), Tharinya Supasa (Agora Thailand), Siripha Junlakarn (Energy Research Institute, Chulalongkorn University), Aksornchan Chaianong (independent consultant), Nuttawat Suwattanapongtada (GIZ Thailand), Kwanpadh Suddhi-Dhamakit and Daniel Anthony McGree (World Bank), Suchai Buranavalahok, Santikorn Pakdeesettakul, Marine Chalons and Tero Raassina (Global Green Growth Institute), MK Balaji (USAID Southeast Asia Smart Power Program) and Jirawat Panpiemras (Bangkok Bank). The Roadmap had also been reviewed by representatives of the Electricity Generating Authority of Thailand and the Securities and Exchange Commission of Thailand. The authors are grateful to Sabine Laurent (Climate Bonds Initiative) for providing data on green bonds.

# Table of contents

**Tables**

## Figures

## Boxes

# Abbreviations and acronyms

| | |
|---|---|
| **AC** | Air conditioner |
| **ADB** | Asian Development Bank |
| **AEDP** | Alternative Energy Development Plan |
| **ASEAN** | Association of Southeast Asian Nations |
| **BAU** | Business-as-usual |
| **BEF** | Building energy code |
| **BNEF** | BloombergNEF |
| **BOI** | Board of Investment |
| **BOT** | Bank of Thailand |
| **CASE** | Clean, Affordable and Secure Energy for Southeast Asia |
| **CBI** | Climate Bonds Initiative |
| **CCUS** | Carbon capture, utilisation and storage |
| **CEFIM** | Clean Energy Finance and Investment Mobilisation |
| **$CO_2$-eq** | Carbon dioxide-equivalent |
| **COD** | Commercial Operation Date |
| **COE** | Council of Engineers Thailand |
| **DNSH** | Do No Significant Harm |
| **CSO** | Civil society organisation |
| **DC** | District cooling |
| **DEDE** | Department of Alternative Energy Development and Efficiency |
| **DFI** | Development finance institution |
| **DSD** | Department of Skill Development |
| **DSM** | Demand side management |
| **ECP** | Energy Conservation Promotion |
| **EE** | Energy efficiency |
| **EGAT** | Electricity Generating Authority of Thailand |
| **EEP** | Energy Efficiency Plan |
| **EERF** | Energy Efficiency Revolving Fund |
| **EETL** | Energy Efficient Technology List |
| **EI** | Energy intensity |
| **EMDE** | Emerging market and developing economy |
| **ENCON** | Energy Conservation Promotion |
| **EPC** | Energy Policy Committee |
| **EPOC** | Environment Policy Committee |
| **EPPO** | Energy Policy and Planning Office |
| **ERC** | Energy Regulatory Commission of Thailand |
| **ESCO** | Energy service company |
| **ESG** | Environmental, social and governance |
| **ESI** | Energy saving insurance |
| **EU** | European Union |
| **FEC** | Final energy consumption |
| **FiT** | Feed-in-tariff |
| **$gCO_2e/kWh$** | Grams of carbon dioxide equivalent per kilowatt-hour of electricity generated |

| | |
|---|---|
| **GHG** | Greenhouse gas |
| **GSS** | Green, social, and sustainability |
| **GTFS** | Green Technology Financing Scheme |
| **GW** | Gigawatt |
| **GWh** | Gigawatt hours |
| **HVAC** | Heating Ventilation and Air Conditioning |
| **ICMA** | International Capital Market Association |
| **IEA** | International Energy Agency |
| **IIP** | Independent Power Producers |
| **KBank** | Kasikornbank |
| **Ktoe** | Tonnes of oil equivalent (ktoe) |
| **kWh** | Kilowatt-hour |
| **LCOE** | Levelised cost of electricity |
| **LT-LEDS** | Long-Term Low Emissions Development Strategy |
| **M-T** | Medium-term |
| **MDB** | Multilateral development bank |
| **M&V** | Measurement and verification |
| **MEA** | Metropolitan Electricity Authority |
| **MEPS** | Minimum energy performance standards |
| **MOEN** | Ministry of Energy |
| **MOF** | Ministry of Finance |
| **MOIN** | Ministry of Industry |
| **MONRE** | Ministry of Natural Resources and Environment |
| **MSMEs** | Micro, Small and Medium Enterprises |
| **Mt** | Million tonnes |
| **MW** | Megawatts |
| **NEP** | National Energy Plan |
| **NEPC** | National Energy Policy Council |
| **NDC** | Nationally Determined Contribution |
| **OBF** | On-bill financing |
| **OECD** | Organisation for Economic Co-operation and Development |
| **OIC** | Office of Insurance Commission |
| **PAYG** | Pay-as-you-go |
| **PDP** | Power Development Plan |
| **PEA** | Provincial Electricity Authority |
| **PPA** | Power purchase agreement |
| **PV** | Photovoltaic |
| **PAYG** | Pay-As-You-Go |
| **RE** | Renewable energy |
| **R&D** | Research and development |
| **S-T** | Short-term |
| **SEC** | Securities and Exchange Commission |
| **SET** | Stock Exchange of Thailand |
| **SHS** | Solar home system |
| **SPP** | Small Power Producer |
| **SPV** | Special Purpose Vehicle |
| **TBA** | Thai Bankers' Association |
| **TGC** | Thai Credit Guarantee Corporation |
| **THB** | Thai Baht |
| **TPQI** | Thailand Professional Qualification Institute |
| **TWh** | Terawatt-hours |
| **UGT** | Utility Green Tariff |
| **USD** | United States dollar |
| **VSPP** | Very Small Power Producer |
| **WPFIEG** | Working Party on Finance and Investment for Environmental Goals |

# Executive Summary

Thailand has adopted ambitious clean energy targets to meet its long-term climate goals, committing to reach carbon neutrality by 2050 and net zero greenhouse gas (GHG) emissions by 2065. Transforming Thailand's energy system is critical to meet Thailand's climate goals, as the energy sector accounted for 69% of Thailand's total GHG emissions in 2018, as well as broader development objectives, including access to affordable energy and job creation. To achieve its climate goals, Thailand's Long-Term Low Emissions Development Strategy (LT-LEDS) includes a target to reach 50% of new power generation capacity from renewables by 2050. Thailand's LT-LEDS estimates that the share of renewable electricity will be 68% of total electricity generation by 2040 and 74% by 2050. The country's share of renewable energy was about 13% of total generation in 2022.

Thailand's clean energy targets as well as broader development objectives will require a rapid acceleration of finance and investment in renewable power and energy efficiency. It is estimated that the investment needs in new renewable power during 2022 - 2037 will amount to Thai Baht (THB) 779 billion (USD 22 billion), whereas investment needs in energy efficiency improvements in industrial, commercial, residential and agricultural sectors are predicted to reach THB 974 billion (USD 28 billion), over the same period.

This Clean Energy Finance and Investment Roadmap of Thailand ("the Roadmap") outlines critical actions that the Government of Thailand could consider to unlock finance and investment in two clean energy sectors: (i) renewable power, with a special attention to small-scale renewable power systems; and (ii) energy efficiency in buildings, with a focus on cooling applications. The two sectors were selected in close consultation with the Department of Alternative Energy Development and Efficiency (DEDE) of the Ministry of Energy of Thailand.

While Thailand has made important strides to deploy large-scale renewable power capacity over the past decade, significant progress remains needed to unlock financing for small-scale renewable power systems. Deployment of small-scale renewables systems can increase energy security, deliver energy cost savings, provide green jobs for local businesses and improve access to clean power in underserved rural communities and off-grid islands. Limited policy support and the lack of availability of innovative financing models and instruments for small-scall renewable systems have hampered their development. Key recommendations to scale up finance and investment for small-scale renewable power in Thailand include:[4]

- Strengthening policy planning, increasing policy predictability and setting region-specific targets on small-scale renewable power over the near- and long-term, in line with Thailand's net-zero target.
- Simplifying renewables licensing and permitting processes, and requirements for small power producers.
- Reviewing and strengthening existing public financial incentives to prioritise the acceleration of small-scale and community-based renewable power models.
- Piloting a green credit guarantee scheme for small-scale renewable power projects, for example of small- and medium-sized energy service companies (ESCOs).

- Providing financial support to Pay-As-You-Go models to expand off-grid, community-based renewable energy.

Mobilising finance and investment in energy efficiency (EE) is another key priority for Thailand to achieve its climate targets. Thailand made progress towards reducing its energy intensity in the past two decades. However, further efforts are needed to reach Thailand's 30% energy intensity reduction target by 2037 (compared to 2010 levels), under its draft Energy Efficiency Plan (EEP).

Unlocking financing for EE in public and commercial buildings, including in cooling appliances, is a priority for Thailand. The building sector represented on average approximately 25% of the total electricity consumed in Thailand in 2019. Improving the EE of cooling applications of Thailand's building stock is a critical priority, as cooling made up for over half of the Thai commercial building sector's electricity consumption and 20% of its GHG emissions.

The Government of Thailand is committed to accelerate finance and investment in EE projects in the Thai building sector. Thailand is one of the leading EE markets in Southeast Asia thanks to the early introduction and public support for financing schemes such as the Thai Energy Efficiency Revolving Fund (EERF), and is also a hub for cooling technology manufacturing. Thailand has a vibrant and fast-growing private ESCO market, although it is still nascent and requires further support to achieve greater scale. ESCOs still face severe barriers in accessing affordable financing for EE projects, which are often perceived as too risky by commercial banks. Key priorities to accelerate financing for EE of buildings and cooling applications in Thailand include:[5]

- Enhancing building codes and minimum energy performance standards for buildings and cooling applications.
- Conducting ex-post evaluations of the EERF and the ESCO Fund and using the evaluation's findings to support decision-making on the need for financial incentives to promote the ESCO market, specifically for EE projects in the building sector.
- Establishing a bulk procurement model for energy-efficient cooling appliances and piloting an energy saving insurance model.
- Developing an Energy Efficient Technology List and collaborating with financial institutions to provide financial incentives to the listed technologies.
- Strengthening the policy framework for district cooling.

For both clean energy sectors analysed in the Roadmap, enhancing cross-government collaboration and co-ordination emerges a as key priority to streamline policy planning and implementation. Furthermore, increasing capacity building, fostering data collection and awareness-raising, with support of international development partners, are indispensable to ensure that the workforce is well-trained and local communities are informed about the benefits and opportunities of the clean energy transition as well as latest products available in the market.

# Roadmap Action Plan

This Action Plan of the Clean Energy Finance and Investment Roadmap of Thailand ("the Roadmap Action Plan") provides an overview of a strategic framework to unlock finance and investment in clean energy in Thailand. It outlines critical actions that the Government of Thailand could consider to mobilise financing in two main sectors: (i) renewable power, with a special attention to small-scale systems; and (ii) energy efficiency in buildings, with a focus on cooling applications.

This chapter serves as a detailed summary guidance of the key recommendations and suggested actions that the Government of Thailand, financial institutions, Energy Service Companies (ESCOs), and academia as well as the international development community active in the country could undertake to foster clean energy investments in Thailand. The recommendations on small-scale renewable energy as well as on energy efficiency are further detailed and explained at the end of the two thematic chapters (chapter 3 and chapter 4, respectively).

## Unlocking finance and investment for small-scale renewables power

While Thailand has made important strides in the development of large-scale renewable power capacity over the past decade, significant progress is still needed to unlock financing for small-scale renewable power systems. By the end of 2022, a total renewable electricity generation capacity of 12 666 megawatts (MW) was installed (including large hydropower), a doubling over the past decade (EPPO, 2024[1]). This capacity generated a total of around 39 terawatt-hours (TWh) electricity in the same year, covering around 13% of the total electricity generation. Within this, total small-scale renewable power capacity[6] represents a small share of 10% of total renewable energy (RE), standing at 1 282 MW in 2022. Deployment of small-scale renewable power systems, especially through rooftop solar photovoltaic (PV) systems, can provide productive benefits for local businesses, manufacturing industries and the agriculture sector as well as an opportunity for clean power access for rural communities. Limited policy support and the lack of availability of innovative financing models and instruments for these systems have hampered their development.

To support the Government of Thailand and key Thai stakeholders to promote and de-risk small-scale renewable power investment, the Roadmap proposes recommendations across three key pillars: (i) financial support; (ii) policy, regulation and governance; and (iii) capacity building, data collection and awareness-raising – summarised below. Table 1 below provides an indication of the tentative timing and potential actors involved in the implementation of the recommended measures.

### *Financial support*

*Reviewing and strengthening existing public financial incentives to prioritise the acceleration of small-scale and community-based renewable energy models*

- Thai energy policymakers and regulators could regularly monitor the up-take of the ongoing feed-in-tariff (FiT) scheme, review and adjust FiT tariff rates to encourage small-scale and community-based renewable energy projects if their uptake is low.

- The FiT policy can facilitate the development of small-scale solar, for example by developing and disseminating template contracts for solar power purchase agreement (PPA), solar roof rental and community-ownership models.

*Improving conditions of green loan programmes for Micro, Small and Medium Enterprises (MSMEs)*

- The government, through the Ministry of Energy and Ministry of Finance, could consider continuing incentives or subsidies to encourage banks to offer green loans to MSMEs at more favourable terms, e.g. in the form of tax incentives or subsidies for interest rate differentials. Credit guarantees can also help to de-risk small-scale projects and to mitigate banks' risks associated with green lending.
- Implementing risk mitigation measures, for example through credit guarantees, can help lower the risk of small-scale projects and MSMEs, increase the confidence of lenders, which can, in turn, improve terms and conditions of existing green loan programmes for small-scale renewable energy projects and MSMEs (e.g. through favourable interest rates, lower collateral requirements, longer tenures and flexible repayment schedules).
- Within the loan origination process, financial institutions could apply adequate and proportionate reporting and verification standards for MSME green loans.
- Simplifying and streamlining application and approval processes for green MSME loans could also help to ease MSMEs access to financing for renewable energy projects.

*Piloting a green credit guarantee scheme for small-scale renewable energy projects*

- The government could consider supporting the pilot of a green credit guarantee scheme to de-risk small-scale renewable projects and MSMEs, designing it to cover grid connected solar rooftops and other renewable energy technologies as well as off-grid renewable energy solutions.
- The Thai Credit Guarantee Corporation (TCG) could act as guarantor, given its mandate and ability to extend and process guarantees.
- Concessional financing from the government and support by donors, multilateral development banks (MDBs) and Development Finance Institutions (DFIs) might be required to partially offset guarantee fees and service costs, especially at the onset of the programme, to lower the guarantee fee for MSMEs and mobilise commercial capital for small-scale renewable projects.
- As a first step, a feasibility study could be conducted, consulting all relevant stakeholders in the financial industry and energy sector, to inform decisions on key design elements, namely: (i) the choice between the individual and portfolio guarantee approach; (ii) the coverage ratio (i.e. what portion of a loan can be covered by a guarantee); (iii) the pricing structure for the guarantee fees; (iv) the process for handling defaults and guarantee payouts; and (v) the exit strategy.

*Providing financial support to Pay-As-You-Go (PAYG) models to expand off-grid, community-based renewable energy*

- The primary targets for replicating PAYG models include off-grid communities, especially in remote islands, where extending the grid is not economically viable. Financial support with favourable terms from the government, donors, MDBs and DFIs is necessary at the early stage of innovative PAYG models, to cover upfront investment and business planning costs.
- Replicating and expanding the PAYG model in remote islands would require significant training to ensure the communities have the necessary technical skills.

*Developing aggregation and securitisation models for small-scale renewable energy projects*

- Blended finance can be used to support bundling and aggregation of multiple small-scale renewable energy projects or assets into larger and rateable financial products or vehicles that are attractive to large institutional investors.
- Small loans for renewable energy projects can be pooled and then sold to a separate legal entity, such as a special purpose vehicle (SPV), to protect the assets from any insolvency of the sponsoring entity or seller. The SPV can then issue marketable securities, typically in tranches with different credit risk.
- To facilitate such structures, donors, DFIs, MDBs and/or the government can provide first loss tranches as credit enhancement to comfort senior tranche investors.
- Grants and technical assistance are necessary to develop large and bankable pipelines of small-scale renewables projects as well as to gather and standardise risk and performance data from small entities.

### *Policy, regulation and governance*

*Strengthening policy planning and setting region-specific targets on small-scale renewable energy over the near- and long-term*

- A clear strategy with near- and long-term targets for small-scale renewable power installed capacity could help to provide policy direction, clarify long-term opportunities for developers and foster the development of a local industry ecosystem.
- Developing clear technology- and region-specific targets will be necessary if the aim is to ensure that all communities have access to reliable, clean and affordable electricity.
- Providing certainty and predictability of the energy policies, plans, targets and related updates.

*Encouraging financial institutions to assess and disclose taxonomy alignment of their portfolios*

- Actual implementation of the taxonomy could be promoted, for example, by setting requirements for financial institutions to assess and disclose the extent of alignment of their portfolios with the taxonomy.
- Such regulatory measures shall clarify the taxonomy alignment reporting requirements and timelines for both financial and non-financial entities.
- Regulatory provisions could also mandate or encourage the use of the taxonomy to identify eligibility criteria of green financial products (e.g. green bonds and loans).
- Developers of small-scale projects would need to incorporate green taxonomy criteria into project design and monitoring systems.
- Adequate capacity building and technical assistance would be necessary for MSMEs to conduct taxonomy alignment assessments.

*Strengthening the regulatory environment for financial securitisation of renewable energy assets*

- Developing the green securitisation market in Thailand in a prudent way requires establishing a favourable local regulatory environment by the Thai financial regulator and supervisor (the Bank of Thailand).
- Such regulation could address the risks inherent to securitisation transactions, for instance, by setting strict risk retention requirements, improving transparency and risk management processes, and enhancing underwriting policies.
- Facilitating the standardisation of contracts and enabling access to issuers' performance data of the underlying assets are key to facilitate due diligence and provide transparency to investors.

- The regulatory framework could also clarify eligibility criteria for renewable energy assets to be securitised, e.g. related to the project size, technology type, track record and revenue generation stability.
- The assessment and rating of renewable energy securitisation transactions by independent credit rating agencies would need to be facilitated. To do so, the financial regulator could collaborate with rating agencies and industry associations to develop rigorous methodologies for assessing creditworthiness.

*Simplifying renewable energy licensing and permitting processes and requirements*

- Processes and requirements for renewable energy licensing and permitting for small or community-owned installations (e.g. construction permits, grid connection authorisations, etc.) could be simplified and streamlined.
- The creation of a single-window service permitting, licensing and information portal (such as an online platform or one-stop service) could significantly reduce administrative barriers and streamline application procedures, especially for small players.

*Improving consistency and harmonisation of grid connection codes*

- The different existing grid connection codes could be harmonised and streamlined across the three responsible organisations (the transmission and distribution utilities), to ensure consistency to accommodate future increase in variable renewable energy.

### Capacity building, data collection and awareness

*Building capacity of MSMEs, financial institutions and technicians, and developing training programmes*

- With grants, technical assistance and support of international development partners, access to information and capacity-building activities for both financial institutions and MSMEs could be increased, in particular by focusing on the following priorities:
  - Enhancing financial institution capacity on conducting climate-related disclosures, applying green standards for their lending and investment products, assessing portfolio alignment with the Thai taxonomy criteria as well as on assessing small-scale renewable energy business models
  - Increasing MSMEs awareness and knowledge on the latest renewable energy opportunities as well as improving their financial literacy
  - Increasing developers' knowledge on designing renewable energy products in line with the Thai taxonomy criteria
  - Developing financial institutions' and regulators' knowledge on securitisation and risk transfer for renewable energy assets, learning from international experience on green securitisation regulation
  - Providing adequate training to solar PV technicians and contractors for them to acquire adequate skills and updated knowledge on latest innovations as well as safety standards.

*Implementing consumer awareness and education campaigns, and fostering community engagement*

- With support from international development partners, awareness campaigns on small-scale, distributed and off-grid renewable technologies can address different target groups.
- Fostering community engagement and raising community awareness about the benefits of PAYG-enabled renewable energy model are necessary to encourage the up-take of these solutions.

- Community engagement activities could therefore promote the outreach and participation of women as well as youth in decision-making processes, to take leadership roles and get involved in project development.

*Fostering data collection on small-scale renewable capacity and financing*

- Increasing the availability of data on the expansion of small-scale energy capacity across different types of renewable energy would be beneficial.
- Financial institutions and investors would benefit from better access to risk and performance data of small-scale renewable projects (e.g. recovery rates, default risks).

**Table 1. Financing for small-scale renewable power: Timing and implementers for key recommendations**

| Key topic area | Recommendations | Timing | Leading agency | Implementers |
|---|---|---|---|---|
| **Financial support** | Reviewing and strengthening existing public financial incentives to prioritise the acceleration of small-scale and community-based renewable energy models | S-T | DEDE | DEDE and MOF |
| | Improving conditions of green loan programmes for MSMEs | S-T | DEDE | DEDE, FIs and ESCOs |
| | Developing aggregation and securitisation models for small-scale renewables | S-T | DEDE | DEDE, FIs, development partners, ESCOs |
| | Providing financial support to PAYG models to expand off-grid RE | S-T | MOEN | MOEN, ESCOs, DFIs, DEDE, electricity authorities and development partners |
| | Piloting a credit guarantee scheme for small-scale renewable energy projects | M-T | DEDE | DEDE, TCG, DFIs, commercial banks, ESCOs and development partners |
| **Policy, regulation and governance** | Strengthening policy planning and setting region-specific targets on small-scale renewable energy over the near- and long-term | S-T | DEDE | DEDE |
| | Enhancing energy policy predictability | S-T | MOEN | DEDE and EPPO |
| | Encouraging financial institutions to assess and disclose taxonomy alignment of their portfolios | S-T | BOT | BOT, SEC and relevant ministries (MONRE, MOF and MOEN) |
| | Simplifying renewable energy licensing and permitting processes and requirements | S-T | ERC | ERC, MOEN, EGAT, MEA and PEA |
| | Improving consistency and harmonisation of grid codes and regulations | M-T | ERC | ERC, EGAT, MEA and PEA |
| | Strengthening the regulatory environment for financial securitisation of renewable energy assets | M-T | BOT | BOT, MOF and MOEN |
| **Capacity building, data collection and awareness** | Building capacity of MSMEs, financial institutions and technicians and developing training programmes | S-T | DEDE | DEDE, TPQI, COE, DSD, academia, research centres, FIs, industry associations, ESCOs and development partners |
| | Implementing consumer awareness and education campaigns and fostering community engagement | S-T | DEDE | DEDE, academia, research centres, ESCOs, CSOs and development partners |
| | Fostering data collection on small-scale renewable capacity and financing | M-T | DEDE | DEDE, utilities, business associations and ESCOs |

Note: BOT = Bank of Thailand; COE = Council of Engineers Thailand; CSOs = civil society organisations; DEDE = Department of Alternative Energy Development and Efficiency of the Ministry of Energy; DFIs = development finance institutions; DSD = Department of Skill Development; EGAT = Electricity Generating Authority of Thailand; ERC = Energy Regulatory Commission of Thailand; ESCOs = Energy Service Companies; FIs = financial institutions; MEA = Metropolitan Electricity Authority; MOEN = Ministry of Energy; MOF = Ministry of Finance; MONRE = Ministry of Natural Resources and Environment; PEA = Provincial Electricity Authority; SEC = Securities and Exchange Commission; TCG = Thai Credit Guarantee Corporation and TPQI = Thailand Professional Qualification Institute.
Note: S-T = short-term; M-T = medium-term
Source: Authors

## Unlocking finance and investment for energy efficient buildings and cooling

Thailand is one of the leading energy efficiency markets in Southeast Asia thanks to the early introduction and public support for financing schemes such as the Thai Energy Efficiency Revolving Fund (EERF). Thailand also has a vibrant private energy service companies (ESCOs) market, although it is still nascent and requires further support to achieve greater scale.

Energy intensity in Thailand decreased from Thai Baht (THB) 8.54 toe/million (0.27 USD) in 2010 to THB 7.6 toe/million (USD 0.21) in 2023, by 12% (DEDE, 2023[2]). Improving the energy efficiency of cooling applications of Thailand's building stock is a critical priority. The building sector represented on average approximately 25% of the total electricity consumed in Thailand in 2019 and cooling applications make up for over half of the Thai commercial building sector's energy consumption (Chumnanvanichkul, Chirapongsananurak and Hoonchareon, 2019[3]). Buildings in Thailand and in other countries of Southeast Asia have been characterised by high cooling demand. In residential buildings alone, the electricity use share of air conditioning (AC) systems is about a quarter of the total. Space cooling electricity demand for large-scale non-residential buildings such as for public and commercial uses is similarly high and relies on equipment with average energy efficiency. Given the country's strategic regional importance as a commercial and manufacturing hub and tourism destination, combined with expected population growth, increasing urbanisation and rising temperatures, electricity demand for cooling will grow, thereby highlighting the importance of scaling up investment in energy efficiency buildings and cooling solutions.

The Government of Thailand is committed to accelerate finance and investment in energy efficiency projects in the Thai building sector and has put in place several supportive policies comprising government regulations, financial incentives and awareness-raising initiatives. This Roadmap provides a set of recommendations to further support Thailand's efforts to mobilise financing for energy efficient buildings and cooling, addressing three main areas: (i) financial support; (ii) policy, regulation and governance; and (iii) capacity building, data collection and awareness-raising. It should be noted that several of the following recommendations can be applied as well to promote energy efficiency across sectors. Table 2 below provides an indication of the tentative timing and potential actors involved in the implementation of the recommended measures.

## *Financial support*

### *Maintaining consistent public support to promote the ESCO market*

- Besides ensuring that market regulations and accounting rules allow for ESCO operations in-country and particularly with regards to their service offerings in the commercial and public buildings sector, the operation of ESCOs can be encouraged with dedicated financial incentives, training programmes as well as the accreditation and certification of qualified ESCOs.
- Favourable financing conditions or de-risking instruments like energy savings insurance models or credit guarantees for ESCOs can help improve access to financing, including for the implementation of energy efficiency measures and small-scale renewable power in large-scale commercial and public buildings.

### *Conducting ex-post evaluations of the Energy Efficiency Revolving Fund and the ESCO Fund*

- Conducting ex-post evaluations of the Energy Efficiency Revolving Fund (EERF) and the ESCO Revolving Fund would allow for the proper assessment of results achieved through these funds over the years of implementation and identify the strengths and weaknesses of these mechanisms, the achieved impact on Thailand's energy efficiency market and remaining gaps.
- The evidence produced by such evaluations could then be used to inform decision-making on the need for future public funding and interventions in the energy efficiency domain.

### *Establishing a bulk procurement model for energy-efficient cooling appliances*

- The government could consider establishing a bulk procurement scheme for energy-efficient cooling appliances. Concessional financing from the government and international development finance providers can cover the upfront costs of the scheme and mobilise investment from commercial sources.

- Building on the existing but still nascent ESCO market in Thailand, a public-private aggregator or Super ESCO with a robust business model could be established to take on the investment risks and costs for bulk procurement, co-ordinate demand and achieve economies of scale, thus reducing prices.

*Implementing an Energy Savings Insurance (ESI) model in Thailand*

- Piloting an Energy Savings Insurance (ESI) model in Thailand could promote the energy efficiency market and unlock Thai ESCOs' potential. When piloting ESI models, Thailand could benefit from the availability of templates, methodologies for standard performance contracts, project investment analysis and verification tools developed in other markets.
- Concessionality could be incorporated into ESI credit lines, thanks to concessional financing and grants extended by international development partners. These concessional elements enable commercial financial institutions to offer preferential financing terms to MSMEs or ESCOs at either longer payback periods or lower rates than available in the commercial market.
- ESI models usually targets MSMEs and aim to help them invest in small-scale energy efficiency projects. For example, ESI models in Thailand could incentivise MSME investment in acquiring energy-efficient appliances such as lighting, Heating Ventilation and Air Conditioning (HVAC) systems, refrigerators as compressed air systems in industrial processes. An enabling insurance regulatory environment as well as a holistic demand creation strategy are necessary for the take-up of ESI models.

*Creating an on-bill financing programme for energy-efficient cooling appliances*

- The government and utilities could contribute to expanding the uptake of energy efficient cooling appliances and equipment in the building sector by creating an on-bill financing (OBF) programme, enabling utility customers to acquire energy efficiency equipment and to pay for it over time through their monthly utility bills.
- For the OBF programme to be successful, adequate investments in consumer awareness shall be planned. Moreover, to ensure that households of all income levels can access OBF loans, financial incentives might be required, such as preferential interest rates for low-income households.

*Fostering issuances of green bonds in the building sector*

- Financial support for green building certification and green bond verification costs can encourage the up-take of this instrument, especially for MSMEs that might not have sufficient resources to pay for certification and verification services.
- Clear criteria on which types of buildings are eligible to be financed through proceeds of green bonds, in line with green building standards, will facilitate issuance in this sector. Eligibility criteria of projects to be financed through green bond proceeds could be anchored to the Thai taxonomy criteria (ADB, 2022[4]).

### *Policy, regulation and governance*

*Incrementally increasing stringency of minimum energy performance standards and expanding AC labelling to large commercial buildings.*

- The scope and stringency of minimum energy performance standards for buildings as well as for appliances (such as air conditioners) could be gradually and periodically increased, to reflect technological advancements and best practices in energy efficiency.
- Green building certifications could also be regularly updated to reflect the latest performance standards.

- AC labelling could be expanded to cover large commercial systems to use higher efficiency systems and labelling implementation could be encouraged.

*Setting up an institutional co-ordination scheme and revising roles and responsibilities of implementing agencies*

- An inter-agency task force could be established to improve co-ordination of the different responsible agencies and oversee enforcement and implementation of energy efficiency standards.

*Strengthening the policy framework for district cooling*

- As demand for district cooling projects is expected to increase, developing District Cooling Guidelines could be developed and disseminated to national, province and district development authorities, developers and investors, to clarify regulatory expectations.
- Integrating stringent energy efficiency standards and encouraging the utilisation of renewable energy sources, such as heat pumps, could be encouraged to enhance the overall sustainability and performance of district cooling systems.

*Developing an Energy Efficient Technology List (EETL) and collaborating with financial institutions to provide financial incentives to the listed technologies*

- The government could consider developing a high-performing Energy Efficient Technology List (EETL), with qualified appliances, installers and solution providers that have been pre-approved as eligible for financing from partnering financial institutions.
- This tool could be made available through an online platform which could offer a shopping-style platform connecting vendors of best-in-class green technologies with businesses and homeowners. Performance requirements for technologies and vendors would be based and assessed against the EETL.

### *Capacity building, data collection and awareness*

*Establishing capacity building and training programmes for financial institutions and ESCOs*

With support of international development partners, tailored capacity building programmes could be established, focusing on the following priorities:

- Training engineers and architects with latest green building design techniques and standards, including by upgrading university curricula
- Training monitoring and verification professionals (e.g. energy auditors)
- Educating and train financial institutions to increase their knowledge and familiarity with energy efficiency projects
- Strengthening measurement and verification (M&V) skills to assess energy savings
- Enhancing institutional capability of agencies responsible for the design, implementation and monitoring of energy efficiency policies.

*Implementing consumer awareness and education campaigns for efficient buildings and cooling*

- With support from international development partners, awareness campaigns on energy-efficient buildings and cooling can be promoted, to focus not only on spreading knowledge on the latest technologies and regulatory changes and standards, but also on the latest developments in terms of financial instruments, both public and private.

*Fostering data collection on energy savings of energy-efficient buildings and cooling systems*

- More and better data on the performance, cost and energy savings of energy efficient buildings and cooling appliances can help inform financing and investment decisions as well as policy design.
- Collecting and publishing data in aggregated form in publicly available dashboards can help to strengthen market confidence in energy efficiency projects.

**Table 2. Financing for energy-efficient cooling in buildings: Timing and implementers for key recommendations**

| Key topic area | Recommendations | Timing | Leading agency | Implementers |
|---|---|---|---|---|
| **Financing** | Piloting on-bill financing and Energy savings insurance (ESI) | S-T | DEDE | DEDE, utilities, FIs, ESCOs and development partners |
| | Establishing a bulk procurement model for energy-efficient cooling appliances | S-T | DEDE | DEDE, utilities, provincial authorities, ESCOs and development partners |
| | Conducting ex-post evaluations of the Energy Efficiency Revolving Fund and the ESCO Fund | S-T | DEDE | DEDE and independent evaluators |
| | Maintaining consistent public support to promote the ESCO market | M-T | DEDE | DEDE, ESCOs and FIs |
| | Fostering the uptake of green bonds in the building sector | M-T | DEDE | DEDE, MOF, SEC and FIs |
| **Policy, regulation and governance** | Incrementally increasing stringency of minimum energy performance standards and expanding AC labelling to large commercial buildings. | S-T | EGAT and DEDE | EGAT, DEDE, MOEN, TISI, research centres and academia |
| | Setting up an institutional co-ordination scheme and revising roles and responsibilities of energy efficiency standards implementing agencies | S-T | MOEN | MONRE, MOF, MOEN and MOIN |
| | Strengthening the regulatory framework for district cooling | M-T | DEDE | DEDE and local authorities |
| | Developing an Energy Efficient Technology List (EETL) and collaborating with financial institutions to provide financial incentives to the listed technologies and providers. | M-T | DEDE | DEDE and financial institutions |
| **Capacity building, data collection and awareness-raising** | Establishing capacity building and training programmes on energy efficiency for the building sector | M-T | DEDE | DEDE, TPQI, COE, DSD, academia, research centres, business associations, ESCOs and development partners |
| | Increasing consumer awareness campaigns for efficient buildings and cooling | M-T | DEDE | DEDE, academia, research centres, business associations, ESCOs and development partners |
| | Fostering data collection on energy savings of energy-efficient buildings and cooling systems | M-T | DEDE | DEDE, business associations and ESCOs |

Note: COE = Council of Engineers Thailand; CSOs = civil society organisations; DEDE = Department of Alternative Energy Development and Efficiency of the Ministry of Energy; DFIs = development finance institutions; DSD = Department of Skill Development; EGAT = Electricity Generating Authority of Thailand; ESCO = Energy Service Companies; FIs = financial institutions; MOEN = Ministry of Energy; MOF = Ministry of Finance; MOIN = Ministry of Industry; MONRE = Ministry of Natural Resources and Environment; SEC = Securities and Exchange Commission; and TPQI = Thailand Professional Qualification Institute.
Note: S-T = short-term; M-T = medium-term
Source: Authors

## References


ADB (2022), *Green Bond Market Survey for Thailand*, https://www.adb.org/sites/default/files/publication/801601/green-bond-market-survey-thailand.pdf. [4]

Chumnanvanichkul, P., P. Chirapongsananurak and N. Hoonchareon (2019), "Three-level Classification of Air Conditioning Energy Consumption for Building Energy Management System Using Data Mining Techniques", *2019 IEEE PES GTD Grand International Conference and Exposition Asia (GTD Asia)*, https://doi.org/10.1109/gtdasia.2019.8716004. [3]

DEDE (2023), *Performance on Energy Efficiency Policy*, https://www.dede.go.th/uploads/GDP_EI_4_2566_edit_5a8f948e8c.pdf?updated_at=2024-04-04T03:32:13.061Z. [2]

Energy Regulatory Commission of Thailand (2009), *Royal Decree: Specifying the Types, Sizes, and Characteristics of Energy Businesses Exempted from the Requirement to Apply for an Energy Business License*, https://www.erc.or.th/web-upload/200xf869baf82be74c18cc110e974eea8d5c/m_laws/8834/2526/file_download/4dcd9abecd274411a3e7a343cc4d44ae.pdf. [5]

EPPO (2024), *Electricity*, https://www.eppo.go.th/epposite/index.php/th/energy-information/static-energy/static-electricity?orders[publishUp]=publishUp&issearch=1. [1]


## Notes

[1] Colombia, Egypt, India, Indonesia, the Philippines, South Africa, Thailand and Viet Nam. Please visit Clean Energy Finance and Investment Mobilisation - OECD for more information.

[2] In the past, the same model has been applied as part of the following studies: (i) Financing Thailand's Climate Actions in NDC and NAP under GIZ's Thai-German Climate Programme (2020); (ii) Ambition to Action's Domestic Expenditure and Employment Impacts of Power Sector Development in Thailand (A2A, 2019); and (iii) Affordable and Secure Energy for Southeast Asia (CASE) on *Towards a collective vision of Thai energy transition: National long-term scenarios and socioeconomic implications* (2022).

[3] Further details on the stakeholder consultation workshops can be found at: Clean energy finance and investment roadmap - OECD.

[4] The recommendations and suggested actions to incentivise financing for small-scale renewable energy are outlined in the "Roadmap Action Plan" below and further detailed at the end of Chapter 3.

[5] The recommendations and suggested actions to unlock financing for energy efficient buildings and cooling are outlined in the "Roadmap Action Plan" below and further detailed at the end of Chapter 4.

[6] In the context of this Roadmap, small-scale renewable power refers to power generation by renewable energy sources with a total capacity of less than 1 000 kW. The threshold represents the amount below which a business is exempted from the requirement to apply for an energy business license as per the Royal Decree following the Energy Industry Act B.E.2550 (Energy Regulatory Commission of Thailand, 2009[5]). The full range of small-scale, low-carbon energy solutions in industry, agriculture, transport and other sectors were not considered within the scope of the report. The report mainly considered distributed renewable energy technologies such as small-scale solar PV, solar home systems and mini grids, which provide clean energy to households, industry and commercial users, independently from centralised systems.

# 1 Introduction: key trends and policies for financing renewable energy and energy efficiency in Thailand

This chapter presents Thailand's economic context, emissions profile and its climate and energy ambitions and targets. It describes the governance and institutional context of Thailand's energy policy as well as the structure of its electricity market, renewable energy potential and the main characteristics of its power mix. Finally, the chapter examines the renewable energy finance and investment landscape, focusing on policies and financial incentives on renewable energy as well as on sustainable finance, including analysis of Thailand's sustainable finance taxonomy. The chapter ends with an overview of the latest trends on renewable energy investments in Thailand.

## Thailand's economic context and clean energy ambitions

Thailand has achieved significant economic and social progress since the 1960s, with fast continuous growth until the 2010s, when Thailand's growth started to lose momentum compared to other countries in Southeast Asia. The already softer growth momentum was further weakened by the economic downturn from the pandemic (OECD, 2023[1]).

The Thai economy has experienced a later and weaker recovery from the pandemic than other countries in the region. Thailand's economy was heavily affected by rising energy and food prices, which caused a cost-of-living crisis and a delay in structural reforms (OECD, 2023[1]). After a severe downturn, the recovery picked up rapidly, bolstered by the strong rebound of inbound tourism, and the increase in exports and domestic demand. According to the OECD (2023[1]), as the Thai economy is recovering, Thailand will now need to address several key structural issues, such as the decrease in the economy's productivity, population ageing, the digital transition, reconfigurations of global value chains and the green transition.

Thailand has increased efforts to decarbonise its economy in recent years. The country submitted its second updated Nationally Determined Contribution (NDC) and its revised long-term low greenhouse gas emissions development strategy (LT-LEDS) in November 2022, committing to reduce its greenhouse gas (GHG) emissions by 30% from the projected business-as-usual (BAU) level by 2030, using 2005 as a baseline year (UNFCCC, 2022[2]; UNFCCC, 2022[3]). The NDC targets emission reductions of up to 40%, subject to adequate and enhanced access to technology development and transfer, financial resources and capacity building support. Furthermore, Thailand committed to meet the long-term goal of carbon neutrality (net-zero $CO_2$) by 2050 and net-zero GHG emission by 2065 (Figure 1.1).

### Figure 1.1. Thailand's long-term GHG emission reduction target

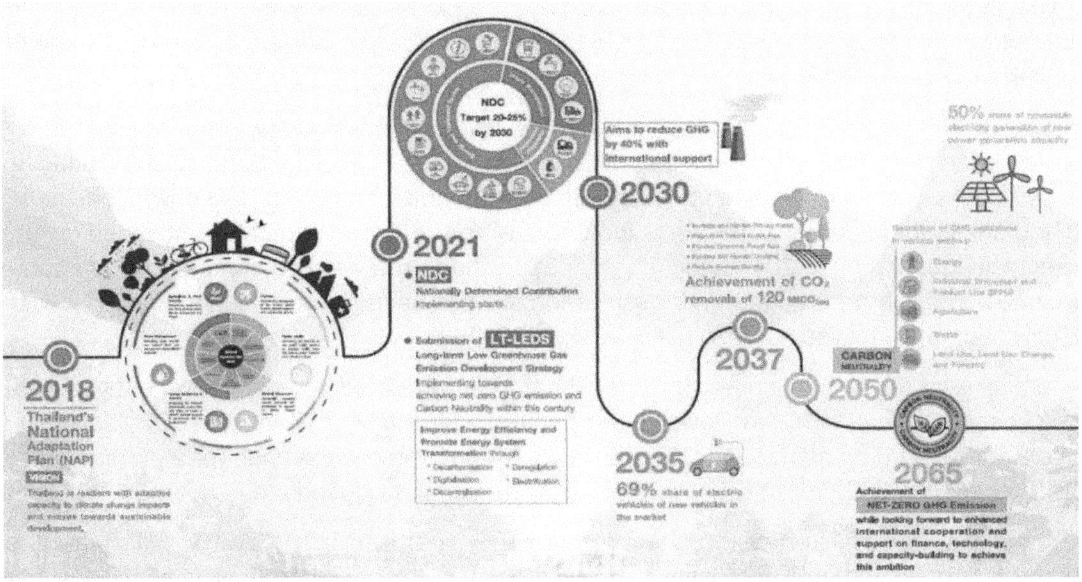


Source: CASE, (2022[4]), Towards a collective vision of Thai energy transition: National long-term scenarios and socioeconomic implications, https://newclimate.org/sites/default/files/2022-11/2022-11-08_th_ltes_-_full_report.pdf.

The transformation of Thailand's energy system will be critical in realising Thailand's long-term climate goals, as the energy sector accounted for 69% of Thailand's total GHG emissions of 372 million tonnes (Mt) carbon dioxide-equivalent (CO2-eq) in 2018 (Thailand's Ministry of Natural Resources and Environment, 2022[5]). The remaining 31% was split between agriculture (15.7%), industrial process and product use (IPPU) (10.8%), and the waste sectors (4.5%) (Figure 1.2). Within the energy sector, most total direct GHGs came from fuel combustion (40%), followed by transport (29%), manufacturing industries and construction (20%), other sectors (nearly 7%) and fugitive emissions from fuel (just over 4%).

## Figure 1.2. Thailand's GHG emission profile

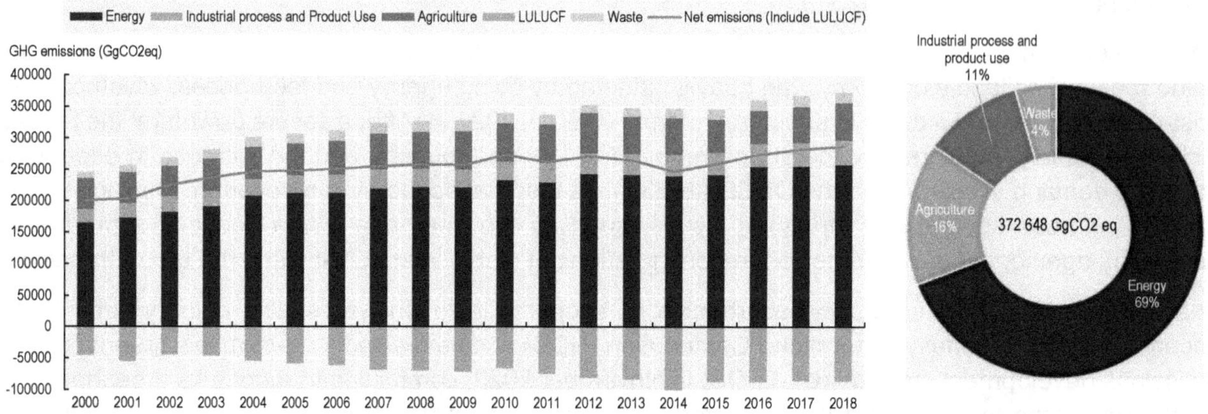


Source: Thailand's Ministry of Natural Resources and Environment (2022[5]), Thailand's Long-term Low Greenhouse Gas Emission Development Strategy, https://unfccc.int/sites/default/files/resource/Thailand%20LT-LEDS%20%28Revised%20Version%29_08Nov2022.pdf.

StatLink https://stat.link/7s32t5

Currently, the Energy Policy and Planning Office (EPPO) of Thailand's Ministry of Energy (MOE) is in the process of finalising its new National Energy Plan (NEP) with the goal of achieving its long-term climate targets. The forthcoming NEP will integrate five key sub-plans, namely the Power Development Plan (PDP), the Alternative Energy Development Plan (AEDP), the Energy Efficiency Plan (EEP), the Gas Plan and the Oil Plan.

The forthcoming NEP is being revised to align with the revised long-term low greenhouse gas emissions development strategy (LT-LEDS). Thailand's 2022 revised LT-LEDS also states that to achieve carbon neutrality in 2050, the country aims to phase out oil power plants by 2025, phase down coal power plants by 2040 and phase them out by 2050, while the share of renewable electricity is estimated to reach 68% of total electricity generation in 2040 and 74% in 2050, with the rest being a combination of imports, best-in-class combined cycle natural gas and fossil- and biomass-based power plants equipped with carbon capture, utilisation and storage (CCUS) (UNFCCC, 2022[2]).

This Roadmap was developed based on three latest plans related to renewable energy and energy efficiency. These plans include the Power Development Plan 2018 – Revision (PDP 2018 Rev.1), the Alternative Energy Development Plan 2018 (AEDP 2018) and the draft version for a public hearing of the Energy Efficiency Plan 2022 (draft EEP 2022). The three plans are described in detail in Chapter 2.

Thailand's acceleration of renewable generation capacity and energy efficiency will contribute to the country's overall development, not only in terms of economic growth but also social wellbeing and environmental protection. The clean energy transition will not only reduce import dependency on fossil fuels, thereby increasing energy security and mitigating climate change by reducing GHG emissions, but also contribute to socio-economic development, such as by creating new green jobs and environmental sustainability, e.g. by reducing air pollution.

## Governance and institutional context of Thailand's energy policy

The Ministry of Energy (MOE) governs the energy and electricity sector in Thailand and has the main responsibility over renewable energy and energy efficiency policies. Several agencies within the MOEN support this work, including the Department of Alternative Energy Development and Efficiency (DEDE), which designs and implements renewable energy and energy efficiency policymaking and the Energy Policy and Planning office (EPPO), which recommends economy-wide energy policy and planning.

Energy policies and plans are developed under a co-ordination process between several decision-making bodies. The MOE proposes and drafts policies that are reviewed by the Energy Policy Committee (EPC), the National Energy Policy Council (NEPC) and finally the Cabinet, before finalisation and implementation by the MOEN and its departments (Figure 1.3).

### Figure 1.3. Thailand's national energy policy: decision-making bodies

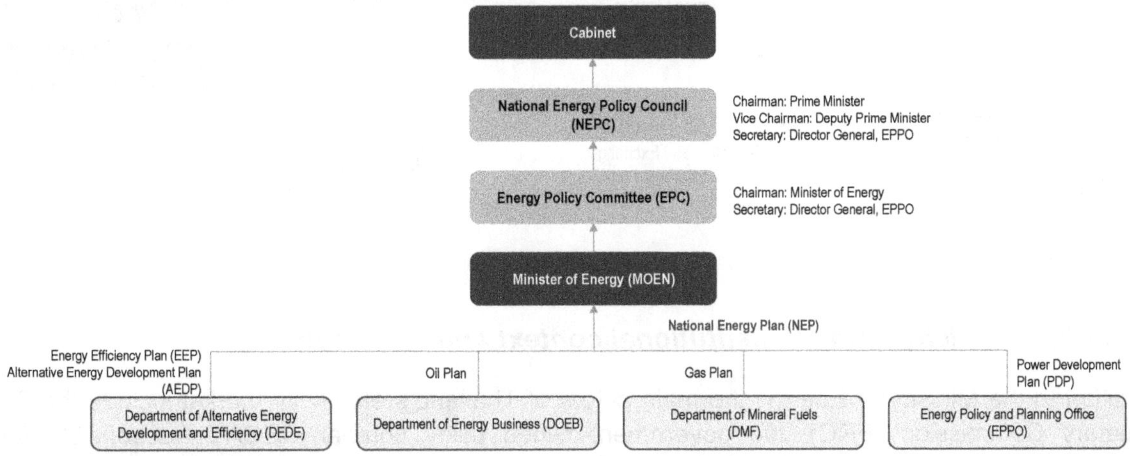


Source: Authors, based on EPPO (2021[6]), https://www.eppo.go.th/epposite/index.php/th/petroleum/oil/link-doeb/item/17093-nep and Ministry of Energy (2024[7]), https://energy.go.th/th/official-structure.

Several other institutions are responsible for areas related to clean energy finance and investment regulations in Thailand (see Figure 1.4 below):

- The Electricity Generating Authority of Thailand (EGAT) is a state-owned enterprise under the supervision of the Ministry of Energy and Ministry of Finance.
- The Energy Regulatory Commission (ERC) of Thailand is an independent agency whose mission is to regulate energy industry operations, including the electricity industry, the natural gas industry and the energy network.
- On the investment side, the Board of Investment (BOI) is a government agency under the Office of the Prime Minister, which promotes inward and outward-bound investments, including for energy-related sectors.
- The Bank of Thailand (BOT) is Thailand's central bank, which formulates and implements monetary policies, supervises and regulates financial institutions, and manages foreign exchange.
- The Securities and Exchange Commission (SEC) aims to ensure an efficient, dynamic and inclusive functioning of Thailand's capital market.

**Figure 1.4. Thailand's clean energy finance: Institutional context**

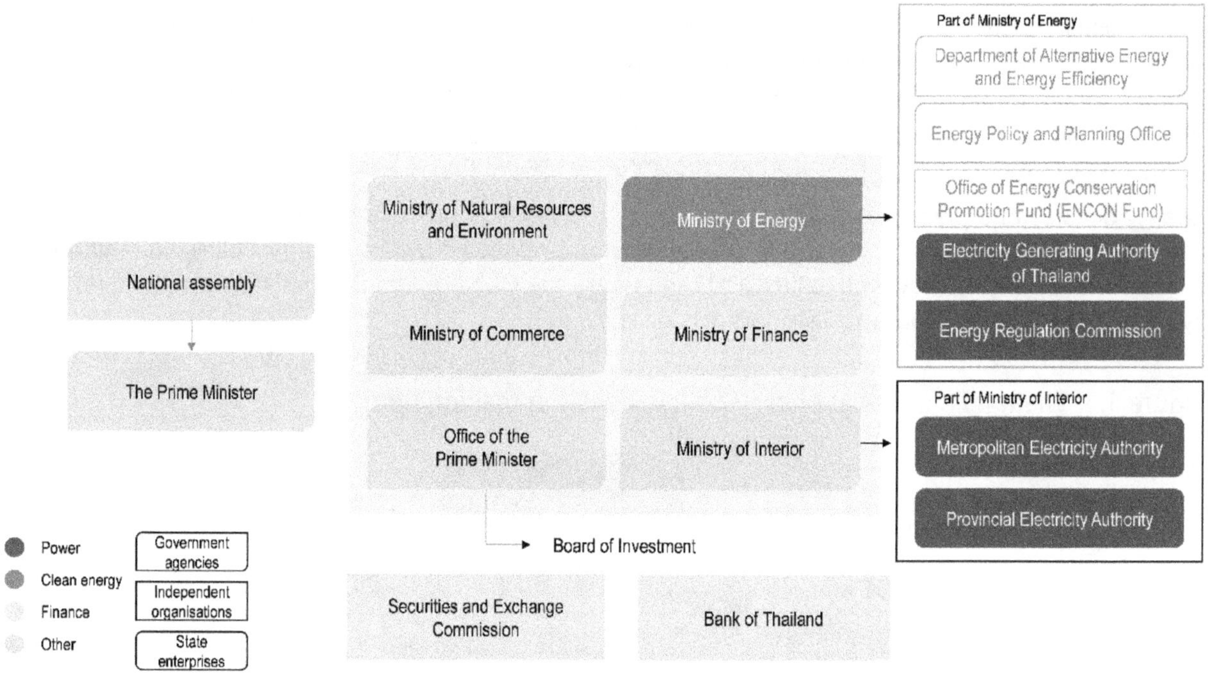


Source: Authors

## *Thailand's electricity market: institutional context and structure*

In addition to the Ministry of Energy, the main actors of Thailand's electricity market include the Energy Regulatory Commission (ERC), the government-owned utility company EGAT (responsible for the transmission grid and 34.5% of total electricity generation), the distribution utility companies, namely the Metropolitan Electricity Authority (MEA) and the Provincial Electricity Authority (PEA), as well as private power producers (see Figure 1.5). The power utility EGAT plans and operates the power system. EGAT sells wholesale electricity to MEA and PEA, as well as to a few industrial clients and utilities in neighbouring countries. The MEA supplies consumers in Bangkok and the metropolitan area, while the PEA supplies the rest of the country (IEA, 2023[8]).

The structure of the power system in Thailand is an enhanced single-buyer system, whereby the vertically integrated state-owned utility EGAT purchases electricity from both its own generation assets and from private power producers. Private power producers can sell electricity to the grid under three power purchase programmes, i.e. (i) Independent Power Producers (IPP), (ii) Small Power Producers (SPP), and (iii) Very Small Power Producers (VSPP). The generation assets are owned by EGAT (30%) and IPPs (33%), SPPs (18%) and VSPPs (8%) (EPPO, 2024[9]). The remaining 16% of installed capacity is sourced from outside the country and is delivered to Thailand through electricity imports. Renewable energy generation capacity is mainly owned by EGAT and VSPPs through the feed-in-tariff and -premium programmes.

The regulations on SPPs and VSPPs were significantly amended in 2007 to be more investor-friendly and practical, including changes to the criteria for qualifying facility, calculation of the avoided cost and interconnection requirements. The practical regulations, together with the higher tariff granted to SPPs and VSPPs producing electricity from renewable energy, have allowed rapid expansion since 2007. However, the regulated power set-up contributes to a lock-in of fossil fuel technologies and the overall inflexibility of the power system, hindering renewable energy uptake (World Bank Group, 2023[10]).

**Figure 1.5. Overview of the electricity market and institutional context in Thailand**

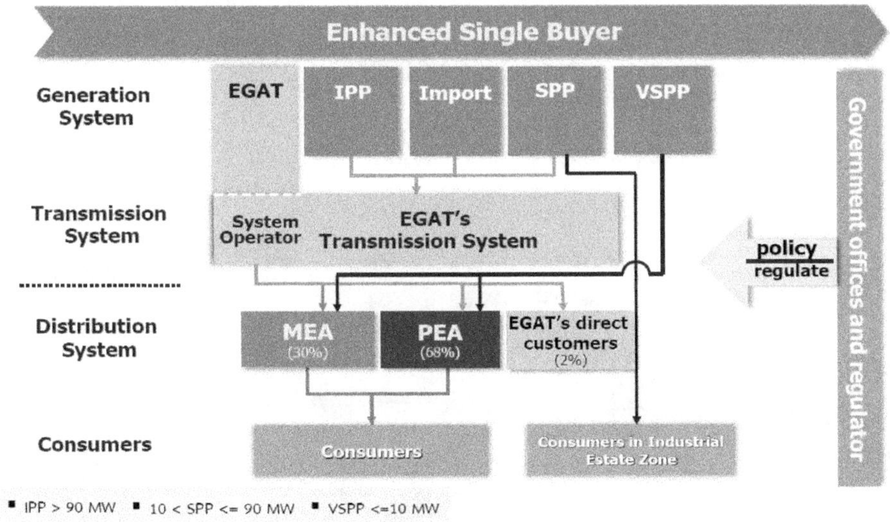


Note: IPP > 90 MW; 10 MW < SPP <= 90 MW; VSPP <= 10 MW

Source: EPPO (2017[11]), Public-private partnership in energy sector, https://slidetodoc.com/asean-summit-publicprivate-partnership-public-private-partnership-in/.

## Thailand's power sector

By end of 2022, Thailand's final energy consumption totalled 75 874 thousand tonnes of oil equivalent (ktoe), increasing at an annual rate of 2.8% since 2002. According to EPPO's data, in 2022 petroleum products accounted for 53% of total energy consumption, while electricity accounts for 22% (EPPO, 2024[12]). Compared to 2021, the final energy consumption increased by 9.3% in 2022, resuming the upward trend after the COVID-19 pandemic. Total final energy consumption has increased for all sources except coal, indicating a growing effort to reduce GHG emissions (Figure 1.6).

**Figure 1.6. Thailand's final energy consumption by fuel type (2002 – 2022)**

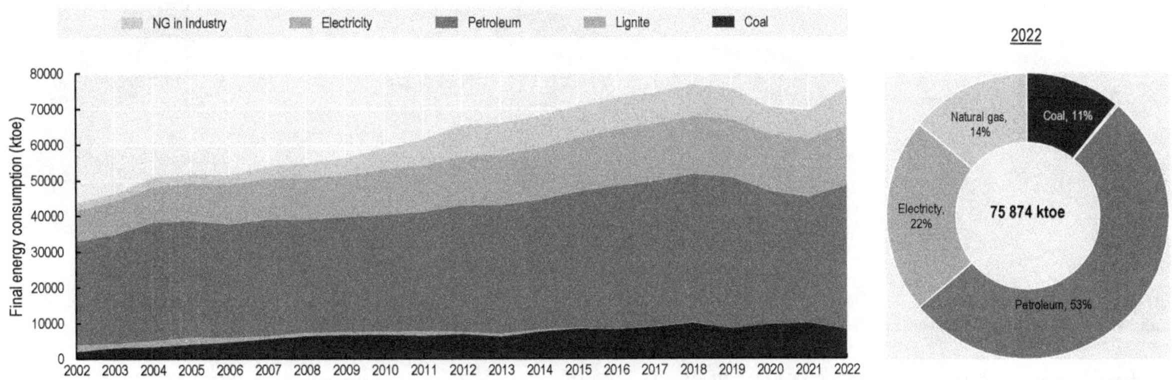


Source: Authors based on data from EPPO (2024[12]), Energy Overview, https://www.eppo.go.th/epposite/index.php/th/energy-information/static-energy/summery-energy.

StatLink https://stat.link/w2tud3

In 2022, electricity accounted for the second-largest share of energy consumption (23%), following petroleum products. As of 2022, the consumption of electricity has reached 197 256 Gigawatt hours (GWh) and has been increasing at an annual rate of over 3% since 2002. The industrial sector consumes the highest share of electricity at 45%, followed by the residential and commercial sectors at 27% and 23% respectively (Figure 1.7). The rise in electricity consumption by the residential sector during 2020-2021 was attributed to remote working practices adopted due to the COVID-19 pandemic.

### Figure 1.7. Electricity consumption by sector (2002 – 2022)

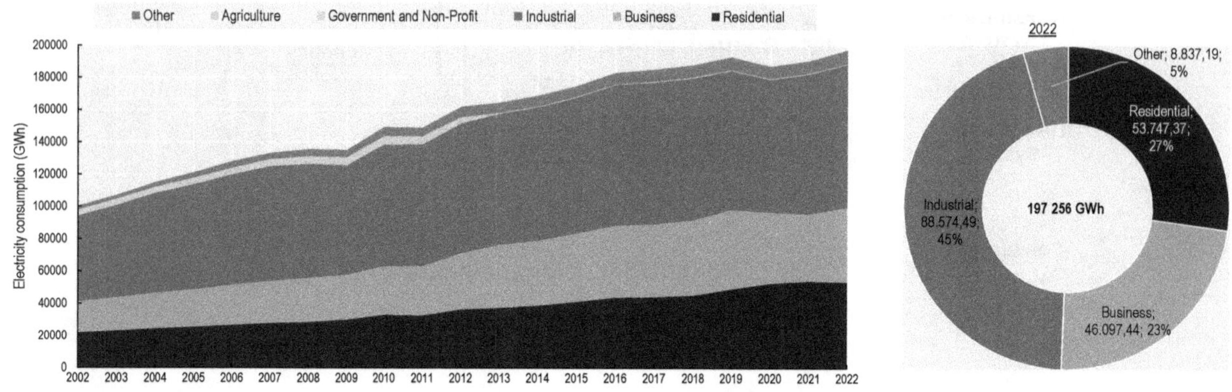


Source: Authors based on data from EPPO (2024[13]), Electricity, https://www.eppo.go.th/epposite/index.php/th/energy-information/static-energy/static-electricity?orders[publishUp]=publishUp&issearch=1.

StatLink https://stat.link/9sg3yc

Thailand's electricity generation primarily relies on natural gas, constituting 53% of total generation in 2022. Coal and lignite accounted for 17%, while imported electricity for 16%. According to data from EPPO, renewable energy sources made up 10% of total generation in 2022, equivalent to 21 876 GWh, marking an 18% annual increase since 2002 (Figure 1.8). Hydro made up 3% of total electricity generation in 2022, at 6 599 GWh. This implies that efforts to increase the share of renewables in electricity generation need to be scaled up significantly to achieve the renewable energy target.

### Figure 1.8. Electricity generation by fuel type (2002 – 2022)

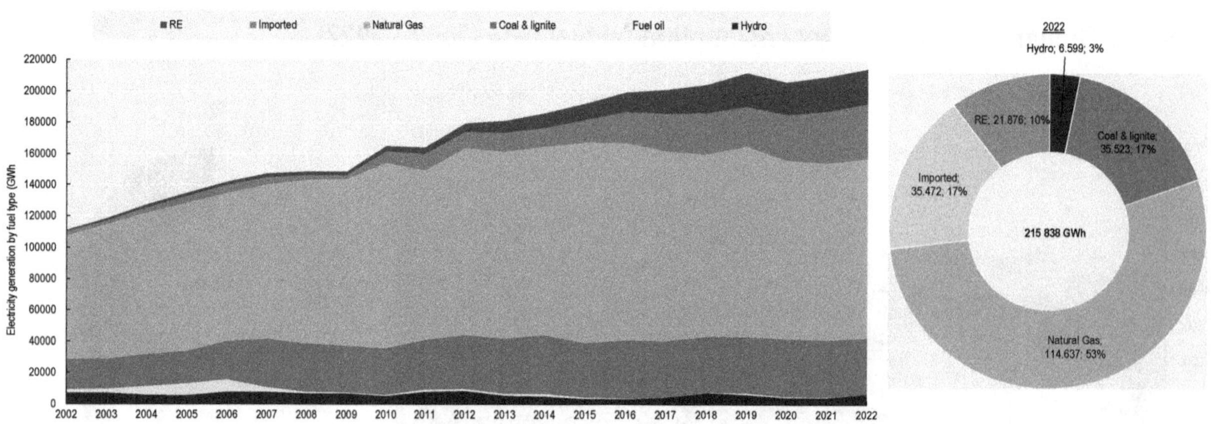


Source: Authors based on data from EPPO (2024[13]), Electricity, https://www.eppo.go.th/epposite/index.php/th/energy-information/static-energy/static-electricity?orders[publishUp]=publishUp&issearch=1

StatLink https://stat.link/ruzhp3

Due to a large share of gas in electricity generation, Thailand has a lower $CO_2$ emission intensity compared to other Southeast Asian countries, such as Indonesia and Viet Nam, that mainly rely on coal to generate electricity. Thailand's average $CO_2$ emission intensity in 2022 stood at 409 grammes $CO_2$ per kilowatt-hour (kWh). This compares with a carbon intensity of 756 g $CO_2$/kWh in Indonesia, where coal represented 61% of its power mix in 2021, while Lao PDR reached a carbon intensity of 309 g $CO_2$/kWh thanks to the higher share of renewable electricity (74% in 2021) (IEA, 2023[8]). At the same time, gas reliance raises security concerns in Thailand, particularly during 2022 when domestic gas production dropped, and imports have been hampered by supply disruptions and high gas prices. This led to extension of the lifetime of some coal assets and resulted in an increase in electricity prices. Gas continues to play an important role in the country as a new gas-fired power plant comprising 4 units of 660 megawatts (MW) capacity is planned to start full operation in Rayong and Chonburi by 2024 (Enerdata, 2023[14]).

Historically, Thailand was a self-sufficient natural gas producer until the 1990s but as demand increased significantly and the production from gas fields in the Gulf of Thailand dropped, share of imports in total consumption has increased. Additionally, Thailand is a net importer of electricity, as it relies on a mix of fossil fuel and hydropower-based electricity from its neighbours, mostly from the Lao People's Democratic Republic (PDR), but also Cambodia, Malaysia and Myanmar (IEA, 2023[8]).

Thailand is endowed with solar, wind and biomass resource availability. The entire geography of Thailand receives high solar irradiance, especially in the central region of the country. A recent study by the Clean, Affordable and Secure Energy (CASE) for Southeast Asia estimated that Thailand has large solar technical potential, at over 300 GW when considering only high irradiance (>1,850 kWh/m2) which only takes up to less than 2% of total land area (CASE for Southeast Asia, 2022[4]). This provides a good opportunity for utility-scale and grid-connected solar photovoltaic (PV) systems as well as small-scale distributed solar, such as rooftop PV. IEA analysis demonstrated that if 10% of the available estimated rooftop surface was used for distributed solar PV, the capacity hosted would be larger than the system's peak demand (IEA, 2018[15]). As for wind power, the largest potential exists in the Northeastern region of Thailand, with an average wind speed of 6 metres per second measured at a height of 90 metres (IRENA, 2017[16]). Most of the hydropower plants are in the northwestern regions of Thailand. However, these resources are far from country's demand locations that are closer to central Thailand (IEA, 2023[8]). Thailand also has biomass power generation potential. Biomass and agricultural residues are available from crops including sugar cane, paddy, cassava, maize and oil palm with variations in seasonal availability. For instance, bagasse, a by-product of the sugar cane industry that can be used for electricity and heat generation is available between December and April (Visvanathan and Chiemchaisri, 2019[17]). Availability of biomass resources is location specific where agricultural activity is present, namely in northern and southern parts of Thailand (DEDE, 2024[18]).

In tropical climates, solar, wind and hydropower supply differs substantially from other climates. For example, during the rainy season, hydropower is more available in Thailand, whereas both wind and solar PV availability generally drops (IEA, 2023[8]). Moreover, hydropower is sometimes restricted by water management to ensure water resource availability for other uses (e.g. irrigation), so hydropower plants do not always produce more hydroelectricity in the wet season than in the summer and winter.

Based on DEDE statistics, the total installed capacity of off-grid and on-grid renewable energy generation in 2022 was 12 666 MW, increasing by slightly over 2% from 2021. The primary sources were biomass (30%), hydro (25%, mainly large projects) and solar (25%), as illustrated in Figure 1.9 below. The renewable mix remained the same over 2020-2022. Regarding solar, most of the grid-connected solar power capacity comes from utility-scale installations of size greater than 1 MW (Tongsopit et al., 2016[19]).

**Figure 1.9. Electricity generation by renewable fuel type (2020 – 2022)**

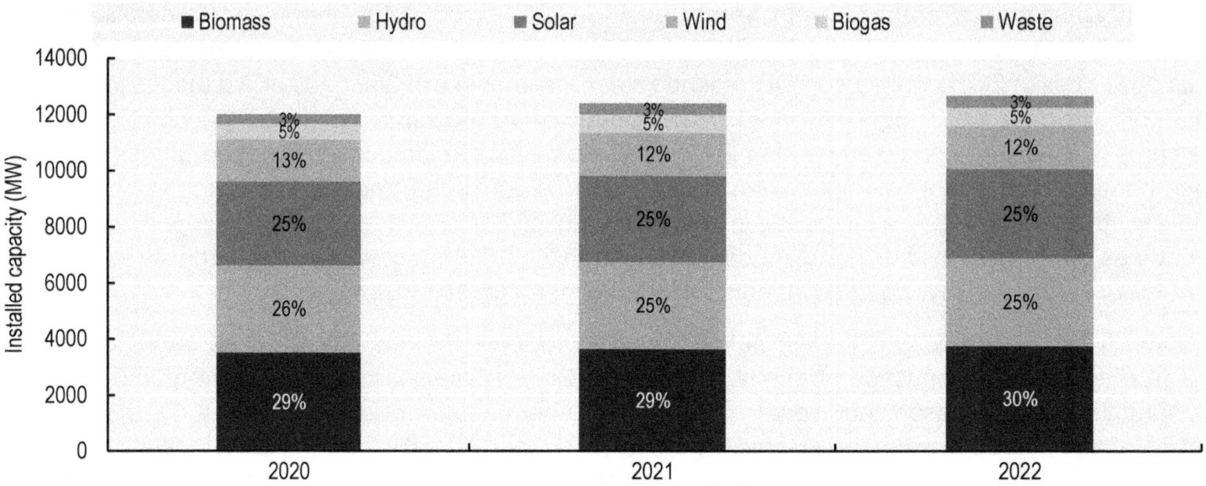


Note: Waste includes municipal solid and industrial waste. Hydro includes both large and small hydro power.
Source: Authors based on data from DEDE (2023[20]), Renewable Energy Performance, https://www.dede.go.th/articles?id=450&menu_id=1.

StatLink https://stat.link/gifx08

### *Thailand electricity pricing*

Electricity in Thailand benefits from a national uniform tariff policy and cross-subsidisation for certain types of user groups (Sirasoontorn and Koomsup, 2017[21]). Residential electricity tariffs range between 2.4 and 4.2 Thai Baht (THB) per kWh (0.06 – 0.11 USD/kWh), which need to be added to a monthly service charge of 8.2 to 38.2 THB/month (0.22 – 1.04 USD/month). Low-income households can have access to electricity subsidies if they exceed 150 kWh per month (SIPET, 2024[22]). On average, Thai households pay between 1.1% and 3.7% of their income on electricity, which is relatively low when compared to other ASEAN countries.

Electricity prices in Thailand are based on two components: a base rate and a variable tariff (Ft rate). The former is the fixed costs of generating electricity and the latter is flexible costs taking into account the variability in fuel and other costs and reviewed by the ERC every four months. Increases in fossil fuel prices over the past two years have been reflected onto consumers through a higher Ft rate (The Diplomat, 2023[23]). For instance, in the beginning of 2022, electricity prices increased by 4.6% as a result of the war in Ukraine (ESCAP, 2022[24]) and averaged 4.18 baht (USD 0.12) per kWh throughout 2022 (Kasikorn Research Center, 2022[25]). Long-term gas import contracts that are on the basis of take or pay from Malaysia and Myanmar alleviate concerns about increase in electricity prices due to the upward trend in fossil fuel prices, coupled with the reduction in subsidised electricity prices. Higher electricity prices would have an impact on competitiveness of businesses and the welfare of the population. Recent analysis estimates that every 1% increase in average electricity prices in Thailand increased the average cost of business by about 0.02% in 2022-2023, when electricity costs for some sectors (e.g. textile and hospitality) represented more than 10% of the total business costs (Kasikorn Research Center, 2022[25]).

### *Electricity supply and demand profile, and grid infrastructure*

Thailand consumed a total of 197 terawatt-hours (TWh) of electricity annually in 2022 (EPPO, 2024[13]). An additional 17 TWh per year was for auxiliary uses in power plants and related to losses in the transmission and distribution grids. Consumption by industry and buildings is roughly on par, as they collectively consumed a total of 182 TWh of electricity.

In Thailand, electricity demand is affected by variations in seasonal changes, which have an impact on industry sectors like food and tobacco as well as in the buildings sector. The summer season experiences a higher electricity load than the wet season due to higher cooling demand (IEA, 2023[8]). There are three peak demands throughout the day where evening peak is higher than the morning and afternoon peaks.

Thailand's transmission grid that connects multiple supply and demand centres ensures a secure and reliable operation of the power system (OECD/IEA, 2018[26]) (Figure 1.10). So far it has served as a major source of flexibility for the power system, particularly as solar and wind energy penetration has been increasing over the past two decades. Other sources of flexibility have been the natural gas-based power plants and hydropower. Additionally, Thailand shares large transmission interconnections with its neighbours, including Myanmar in the west, the Lao People's Democratic Republic and Cambodia in the east, and Malaysia in the south. An important asset for Thailand's power system flexibility is the single 1-gigawatt (GW) size (4 x 250 MW) pumped hydro storage plant in Lam Takhong. The plant located in northeast Thailand represents a quarter of the country's total installed hydropower capacity and is the largest plant in the Southeast Asia region.

While Thailand's power system has latent flexibility and a high reserve margin, as the share of renewable energy increases, higher system flexibility will be required. Results from an IEA study suggest that 15% share of variable renewable energy in the power system can be integrated by 2030 with no additional technical and contractual feasibility measures (IEA, 2021[27]). However, barriers concerning power and fuel procurement often prevent that flexibility from being accessed. IEA analysis also shows that Thailand could pursue a full suite of flexibility options, including energy storage, flexible power plants, investments to enhance the grid infrastructure and demand-side responses. For example, demand-side management programs applied to buildings cooling loads can have a key role to improve the security of the power grid (Mugnini, Polonara and Arteconi, 2021[28]). Moreover, greater flexibility could be achieved by renegotiating or converting contracts to reduce contractual barriers resulting from take-or-pay fuel supply contracts (IEA, 2023[8]). Better management of small-scale and distributed renewable power system can enhance the potential to provide flexibility within the energy system, helping to balance supply and demand and enhance overall reliability and efficiency.

**Figure 1.10. An overview of Thailand's main transmission system**

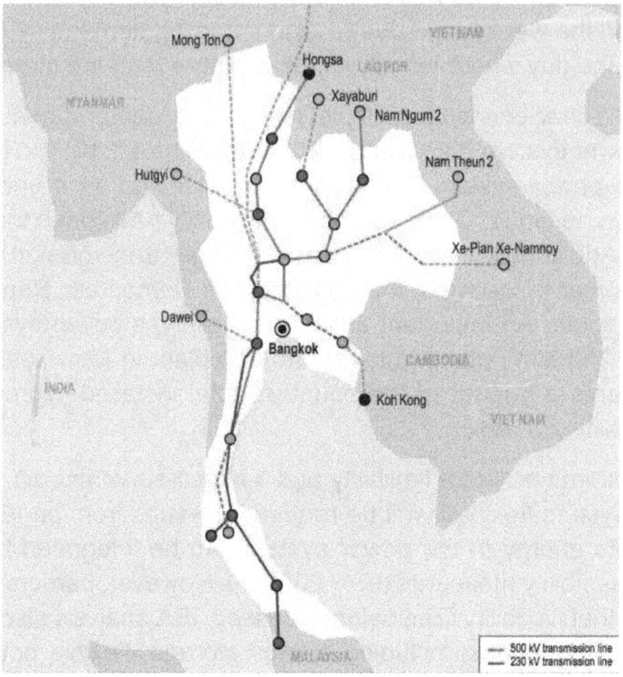


Source: OECD/IEA (2018[26]), Thailand Renewable Grid Integration Assessment, https://iea.blob.core.windows.net/assets/c41cd30d-5f69-4b12-9502-3e7caaca294e/Partner_Country_Series_Thailand_Grid_Renewable_Integration_Assessement.pdf.

## Renewable energy finance and investment landscape in Thailand

### *Policies and incentives promoting renewable energy investment*

The Government of Thailand has been a key driver of the country's renewable energy development. The government's incentives, such as tax exemptions and higher tariffs for electricity generated from renewable sources, significantly contributed to attracting private sources of financing (domestic and international).

Since 2006, Thailand has put in place a suite of feed-in-tariff (FiT) schemes to boost the development of renewable energy in its electricity sector. The first incentive scheme was called the "adder", a feed-in premium, whereby for every kWh of electricity produced, the power producer received an adder rate on top of the utility electricity price for 7-10 years from the Commercial Operation Date (COD) depending on renewable energy type. The adder rates varied depending on the installed capacity of the SPPs or VSPPs and the type of renewable power plant. The scheme was put into effect in 2011 and stopped in 2014 for new projects. With declining costs across various renewable energy technologies, especially for solar installations, in 2015, the government replaced the "adder" with a competitive bidding FiT set as the ceiling price. Thailand's FiT for solar PV decreased continuously from 11.50 baht/kWh (normal tariff at 3.50 baht/kWh plus the "adder" at 8 baht/kWh) in 2006 to 4.16 baht/kWh in 2016 as a result of the rapid global decline in the price of photovoltaic (PV) systems and changing market conditions (Sagulpongmalee, Therdyothin and Nathakaranakule, 2019[29]). In 2022, Thailand introduced a new quota of 5 GW under the FiT scheme for the period between 2022 and 2030 (Watson Farley & Williams, 2022[30]). This quota is exclusively for ground-mounted solar, wind power, battery storage and biogas from wastewater and waste. Further details on the FiT programme for small-scale renewables can be found in Chapter 3.

In addition to the FiT scheme, the Board of Investment (BOI) provides investment incentives for renewable energy and energy efficiency projects. These include a wide range of incentives such as up to eight years of corporate income tax exemptions, import duty exemptions for machinery and raw materials used in research and development (R&D), an immigration fast track for foreign workers, and permission to own land (Thailand Board of Investment, 2023[31]).

The incentive measures discussed above contributed to the increase in and acceleration of solar deployment in Thailand and to the decrease in solar PV total installed costs. In Thailand, the solar PV total installed cost in the residential and commercial sectors decreased by almost 67%, from 4 065 USD/kW in 2013 to 1 354 in 2020 (IRENA, 2021[32]).

In 2022, Thailand introduced the concept of the Utility Green Tariff (UGT) scheme to allow power consumers to purchase renewable electricity at a special utility tariff rate. The main objective of the UGT programme is to promote the development of renewable energy power plants while ensuring that the general public is not overburdened. The Energy Regulatory Commission (ERC) has proposed two price structures for the UGT program, one for existing renewable energy power plants from unspecified renewable sources, and the other for new or existing plants from specified sources. These price structures and related criteria were released for public hearing in January 2024.

### *Sustainable finance initiatives*

Thailand's financial sector and banking system appear sound and mature, with local commercial banks showing high capital adequacy and high liquidity coverage ratios (OECD, 2023[1]). However, private debt remains relatively high, which can weigh on domestic demand especially with the current context of high interest rates. Moreover, current licensing requirements remain burdensome for some businesses to access financing. Easing license requirements and assisting businesses with compliance would ease their access to loans.

Thailand made significant progress on sustainable finance and investment, with a growing local green and sustainable bond market and increasing investor awareness towards climate- and sustainability-related risks and opportunities (ADB, 2022[33]). Outstanding green, social, and sustainability bonds (GSS) in Thailand were worth United States Dollars (USD) 9.5 billion as of 2022, with private issuances leading the way and green bonds being the most common bond type (ESCAP, 2023[34]). Most GSS bonds were issued in Thai baht, showing the maturity of the local currency bond market. However, the GSS bond market in Thailand remains relatively small, compared to the standard local currency bond market (ADB, 2022[35]).

Thailand was one of the first countries in the world to issue a sustainability bond. In 2020, the Government of Thailand issued a 15-year bond to finance a range of green and social projects, which paved the way for a follow-up sovereign issuance, bringing the total amount raised to THB 247 billion (approximately USD 7.1 billion) as of 2022 (Ministry of Finance of Thailand, 2022[36]). Of the first sustainability bond proceeds, only 17% was allocated to green projects (mainly for clean transportation), while the rest was used to support COVID-19 recovery packages. The sustainability bond issuance was based on the Sustainable Financing Framework, which the Government of Thailand developed to issue green, social and sustainability financing instruments (Kingdom of Thailand, 2020[37]).

In 2019, the Thai Sustainable Finance Working Group was established within the "Three Regulators Steering Committee", composed of representatives of the Bank of Thailand (BOT), the Securities and Exchange Commission (SEC), the Office of Insurance Commission (OIC) and the Ministry of Finance (MOF). The Working Group has the mandate to foster and monitor a culture of sustainable finance within the Thai financial sector. In 2022, the Working Group laid down the key priorities on sustainable finance for Thailand in its document titled "Sustainable Finance Initiatives for Thailand" (Thailand Working Group on Sustainable Finance, 2021[38]), which include:

- **Developing a practical national sustainable finance taxonomy** to promote inward investment flows across Thailand's financial subsectors from domestic and international investors and support better informed and more efficient decision-making and responses to investment opportunities that contribute to achieving national sustainable development objectives.

- **Improving the data environment** to encourage the flourishing of new products and markets which meet the sustainability criteria of a wider and more diverse range of investors and position Thailand against other sustainable finance centres.
- **Implementing effective incentives** to facilitate and promotes policies and mechanisms that incentivise financial flows towards sustainable development, including fiscal and prudential policies as well as viable non-financial approaches.
- **Creating demand-led products and services** in order to build real underlying demand for sustainable products and services.
- **Building human capital** to improve the quality of day-to-day interactions among relevant stakeholders by enhancing the skills, competences, values, and behaviours of the management and staff of the financial sector.

In recent years, financial authorities in Thailand have developed a wide range of sustainable finance policies, guidelines and codes, in addition to industry guidelines and platforms developed by industry associations. For example:

- The Securities and Exchange Commission of Thailand (SEC) developed Sustainability Reporting Guidelines, which are mandatory for publicly listed companies, as well as Green, Social and Sustainability (GSS) Bond Issuance Guidelines, and Guidelines on Management and Disclosure of Climate-related Risk by Asset Managers.
- In 2019, the Thai Bankers' Association (TBA) developed the Sustainable Banking Guidelines for Responsible Lending, which were adopted by all TBA members.
- The Stock Exchange of Thailand (SET) also promotes the disclosure of environmental, social and governance (ESG) data of the Thai listed companies, including sustainability assessment results and a list of sustainable stocks.
- In 2019, the SEC waived approval and filing fees for GSS bonds issued between May 2019 and May 2025.
- The SEC also launched the Investment Governance Code, which contains guidance reflecting internationally accepted standards for responsible investment.
- In addition, the SEC and the Thai Bond Market Association collaborated to design and launch the Sustainable Information Platform to serve as an information centre for GSS bonds.
- Moreover, in 2022, the SEC issued regulations for the disclosure standards of the Sustainable and Responsible Investing Fund to widen access for retail investors.
- In 2023, The Association of Southeast Asian Nations (ASEAN) stock exchanges, including Thailand's, agreed on a common set of ESG metrics to encourage the disclosure of consistent ESG information across the region.
- In the insurance space, the Office of the Insurance Commission (OIC) is also promoting good ESG practices among insurance companies.

In addition, in 2023, the BOT issued a policy statement on "Internalizing Environmental and Climate Change Aspects into Financial Institution Business". The policy statement contains expectations for financial institutions to systematically assess the environmental impact both in terms of opportunities and risks in the decision-making process and operations, governance, strategy, risk management as well as disclosure. The BOT requested financial institutions to apply this policy statement in accordance with their organisational structure and size, as well as the materiality of environmental risks on their business (Bank of Thailand, 2023[39]).

Most notably, in 2023, the Thailand Taxonomy Board, composed of representatives of the BOT and the SEC, developed the first phase of a transition taxonomy to classify economic activities and facilitate the development of green, transition and sustainable finance products (Thailand Taxonomy Board, 2023[40]).

The Thai taxonomy is designed to cover six environmental objectives: climate change mitigation; climate change adaptation; sustainable use and protection of marine and water resources; protection and restoration of biodiversity and ecosystems; pollution prevention and control; and resource resilience and transition to a circular economy. The first version of the Thai Taxonomy developed screening criteria and thresholds only for the climate change mitigation objective, as a start, and it incorporates the principles of Do No Significant Harm (DNSH) to the other five objectives, i.e. activities that are in line with mitigation thresholds shall comply with generic DNSH requirements to ensure no damage to the other environmental objectives. Any activity eligible for the Thai taxonomy also needs to ensure that it does not generate a negative social impact and observes minimum social safeguards, based on a list of local and international policies and principles.

The Thai taxonomy employs a traffic light system that distinguishes between green, amber (transitional) and red activities depending on their contribution to mitigation objectives. As part of the first phase, the Thai taxonomy established green, amber and red quantitative thresholds to classify activities in the energy and transportation sectors. All thresholds are subject to review every three to five years in accordance with new data and technological development. The second phase of the Thai taxonomy – currently under development – will cover manufacturing, agriculture, real estate, construction and waste (Thailand Taxonomy Board, 2023[41]).

The green threshold of energy activities in the Thailand Taxonomy has been established as 100 grams of carbon dioxide equivalent per kilowatt-hour of electricity generated ($gCO_2e/kWh$) until 2040 and will decline to 50 $gCO_2e/kWh$ afterwards. This threshold is in line with international good practice, such as the Climate Bonds Initiative (CBI) and European Union (EU) taxonomies. The amber threshold is applicable to "transitional" activities, i.e. those that have not yet achieved net-zero emissions but are on a credible decarbonisation pathway. The amber threshold is applicable only to existing activities (e.g. retrofits of existing assets), whereas new activities are supposed to adopt purely green technologies. 2040 is established as a sunset date for the amber threshold. After this date, all activities need to achieve the green threshold. The sunset date may be subject to change based on new technological and scientific developments. The amber thresholds are based on Thailand's NDC pathways and the Long-Term Low Greenhouse Gas Emission Development Strategy. Table 1.1 below summarises the main thresholds for energy activities under the first phase of the Thai taxonomy, but it is worth noting that the taxonomy includes additional quantitative and qualitative thresholds for every energy activity.

### Table 1.1. Summary thresholds for energy sector activities according to the Thai taxonomy (gCO2e/kWh)

| | 2022-2025 | 2026-2030 | 2031-2035 | 2036-2040 | 2041-2045 | 2046-2050 |
|---|---|---|---|---|---|---|
| **Green Activities** | 100 | 100 | 100 | 100 | 50 | |
| **Amber Activities** | 381 | 225 | 191 | 148 | N/A | N/A |
| **Red Activities** | >381g | >225g | >191g | >148g | >50g | >50g |

Note: After 2040, the sunset date, the amber classification is no longer available (amber activities will have reached the green threshold by then).
Source: Thailand Taxonomy Board (2023[40]), Thailand Taxonomy Phase I, https://www.bot.or.th/content/dam/bot/financial-innovation/sustainable-finance/green/Thailand_Taxonomy_Phase1_Jun2023_EN.pdf.

Renewable energy activities (solar, wind, marine energy generation) all classify as green, whereas hydropower, geothermal, bioenergy generation, energy production from natural gas and renewable non-fossil gaseous and liquid fuels (including hydrogen), and co-generation of heating and cooling using renewables can be classified as either green, amber or red, depending on their mitigation performance. Energy efficiency measures are covered under these energy sector criteria by means of establishing thresholds using emission intensity ($gCO_2$ per unit of production). In order to achieve a certain threshold, an energy activity must reduce its emission intensity, including by implementing measures to improve efficiency as an option.

The Thai Taxonomy is closely aligned with the ASEAN Taxonomy for Sustainable Finance (ASEAN taxonomy), which is a guide designed to promote the development of sustainable finance taxonomies across ASEAN member states (ASEAN Taxonomy Board, 2023[42]). The ASEAN taxonomy allows for both a principle-based assessment and a threshold-based classification of activities with different "tiers" (i.e. levels of performance), to accommodate for differences in levels of development and starting points of ASEAN countries. The ASEAN taxonomy sets technical screening criteria for some priority sectors (electricity, gas, steam and air conditioning (AC) supply). Criteria for other sectors will be developed in subsequent versions of the Taxonomy. Overall, for the energy sector, the green thresholds of the Thai taxonomy are broadly aligned with the ASEAN taxonomy, whereas amber thresholds under the Thai taxonomy are more ambitious than the ASEAN taxonomy.

Feedback from the stakeholder consultation workshops conducted for this report also revealed that while the financial sector has grown accustomed to energy efficiency financing and Thailand's taxonomy has emerged as a significant driver for financial institutions to support green activities, undertaking technical assessments of taxonomy alignment remains complex.

### *Estimated trends on finance and investment for renewable energy in Thailand*

Despite increases in renewable energy investments in Thailand from 2013 until 2017, outstanding policy unpredictability and overcapacity issues might have hindered renewables investments in Thailand until today (IRENA and CPI, 2023[43]). According to data from BloombergNEF (BNEF), Thailand attracted over USD 11 billion of renewable energy investment from 2014 to 2023. In terms of cumulative volume, when compared to other Southeast Asian countries, renewable energy investment in Thailand over the 2014-2023 period are approximately on par to those in the Philippines. Renewable energy investments in Thailand saw a peak in 2017, when they reached over USD 3 billion, and declined since then (Figure 1.11). According to IRENA and the Climate Policy Initiative (CPI), this is partially explained by the overcapacity in the system where the installed capacity exceeded demand by 40%. Additionally, policy uncertainty might have hindered renewable energy investment by the private sector (2023[43]).

**Figure 1.11. Renewable energy investments in selected Southeast Asian countries (2014-2023)**

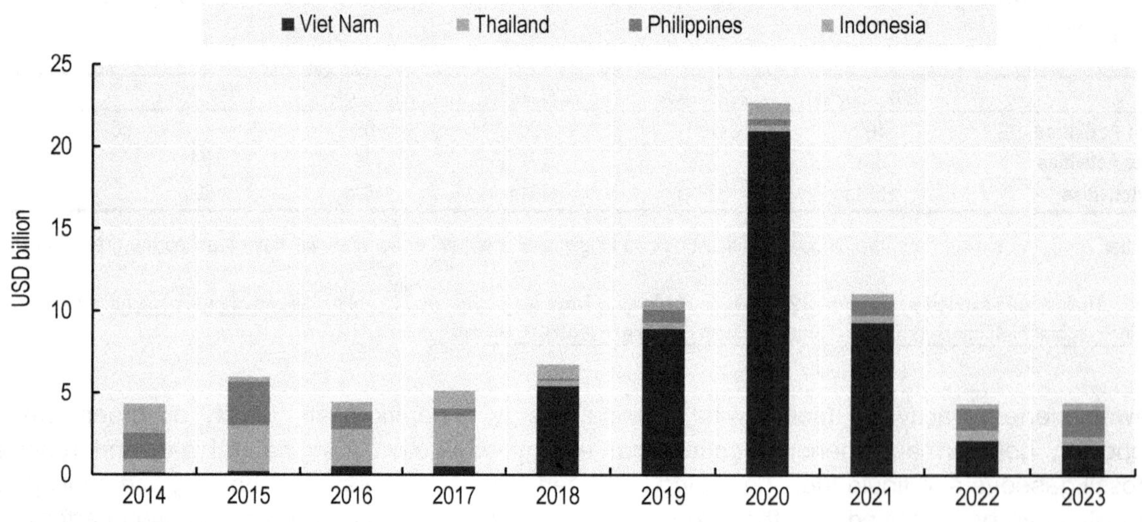


Note: This data includes new investments only.
Source: Authors, based on data on renewable energy investment data from BloombergNEF (BNEF).

### *Domestic public finance for renewable energy and energy efficiency*

The main sources of domestic public finance for clean energy in Thailand include (Frankfurt School - UNEP Collaborating Centre for Climate & Sustainable Energy Finance, 2012[44]; Parliamentary Budget Office, 2022[45]):

- **National budget**: The Thai government has allocated resources for the development of renewable energy in Thailand from its national budget. The budget for renewable energy development is primarily allocated to the Ministry of Energy and, in 2022, it stood at THB 2.7 billion (USD 77.5 million) whereas THB 1.1 billion (USD 32.6 million) was devoted to promoting competitiveness through the promotion of renewable energy (RE), energy efficiency (EE), enhanced energy security and regulating energy prices.
- **Energy Conservation Promotion Fund (ENCON Fund)**: Established under Thailand's Energy Conservation and Promotion Act, this fund has been the Thai government's key financial mechanism for supporting renewable energy and energy efficiency development. A budget of THB 3 billion (USD 99 million) from the ENCON Fund was allocated for the promotion of renewable energy and energy efficiency during 2022 – 2024 to encourage both public and private investments. Various financial instruments including grants, low-cost project debt, and project-level equity have been applied. The ENCON Fund is also the main funding source for the direct subsidies programme for clean energy. The ENCON Fund is split into two main funds (see Figure 1.12):
    - The **Energy Efficiency Revolving Fund (EERF)**: The EERF was initiated in 2003 to provide companies access to low-interest loans for renewable energy and energy efficiency projects, through nine rounds of implementation, running from 2003 until 2019. The EERF provided a low-cost source of funding (0% - 0.5% interest rate) to private Thai banks, who could then on-lend these funds to companies at a lower-than-market interest rate—not higher than 4% (Asia Clean Energy Partners, 2022[46]). The EERF targeted owners of private buildings and factories interested in installing energy efficiency technologies. The EERF disbursed USD 235 million from 2003 to 2012 and mobilised USD 284 million in debt financing from 13 local banks, which resulted in 294 projects mainly involving the replacement of chillers and the installation of biogas facilities (Asian Development Bank, 2022[47]). Funding was eligible for medium size projects with an installed capacity at least 1 MW.
    - The **ESCO Revolving Fund** was established to encourage private investments in viable renewable energy and energy efficiency projects, including through ESCOs (Energy For Environment Foundation, 2011[48]). The fund was implemented during 2008 – 2019 during which a total of THB 1 500 million (USD 46 million) was allocated to two fund managers, i.e. the Energy for Environment Foundation (EforE) and the Energy Conservation Foundation, Thailand (ECFT). During the first two phases, the fund amounting THB 550 million (USD 17 million) was allocated to EforE who financed 63 renewable energy and energy efficiency projects. The ESCO Fund included six financing mechanisms: equity; venture capital; equipment leasing; partial credit guarantees; carbon credit trading; and technical assistance. Venture capital investments are conducted through a sub-fund, the ESCO Venture Capital Fund.
- **Power Development Fund**, established in 2010, aims to enhance the livelihood and quality of life of communities nearby power plants as well as to support the development of Thailand's power sector by providing financing for renewable power projects. In 2022, a budget of THB 341 million (approximately USD 10 million) was allocated to promote RE.

**Figure 1.12. Structure of the Energy Conservation Promotion Fund (ENCON Fund)**

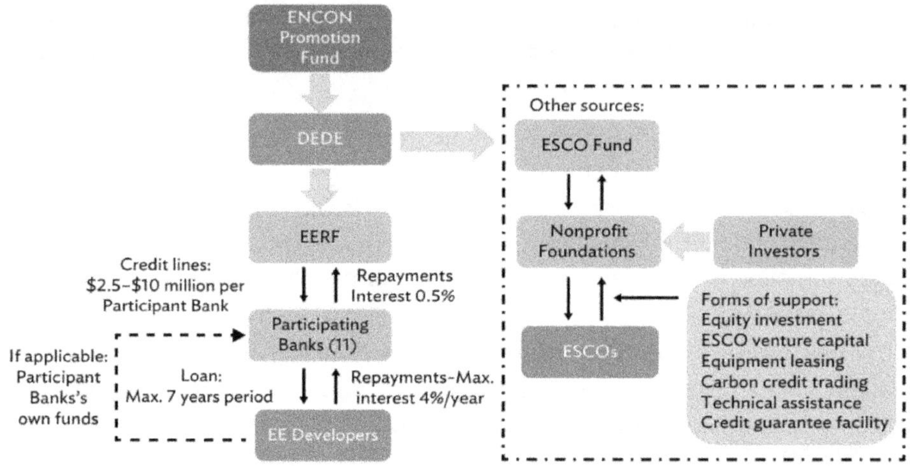


Source: ADB (2022[47]), Financing Clean Energy in Developing Asia—Volume 2, https://dx.doi.org/10.22617/TCS220368-2.

The ENCON Fund has been a major source of subsidies for energy efficiency projects in Thailand. The ENCON Fund's Direct Subsidy Scheme offers grant contributions of 20%, 30% or 40% of the total energy efficiency equipment costs, with the minimum and maximum funding amounts in 2018 being THB 30 000 (USD 928) and THB 1.5 million (USD 46 729), respectively (ACE and GIZ, 2019[49]). The ENCON Fund also has performance-based grants, i.e. financial support determined by the financial savings resulting from energy efficiency measures. This included notably the demand side management (DSM) bidding programme, which provided subsidies based on actual energy savings through a bidding mechanism, whereby proposals with lower-weighted subsidy rates were subsidised first. The ENCON Fund's grant arm also provided tax incentives offering a total of 25% VAT tax exemptions of the purchasing cost of energy-efficient equipment/machinery, until 2018 (ACE and GIZ, 2019[49]).

### *International development finance for renewable energy*

International development finance has been instrumental to mobilise renewable energy investments in Thailand. Official development finance[1] for energy generation from renewables and mitigation-related energy policy in Thailand is on an upward trend since 2019 and reached a peak of over USD 121 million in 2021 (Figure 1.13). Private finance mobilised by official development finance for the same sectors has been declining since 2019 and stood at USD 46 million in 2021.

A wide range of bilateral and multilateral development finance providers are active in Thailand. Japan, Germany, the United States, Denmark and Canada are among the most active bilateral development finance providers for renewable energy in the country, and the Asian Development Bank (ADB), the International Bank for Reconstruction and Development (IBRD) and the Global Environment Facility (GEF) are the key multilateral providers.

**Figure 1.13. Development finance and private finance mobilised for renewable energy in Thailand**

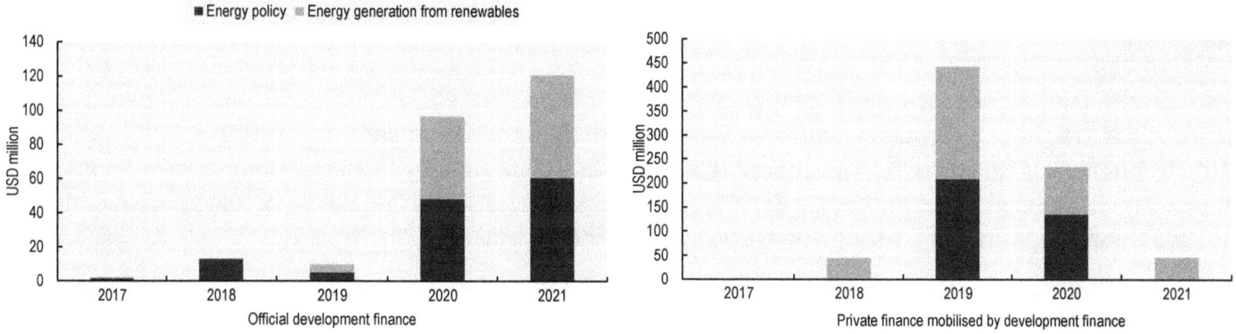


Note: Official development finance data presented include both Official Development Assistance (ODA) and Other Official Flows (OOF), provided by both bilateral and multilateral providers. OOF include: grants to developing countries for representational or essentially commercial purposes; official bilateral transactions intended to promote development, but having a grant element of less than 25%; and official bilateral transactions, whatever their grant element, that are primarily export-facilitating in purpose (OECD, 2024[50]).
Source: OECD (2024[51]), Creditor Reporting System (CRS) database, OECD Data Explorer • Mobilised private finance for development.

StatLink https://stat.link/i6xvs3

*Private financing for green infrastructure and sustainable energy*

Private financing plays a crucial role in the development of renewable energy projects in Thailand, as government funding alone is not sufficient to meet the country's renewable energy targets. Private financing for renewable energy in Thailand takes several forms, including:

- **Project financing**: This involves raising capital for a specific renewable energy project. The financing is typically structured on a non-recourse or limited recourse basis, whereby the lender can claim only the project's assets with no further claim against the borrower's other assets in the event of default (non-recourse) or can have limited claims beyond the project's assets under specific conditions (limited recourse).
- **Corporate financing**: This involves raising capital for a renewable energy company, which can use the funds to develop multiple projects with activities reflected on the sponsor's balance sheet. Unlike project finance, which is confined to specific projects, corporate finance deals with broader financial strategies of an entire organisation.
- **Crowdfunding**: This involves raising small amounts of money from a large number of people through an online platform. Crowdfunding is a relatively new form of financing for renewable energy projects in Thailand.

Typical private financial instruments used for clean energy in Thailand include:

- **Green bonds**: they are any type of bond instrument where the proceeds or an equivalent amount will be exclusively applied to finance or re-finance, in part or in full, new and/or existing eligible green projects (ICMA, 2021[52]). Unlike plain vanilla bonds, the proceeds from green bonds are exclusively used to finance or refinance projects with clear environmental benefits. In Thailand, green bonds are becoming an increasingly popular way to finance renewable energy projects.
- **Green loans**: they are any type of loan instruments and/or contingent facilities (such as bonding lines, guarantee lines or letters of credit) made available exclusively to finance, re-finance or guarantee, in whole or in part, new and/or existing green projects (LMA, 2023[53]).

The standards used to issue a green bond or extend a green loan in Thailand include the Green Bond Principles issued by the International Capital Market Association (ICMA), the ASEAN Green Bond Standards issued by the ASEAN Capital Markets Forum and the Green Loan Principles issued by the Loan

Market Association (LMA) in 2020 (Thailand Working Group on Sustainable Finance, 2021[38]). Thailand's taxonomy can be used to identify eligible projects that can be financed through green bonds or loans (further details on the Thai taxonomy are elaborated later in this chapter) (Thailand Taxonomy Board, 2023[41]).

Thai commercial banks are increasingly setting ambitious targets to promote green financing and sustainability strategies. Bank of Ayudhya, Government Savings Bank and Kasikornbank are signatories of the Principles for Responsible Investment (UNEP FI, 2024[54]). Among Thailand's largest and most active financial institutions in clean energy include the following list and Table 1.2 below provides an overview of the main loan programmes for renewable energy and energy efficiency in Thailand:

- **Kasikornbank (KBank)** is considered one of the green financing leaders in Thailand, with dedicated units working on renewable energy and energy efficiency projects. KBank is committed to a net-zero target for its operations by 2030[2] and to a goal of allocating at least THB 100-200 billion (USD 3-6 billion) in sustainable financing and investment by 2030 (KBank, 2022[55]). To achieve its sustainability goals, KBank offers several loan schemes for renewable energy and energy efficiency projects, such as solar energy, lighting solutions and energy savings, with favourable interest rates.
- **Siam Commercial Bank (SCB)** has commitments to sustainability targets under three pillars – sustainable finance, creating social impact, and a better environmental future. Its sustainable finance targets related to clean energy include: (i) funding and raising THB 53 000 million (USD 1523 million) to support the Sustainable Development Goals (SDGs); (ii) developing at least 100 Environmental, Social, and Governance (ESG) financial products; and (iii) integrating ESG considerations as part of credit and advisory policies and processes (Siam Commercial Bank, 2021[56]).
- **Bangkok Bank (BBL)** has sustainable finance-related targets, such as providing eco-friendly loans and integrating EGS issues into its policies and credit approval processes. The Bank already offers a range of sustainable finance products, such as green loans (especially for RE), sustainability-linked loans, sustainable bonds and sustainable mutual funds (Bangkok Bank, 2022[57]).

Several commercial banks in other countries in the region are also active in financing and supporting clean energy projects in Thailand. One example is the Singaporean bank UOB, which in 2021 launched a financing platform to drive the development and adoption of energy efficiency projects for buildings in Singapore, Malaysia, Thailand and Indonesia (Box 1.1 below).

## Table 1.2. Overview of loan programmes for clean energy offered by Thai banks

| Bank | Loan programme | Objective | Eligibility criteria |
|---|---|---|---|
| Kasikorn Bank (KBank) | K-Energy Saving Guarantee Program | Implementing energy-saving solutions, guaranteed and provided by Energy Service Companies (ESCOs). | - Energy cost (fuel and electricity) > THB 500 000 (USD 14 368) per month.<br>- Services provided by certified ESCO. |
| | K–Energy Saving Guarantee Program (Solar Rooftop) | Installing solar rooftop PV. | - Having owned and conducted businesses for at least three years.<br>- Aiming to reduce the cost of electricity or sell solar electricity back to the grid.<br>- Guaranteed energy savings. |
| | K-Energy Saving Loan under the Revolving fund for energy conservation | Supporting projects with energy savings, with DEDE support. | - Projects certified by DEDE and in line with the Energy Promotion Act<br>- Maximum loan term of 7 years. |

| | | | |
|---|---|---|---|
| | Top-Up Loan for Energy Saving (Lighting Solution) | Implementing energy-efficient lighting solutions, guaranteed and provided by ESCOs. | - Entrepreneurs who use more than 12 hours of electrical lighting per day.<br>- Projects that aim to manage energy efficiency with guaranteed energy savings or a warranty.<br>- The supplier that conducts the project must be an ESCO, approved by the bank.<br>- The project and customer must follow the bank's requirements. |
| **Siam Commercial Bank (SCB)** | SME Go Green | Promoting energy savings and other green businesses. | - Having operated businesses for more than four years.<br>- Annual business sales between THB 75-500 million (USD 2 – 14 million). |
| | Green Forward | Promoting energy efficiency, pollution control and green/sustainable businesses. | - Having operated businesses for more than three years.<br>- Annual business sales of no more than THB 75 million (USD 2 million). |
| **Bangkok Bank (BBL)** | Bualuang Green Loan | To support MSMEs in investing in environmentally friendly solutions. | Debt-to-equity ratio no more than 3. |
| **Krungthai Bank (KTB)** | Environmental Credits (loans) | Supporting MSMEs to invest in waste treatment systems. | - Equipment replacement in air/waste/wastewater control system, up to THB 50 million (USD 1.5 million).<br>- Fermentation plant installation (to produce fertilizer), up to 20 tonnes per day.<br>- Wastewater management system, up to 100 m per day. |
| | Loans for solar rooftop systems | Supporting solar rooftop investments. | N/A |
| **Bank of Ayudhya (Krungsri)** | Solar Roof Lending Program | Supporting entrepreneurs wishing to install a solar roof. | N/A |
| **Exim Bank** | Solar Orchestra by BIZ Transformation Loan | Supporting solar rooftop investment. | - Having businesses operated more than eight years with net positive profits for over two years.<br>- Only for industries that are related to export activities. |
| | EXIM Kill Bill by Biz Transformation | Supporting entrepreneurs' replacement of chillers and use of energy saving equipment, with minimum interest rate of 2.00% per annum and a maximum loan tenor up to 7 years. | N/A |
| **SME Development Bank** | Bio-Circular-Green Economy (BCG) Loan | Supporting BCG businesses. | Having operated businesses more than three years. |
| **Government Savings Bank (GSB)** | GSB for BCG economy | Supporting BCG businesses, such as biodiesel, reusing, recycling, solar rooftop, etc. | Only for BCG businesses. |

Source: Authors

### Box 1.1. U-Energy: An integrated financing platform to drive energy efficiency in Thailand

**Building owners, energy service companies and homeowners are expected to reduce an average of 20% in energy consumption by tapping UOB's green financing for energy efficiency projects.**

In 2022, UOB Thailand launched U-Energy, the first integrated financing platform in Asia, to drive the development and adoption of energy efficiency projects for commercial and residential buildings in the country. With U-Energy, the Bank will help businesses and homeowners save on electricity bills, cut carbon emissions and achieve their sustainability goals.

At launch, the U-Energy platform will have eight energy service companies that customers can tap for energy efficiency projects. These U-Energy partners can support common energy efficiency projects such as improving chiller and air conditioning efficiency, installing solar panels on rooftops, switching to Light Emitting Diode (LED) lights, optimising energy and power management systems and changing the building facade to reflect direct sunlight to reduce heat absorption, as well as replacing elevators with energy-regeneration technology. On average, it is expected that ESCOs on the U-Energy platform will help customers cut down energy consumption by an average of 20%.

The platform offers green finance products with favourable and flexible terms and conditions. Commercial and industrial building owners can opt for a direct purchase of the energy-efficient equipment or system with UOB Thailand's green financing. Under this scheme, building owners may obtain a loan of up to THB 250 million (USD 7 million) with a maximum seven-year loan facility, subject to optimal equipment and system sizing by the U-Energy partners. To enable greater speed to market, loan applications from building owners who are existing UOB Thailand customers will be put on a fast-track approval process. Alternatively, building owners can take up the "energy-as-a-service" model where UOB will provide green loans to U-Energy partners at no upfront cost to building owners.

For homeowners, UOB Thailand offers a zero per cent interest instalment plan of up to 36 months when UOB credit cards are used as the mode of payment for their energy efficiency retrofitting projects.

Source: UOB (2022[58]), UOB Thailand launches U-Energy, Asia's first integrated financing platform to drive energy efficiency, https://www.uob.co.th/investor-en/news/press-news/2022/news-23Mar2022.page.

Several institutions in Thailand have successfully issued green bonds to finance green infrastructure investment, particularly for transport and clean energy. As shown in Figure 1.14 below, green bond issuance in Thailand has been on an upward trend since 2018. Thailand is one of the countries with the highest volume of green bond issuance in Southeast Asia, following Singapore and Indonesia. According to data from Climate Bonds Initiative (CBI), a total of 80 green bonds worth USD 6.2 billion was issued from 2018 to 2023 in Thailand, with the vast majority (85%) being issued in local currency (THB) and the rest in United States dollars or euros, showing high liquidity of the local currency green bond market in Thailand. In 2023, green bond issuances in Thailand were worth USD 1.9 billion. According to data from the Thai Bond Market Association, green bonds in Thailand were mainly issued in the form of long-term corporate bonds (Thai Bond Market Association, 2023[59]). Clean energy and transport accounted for most of the green bond proceeds' allocation (Asian Development Bank, 2022[60]).

**Figure 1.14. Green bond issuances in selected Southeast Asian countries (2018-2023)**

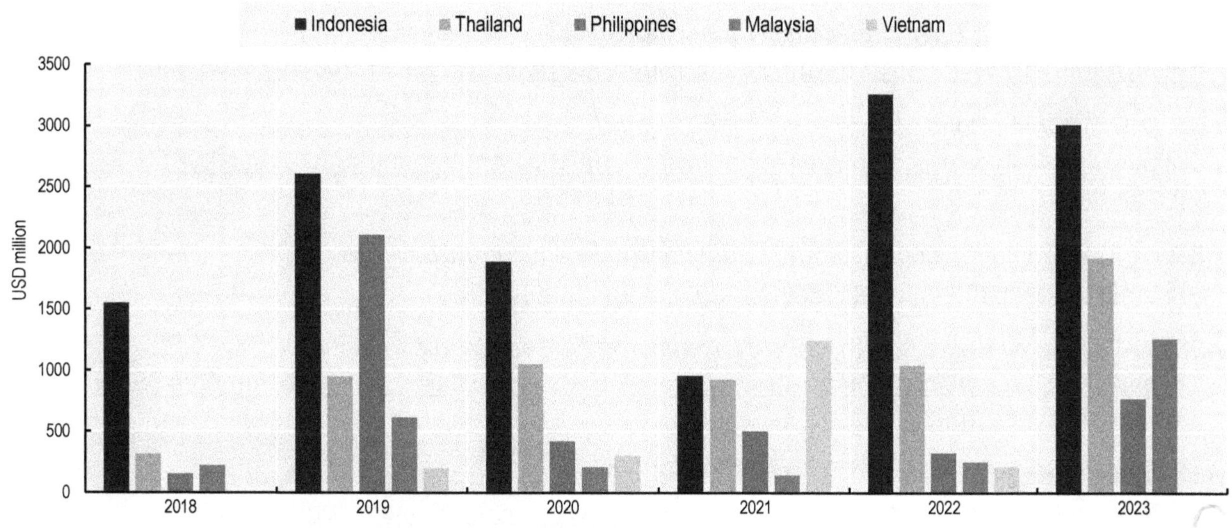


Source: Authors, based on data provided by the Climate Bonds Initiative (CBI).

## References


ACE and GIZ (2019), *Energy Efficiency Financing Guideline in Thailand*, https://agep.aseanenergy.org/wp-content/uploads/2019/05/EEF-Guideline-in-Thailand.pdf. [49]

ADB (2022), *Green Bond Market Survey for Thailand*, https://www.adb.org/sites/default/files/publication/801601/green-bond-market-survey-thailand.pdf. [35]

ADB (2022), *Promoting Local Currency Sustainable Finance in ASEAN+3*, https://www.climatebonds.net/files/reports/asean3_report.pdf. [33]

ASEAN Taxonomy Board (2023), *ASEAN Taxonomy for Sustainable Finance*, https://www.bot.or.th/content/dam/bot/financial-innovation/sustainable-finance/green/ASEAN-Taxonomy_ver2_202306.pdf. [42]

Asia Clean Energy Partners (2022), *Thai Financial Institutions Open A New Era for Energy Efficiency Financing in Thailand*, https://www.asiacleanenergypartners.com/post/thai-financial-institutions-open-a-new-era-for-energy-efficiency-financing-in-thailand. [46]

Asian Development Bank (2022), *Financing Clean Energy in Developing Asia—Volume 2*, Asian Development Bank, Manila, Philippines, https://doi.org/10.22617/tcs220368-2. [47]

Asian Development Bank (2022), *Green Infrastructure Investment Opportunities:*, Asian Development Bank, Manila, Philippines, https://doi.org/10.22617/TCS210495-2. [60]

Bangkok Bank (2022), *Sustainability Report 2022*, https://www.bangkokbank.com/-/media/files/investor-relations/sustainability-report/2022/sr2022_en.pdf. [57]

Bank of Thailand (2023), *Policy Statement of the Bank of Thailand Re: Internalizing Environmental and Climate Change Aspects into Financial Institution Business*, https://www.bot.or.th/content/dam/bot/fipcs/documents/FPG/2566/EngPDF/25660028.pdf. [39]

CASE for Southeast Asia (2022), *Towards a collective vision of Thai energy transition: National long-term scenarios and socioeconomic implications*, Clean, Affordable and Secure Energy (CASE) for Southeast Asia, https://newclimate.org/sites/default/files/2022-11/2022-11-08_th_ltes_-_full_report.pdf. [4]

DEDE (2024), *Biomass Database Potential in Thailand*, https://weben.dede.go.th/webmax/content/biomass-database-potential-thailand. [18]

DEDE (2023), *Performance on Alternative Energy Policy*, https://www.dede.go.th/articles?id=450&menu_id=1. [20]

Enerdata (2023), *Mitsubishi commissions the 2nd turbine of a 2.65 GW CCGT project in Thailand*, https://www.enerdata.net/publications/daily-energy-news/mitsubishi-commissions-2nd-turbine-265-gw-ccgt-project-thailand.html. [14]

Energy For Environment Foundation (2011), *ESCO Revolving Fund*, http://www.efe.or.th/escofund.php?task=&sessid=&lang=en. [48]

EPPO (2024), *Electricity*, https://www.eppo.go.th/epposite/index.php/th/energy-information/static-energy/static-electricity?orders[publishUp]=publishUp&issearch=1. [13]

EPPO (2024), *Electricity by EPPO*, https://public.tableau.com/app/profile/epposite/viz/5_16516658875330/sheet0. [9]

EPPO (2024), *Energy overview*, https://www.eppo.go.th/epposite/index.php/th/energy-information/static-energy/summery-energy. [12]

EPPO (2021), *National Energy Plan*, https://www.eppo.go.th/epposite/index.php/th/petroleum/oil/link-doeb/item/17093-nep. [6]

EPPO (2017), *Public - Private Partnership in Energy Sector*, https://slidetodoc.com/asean-summit-publicprivate-partnership-public-private-partnership-in/. [11]

ESCAP (2023), *Sustainable Finance: Bridging the Gap in Asia and the Pacific*, https://www.unescap.org/kp/2023/sustainable-finance-bridging-gap-asia-and-pacific. [34]

ESCAP (2022), *The role of power system connectivity in times of high energy prices*, https://www.unescap.org/blog/role-power-system-connectivity-times-high-energy-prices. [24]

Frankfurt School - UNEP Collaborating Centre for Climate & Sustainable Energy Finance (2012), *Case Study: The Energy Efficiency Revolving Fund*, https://unfccc.int/files/cooperation_and_support/financial_mechanism/standing_committee/application/pdf/fs-unep_thai_eerf_final_2012.pdf. [44]

ICMA (2021), *Green Bond Principles*, https://www.icmagroup.org/assets/documents/Sustainable-finance/2022-updates/Green-Bond-Principles-June-2022-060623.pdf. [52]

IEA (2023), *Thailand's Clean Electricity Transition*, https://iea.blob.core.windows.net/assets/dd5b10b2-b655-4c7d-8c09-d3d7efe6bd50/ThailandsCleanElectricityTransition.pdf. [8]

IEA (2021), *Thailand Power System Flexibility Study*, https://iea.blob.core.windows.net/assets/19f9554b-f40c-46ff-b7f5-78f1456057a9/ThailandPowerSystemFlexibilityStudy.pdf. [27]

IEA (2018), *Thailand Renewable Grid Integration Assessment*, https://iea.blob.core.windows.net/assets/c41cd30d-5f69-4b12-9502-3e7caaca294e/Partner_Country_Series_Thailand_Grid_Renewable_Integration_Assessement.pdf. [15]

IRENA (2021), *Renewable Power Generation Costs in 2020*, https://www.irena.org/-/media/Files/IRENA/Agency/Publication/2021/Jun/IRENA_Power_Generation_Costs_2020.pdf?rev=c9e8dfcd1b2048e2b4d30fef671a5b84. [32]

IRENA (2017), *Renewable Energy Outlook Thailand*, https://www.irena.org/-/media/files/irena/agency/publication/2017/nov/irena_outlook_thailand_2017.pdf. [16]

IRENA and CPI (2023), *Global landscape of renewable energy finance, 2023*, International Renewable Energy Agency (IRENA), https://www.irena.org/Publications/2023/Feb/Global-landscape-of-renewable-energy-finance-2023. [43]

Kasikorn Research Center (2022), *Electricity price remains on the rise…Businesses are pressed to adapt to rising costs*, https://www.kasikornresearch.com/en/analysis/k-social-media/Pages/Energy-Charge-FB-05-10-22.aspx. [25]

KBank (2022), *Sustainability Report 2022*, https://www.kasikornbank.com/en/sustainable-development/SDAnnualReports/Y2022_SD_EN.pdf. [55]

Kingdom of Thailand (2020), *Sustainable Financing Framework*, https://www.pdmo.go.th/pdmomedia/documents/2020/Jul/KOT%20Sustainable%20Financing%20Framework.pdf. [37]

LMA (2023), *Green Loan Principles*, https://www.lma.eu.com/application/files/8916/9755/2443/Green_Loan_Principles_23_February_2023.pdf. [53]

Ministry of Energy (2024), *Government structure*, https://energy.go.th/th/official-structure. [7]

Ministry of Finance of Thailand (2022), *Sustainability Bond Annual Report 2022*, https://www.pdmo.go.th/pdmomedia/documents/2023/Jan/Cover%20Sus%20bond%20annual%20report-edited.pdf. [36]

Mugnini, A., F. Polonara and A. Arteconi (2021), "Energy flexibility curves to characterize the residential space cooling sector: The role of cooling technology and emission system", *Energy and Buildings*, Vol. 253, p. 111335, https://doi.org/10.1016/j.enbuild.2021.111335. [28]

OECD (2024), *Mobilised private finance for development*, https://data-explorer.oecd.org/vis?fs[0]=Topic%2C1%7CDevelopment%23DEV%23%7COfficial%20Development%20Assistance%20%28ODA%29%23DEV_ODA%23&pg=0&fc=Topic&bp=true&snb=11&df[ds]=dsDisseminateFinalDMZ&df[id]=DSD_MOB%40DF_MOBILISATION&df[ag]=OECD.DCD.FSD&df[vs]=. [51]

OECD (2024), *Other official flows (OOF)*, https://data.oecd.org/drf/other-official-flows-oof.htm#:~:text=OOF%20include%3A%20grants%20to%20developing,are%20primarily%20export%2Dfacilitating%20in. [50]

OECD (2023), *OECD Economic Surveys: Thailand 2023*, OECD Publishing, Paris, https://doi.org/10.1787/4815cb4b-en. [1]

OECD/IEA (2018), *Thailand Renewable Grid Integration Assessment*, https://iea.blob.core.windows.net/assets/c41cd30d-5f69-4b12-9502-3e7caaca294e/Partner_Country_Series_Thailand_Grid_Renewable_Integration_Assessement.pdf. [26]

Parliamentary Budget Office (2022), *Budget analysis report. Fiscal year 2022*, https://www.parliament.go.th/ewtadmin/ewt/parbudget/download/article/article_20210813152628.pdf. [45]

Sagulpongmalee, K., A. Therdyothin and A. Nathakaranakule (2019), "Analysis of feed-in tariff models for photovoltaic systems in Thailand: An evidence-based approach", *Journal of Renewable and Sustainable Energy*, Vol. 11/4, https://doi.org/10.1063/1.5091054. [29]

Siam Commercial Bank (2021), *Sustainability targets [2021 - 2023]*, https://www.scb.co.th/content/dam/scb/about-us/sustainability/documents/2021/x-3-year-sustainability-target-en.pdf. [56]

SIPET (2024), *Thailand Power Sector Snapshot*, https://www.sipet.org/Power-Sector-Snapshot-thailand.aspx#:~:text=Tariffs%20and%20Affordability,-Residential%20electricity%20tariffs&text=Low%2Dincome%20households%20can%20make,of%20their%20income%20on%20electricity. [22]

Sirasoontorn, P. and P. Koomsup (2017), *Energy Transition in Thailand: Challenges and Opportunities*, https://library.fes.de/pdf-files/bueros/thailand/13888.pdf. [21]

Thai Bond Market Association (2023), *Green, Social, Sustainability Bond & Sustainability-linked Bond (ESG Bond)*, https://www.thaibma.or.th/EN/BondInfo/ESG.aspx. [59]

Thailand Board of Investment (2023), *Investment Promotion Guide 2023*, https://www.boi.go.th/upload/content/BOI_A_Guide_EN.pdf. [31]

Thailand Taxonomy Board (2023), *Thailand Taxonomy A Reference Tool for Sustainable Economy*, https://www.bot.or.th/en/financial-innovation/sustainable-finance/green/Thailand-Taxonomy.html. [41]

Thailand Taxonomy Board (2023), *Thailand Taxonomy Phase 1*, https://www.bot.or.th/content/dam/bot/financial-innovation/sustainable-finance/green/Thailand_Taxonomy_Phase1_Jun2023_EN.pdf. [40]

Thailand Working Group on Sustainable Finance (2021), *Sustainable Finance Initiatives for Thailand*, https://www.bot.or.th/en/news-and-media/news/news-20210818.html. [38]

Thailand's Ministry of Natural Resources and Environment (2022), *Thailand's Long-Term Low Greenhouse Gas Emission Development Strategy*, https://unfccc.int/sites/default/files/resource/Thailand%20LT-LEDS%20%28Revised%20Version%29_08Nov2022.pdf. [5]

The Diplomat (2023), *Who Pays and Who Profits From High Energy Prices in Thailand?*, https://thediplomat.com/2023/06/who-pays-and-who-profits-from-high-energy-prices-in-thailand/. [23]

Tongsopit, S. et al. (2016), "Business models and financing options for a rapid scale-up of rooftop solar power systems in Thailand", *Energy Policy*, Vol. 95, pp. 447-457, https://doi.org/10.1016/j.enpol.2016.01.023. [19]

UNEP FI (2024), *Our Members*, https://www.unepfi.org/members/. [54]

UNFCCC (2022), *Thailand's 2nd Updated Nationally Determined Contribution*, https://unfccc.int/sites/default/files/NDC/2022-11/Thailand%202nd%20Updated%20NDC.pdf. [3]

UNFCCC (2022), *THAILAND'S LONG-TERM LOW GREENHOUSE GAS EMISSION DEVELOPMENT STRATEGY (REVISED VERSION)*, https://unfccc.int/sites/default/files/resource/Thailand%20LT-LEDS%20%28Revised%20Version%29_08Nov2022.pdf. [2]

UOB (2022), *UOB Thailand launches U-Energy, Asia's first integrated financing platform to drive energy efficiency*, https://www.uob.co.th/investor-en/news/press-news/2022/news-23Mar2022.page. [58]

Visvanathan, C. and C. Chiemchaisri (2019), *Management of Agricultural Wastes and Residues in Thailand: Wastes to Energy Approach*, https://faculty.ait.ac.th/visu/wp-content/uploads/sites/7/2019/01/Agri-waste2energy-Thai.pdf. [17]

Watson Farley & Williams (2022), *THAILAND'S 5 GW RENEWABLE PPA FIT SCHEME: 2022-203*, https://www.wfw.com/articles/thailands-5-gw-renewable-ppa-fit-scheme-2022-2030/. [30]

World Bank Group (2023), *Thailand Economic Monitor: Thailand's Pathway to Carbon Neutrality: The Role of Carbon Pricing*, https://documents1.worldbank.org/curated/en/099121223123018912/pdf/P5010090ef52cc09d0b46c0af1a43820def.pdf?cid=eap_fb_thailand_en_ext. [10]

## Notes

[1] Official development finance data presented include both Official Development Assistance (ODA) and Other Official Flows (OOF), provided by both bilateral and multilateral providers.

[2] KBank's net-zero target applies to GHG emission scope 1 and 2.

# 2 Estimated finance and investment needs to reach Thailand's clean energy plans

This chapter presents estimates of the finance and investment needed to implement and reach Thailand's clean energy plans. The estimates result from modelling work of the Thai consultancy, The Creagy, which supported the OECD with the research and analysis conducted for this Roadmap. The chapter starts with an overview of Thailand's latest renewable energy and energy efficiency plans as well as its energy outlook to 2037. The chapter then provides an overview of the estimates of the financing needs for both renewable energy and energy efficiency. The chapter also shows estimates of the local share and the supply chain distribution of the required investments in solar PV as well as in high-efficiency cooling systems. The chapter concludes with a summary of the estimated economic impact resulting from the implementation of the current clean energy plans, in terms of value added and job creation.

This chapter provides estimates of finance and investment needs to meet the goals of Thailand's National Energy Plan, as well as the economic benefits of the clean energy transition in terms of green job creation. These models can be updated to reflect the targets of the forthcoming National Energy Plan and a training to achieve this has been delivered to the Department of Alternative Energy Development and Efficiency (DEDE) of the Ministry of Energy of Thailand in 2023. The models have been developed by the Thai consultancy firm The Creagy.[1] Further details on the methodology applied for the modelling work can be found in Annex C.

## Thailand's latest clean energy plans

The Ministry of Energy of Thailand has taken steps to develop a comprehensive National Energy Plan that will integrate five key energy sub-plans, including:

- the Power Development Plan (PDP)
- the Alternative Energy Development Plan (AEDP)
- the Energy Efficiency Plan (EEP)
- Natural Gas Management Plan (Gas Plan)
- Fuel Management Plan (Oil Plan).

The section below outlines the existing drafts available for the PDP, the AEDP and the EEP, which are currently being revised.

### *Power Development Plan (PDP) 2018-2037 (Revision 1), or PDP 2018 (Rev.1)*

The Power Development Plan 2018-2037 (Revision 1) or PDP 2018 (Rev. 1) aims to enhance energy security and improve energy efficiency in Thailand (EPPO, 2020[1]). The plan focuses on three key areas:

- energy security – to meet the increasing demand for power and fuel diversification, aligned with the National Economic and Social Development Plan
- economy – to maintain a proper cost of power generation ensuring long-term economic competitiveness
- environment – to reduce the carbon dioxide footprint of power generation and emphasise renewable energy sources.

The PDP aims for a 36% share of renewable power generation by 2037. According to the plan, a total contracted capacity of 77 211 megawatts (MW) is expected by 2037, out of which 18 696 MW (24%) will come from the contracted capacity of new renewable energy power plants.

### *Thailand's Alternative Energy Development Plan 2018-2037 (AEDP 2018)*

The overall goal of Thailand's current Alternative Energy Development Plan 2018-2037 (AEDP 2018) is to increase the share of renewable energy of total final energy consumption, to 30% by 2037. In 2037, total renewable energy would be consumed across three sectors, namely heating (26 901 thousand tonnes of oil equivalent (ktoe)), power (7 298 ktoe) and biofuels (4 085 ktoe). The share of renewable energy in total final energy consumption as of December 2022 was about 14% (11 524 ktoe), which is significantly below the target.

Realising the AEDP 2018 could reduce dependency on gas imports and put the energy sector on a path aligned with Thailand's long-term climate ambitions. The AEDP aims for an expansion in renewable energy capacity in electricity generation from 12 666 MW in 2022 to a total of 29 411 MW (including large hydro) in 2037 that would represent 23% of the total electricity demand (DEDE, 2023[2]; EPPO, 2020[1]). Solar photovoltaic (PV) would represent by far the largest generation capacity (14.9 GW), followed by biomass (5.8 GW), hydro (3.2 GW) and wind (3 GW) (Figure 2.1).

### Figure 2.1. Total installed electricity generation capacity development according to the AEDP 2018

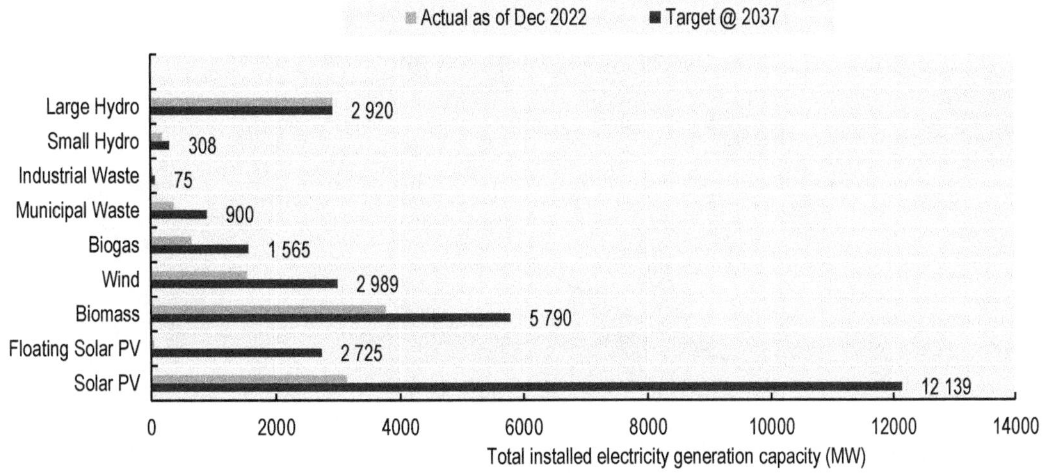


Source: DEDE (2023[2]), Performance on Alternative Energy Policy, https://www.dede.go.th/articles?id=450&menu_id=1.

StatLink https://stat.link/w2o3nc

### *Thailand's draft Energy Efficiency Plan (EEP 2022)*

The draft version of the Energy Efficiency Plan (EEP 2022) is Thailand's latest plan on energy efficiency released for a public hearing by DEDE, aiming to reduce energy intensity[2] by 36% by 2037 (with 2010 as the base year) or to reduce final energy consumption (FEC) by 52 318 ktoe (DEDE, 2023[3]). From 2010 until 2021, the amount of accumulated energy savings was 16 821 ktoe; therefore, approximately 35 497 ktoe reduction of FEC (68%) is targeted under this Plan until 2037.

All sectors are planned to contribute to these savings, with savings in electricity and heat demand split as 8 761 ktoe (25% of the total) and 26 736 ktoe (75%), respectively. The transportation and industrial sectors are two key economic sectors accounting for high shares of the energy efficiency target (48% and 35%, respectively), while the commercial, residential, and agricultural sectors account for 10%, 5%, and 2%, respectively (Table 2.1 below).

### Table 2.1. Energy savings contribution of different sectors towards the target under EEP 2022

| Sector | Total (ktoe) | Share of total energy consumption |
|---|---|---|
| **Industrial** | 12 432 | 35% |
| **Commercial** | 3 542 | 10% |
| **Residential** | 1 774 | 5% |
| **Agriculture** | 710 | 2% |
| **Transportation** | 17 039 | 48% |
| **Total** | 35 497 | |

Source: DEDE (2023[3]), Thailand's Economy Update, https://www.apec.org/docs/default-source/Satellite/EGEEC/Files/60/Economy_Updates_-_Thailand.pdf.

In 2023, Thailand's final energy consumption stood at 83 068 ktoe. This was 9 763 ktoe less than the projection according to the Business-as-Usual (BAU) model (92 831 ktoe). The energy intensity in 2023 was 7.46 ktoe/billion Thai Baht (THB) or 15% decrease from the base year (2010) (see Figure 2.2).

## Figure 2.2. Energy efficiency trends in Thailand (2010-2022)

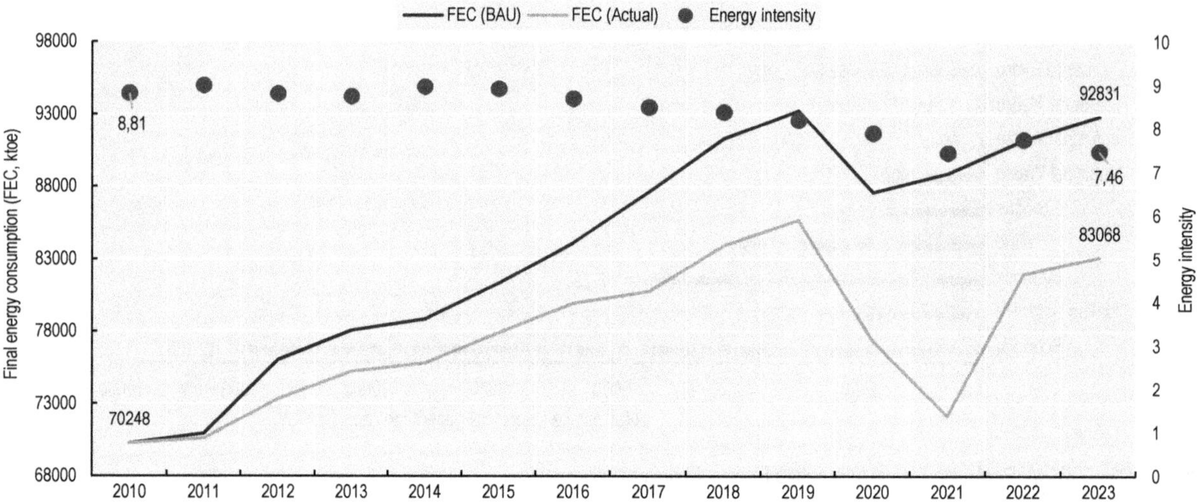


Source: Authors, based on data from EPPO and DEDE (2023[4]), Performance on Energy Efficiency Policy, https://www.dede.go.th/uploads/GDP_EI_4_2566_edit_5a8f948e8c.pdf?updated_at=2024-04-04T03:32:13.061Z.

StatLink https://stat.link/w8dfax

To realise the energy efficiency targets, Thailand's EEP 2022 lays out three strategic measures (compulsory, voluntary, and complementary). Compulsory measures include energy management standards, energy codes (industrial, buildings, residential), energy efficiency resource standards, demand responses and excise taxes (eco-sticker). Voluntary measures include equipment standards and labelling, financial support (grants and subsidies, soft loans, tax incentives and credit guarantees) and innovations (smart building and big data). Complementary measures include human resources development, energy managers, energy auditors, technologies, public relation/awareness, research and development.

The Energy Conservation Promotion Act (ENCON Act) is another key instrument establishing the legal framework for promoting energy conservation in Thailand (see Figure 2.3). This Act introduced several regulations to support the implementation of energy conservation measures in various sectors. The act establishes an Energy Conservation Promotion Fund (ENCON Fund) to support research and development of energy-efficient technologies, as well as to provide financial assistance for energy conservation projects. The act requires large energy-consuming industries and buildings to develop and implement energy conservation plans, including measures such as energy audits, energy-efficient design, and installation of energy-saving equipment. Additionally, the act mandates the labelling of energy-efficient appliances to promote consumer awareness and encourage the purchase of energy-efficient products.

**Figure 2.3. Laws and regulations on energy efficiency in Thailand**

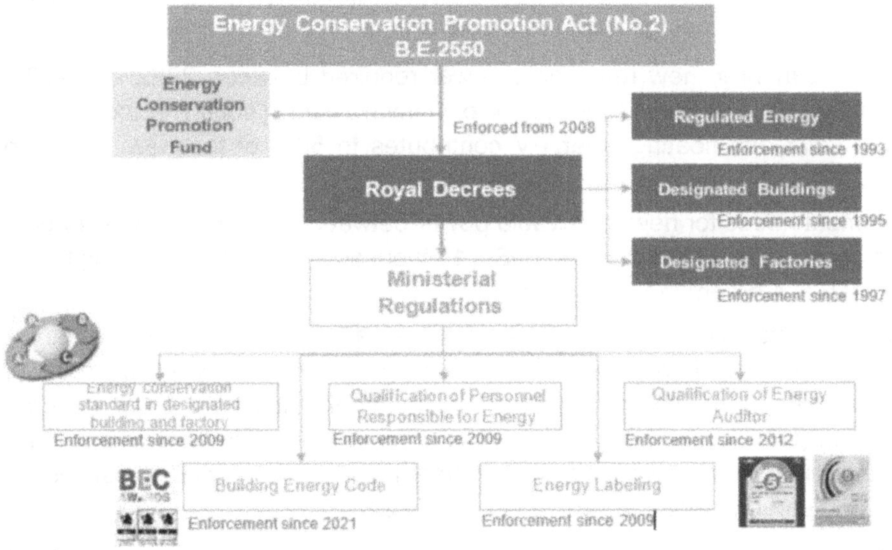


Source: Authors based on (DEDE, 2018[5]), Building Energy Code, Ministry of Energy of Thailand, https://seforallateccj.org/wpdata/wp-content/uploads/ecap17-thailand.pdf.

## Estimating finance and investment needed to meet Thailand's clean energy plans as well as their economic impacts

Thailand is facing the challenges of sustaining economic growth while simultaneously addressing environmental concerns and energy security. Within the development of this Roadmap, the Thai consulting firm The Creagy ran three models to estimate the financing and investment needs to achieve Thailand's current renewable energy and energy efficiency targets. The data and projections presented in this section were drawn from official sources such as the PDP 2018 (Rev.1), the AEDP 2018 and the draft version of EEP 2022, and are based on the energy and power system models developed by the Energy Research Institute, Agora Energiewende, and NewClimate Institute, as part of the Clean, Affordable and Secure Energy for Southeast Asia (CASE) programme (CASE for Southeast Asia, 2022[6]). Further details on the energy targets and projections the models are based on are shown in Annex C.

The models run for this Roadmap aimed to estimate the following elements:

- the investment and financing needs required for implementing the AEDP 2018 and the draft EEP 2022, the level of financial assistance needed by public and private financing sources, as well as the distribution of investment costs across the supply chain for the selected renewable energy and energy efficiency technologies.
- the economic impact, including employment and value added, that would be generated from the implementation of the AEDP 2018 and the draft EEP 2022.

The main findings are presented below and the full methodology used for the three models can be found in Annex C.

### *Estimated finance and investment needs for the implementation of the Alternative Energy Development Plan 2018-2037 (AEDP 2018)*

The goal of the AEDP 2018 is to increase the contractual capability of renewable energy power generation to 29 411 MW by 2037. Out of this, along with the retired capacity of 1 554 MW during 2022 - 2037, approximately 18.6 GW will be required from newly installed systems between 2022 and 2037. The modelling work conducted for this Roadmap estimated the finance and investment needed to reach the goals of the AEDP 2018. Key findings from the model are:

- The total investment in new renewable power required between 2022 and 2037 will amount to approximately THB 779 billion (USD 22 billion). Investment in solar PV, including solar PV rooftop, utility-scale solar and floating solar PV contributes to 56% of the new installations (Figure 2.4 below).
- The investment needs for new renewable power between 2022 and 2037 vary each year, with the lowest amounting THB 370 thousand (USD 11 thousand) in 2025 and the highest amounting THB 130 billion (USD 4 billion) in 2033 (Figure 2.5).
- To finance the installation of new renewable power, a combination of government support, private equity and private debt is needed. The share of government support, private equity and private debt are 4%, 23%, and 72%, respectively. To implement the AEDP 2018, government support of THB 35 billion (USD 1 billion) is needed. The support is likely to be provided mainly through five financial instruments, namely grants, investment and performance subsidies, debt and equity financing, and carbon credits, as shown in Figure 2.6.

The modelling also provided an estimation of the local share of investment for solar PV. Key findings are presented in Box 2.1 below.

## Figure 2.4. New renewable energy installations in the power sector and estimates of related investment needs (2022 – 2037)

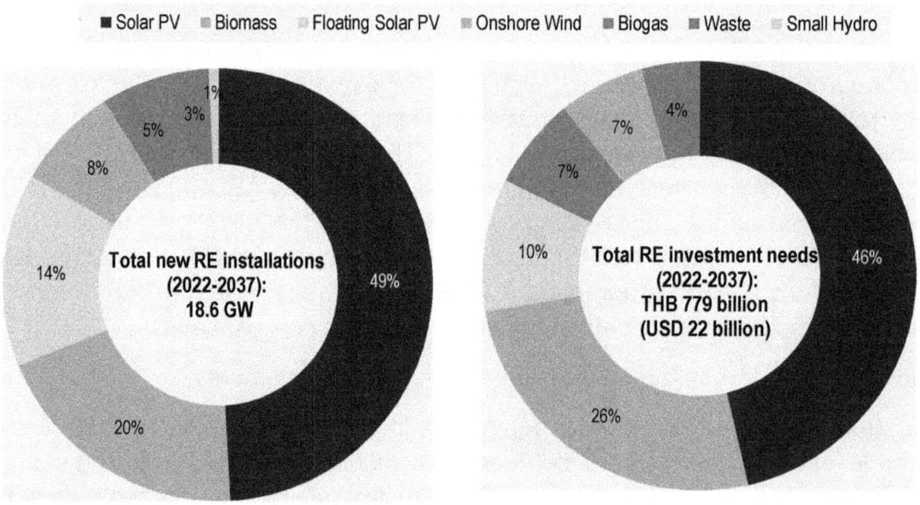


Source: Authors

StatLink https://stat.link/7dgxm2

**Figure 2.5. Estimates of annual investment needs for new renewable energy installations in the power sector (2022-2037)**

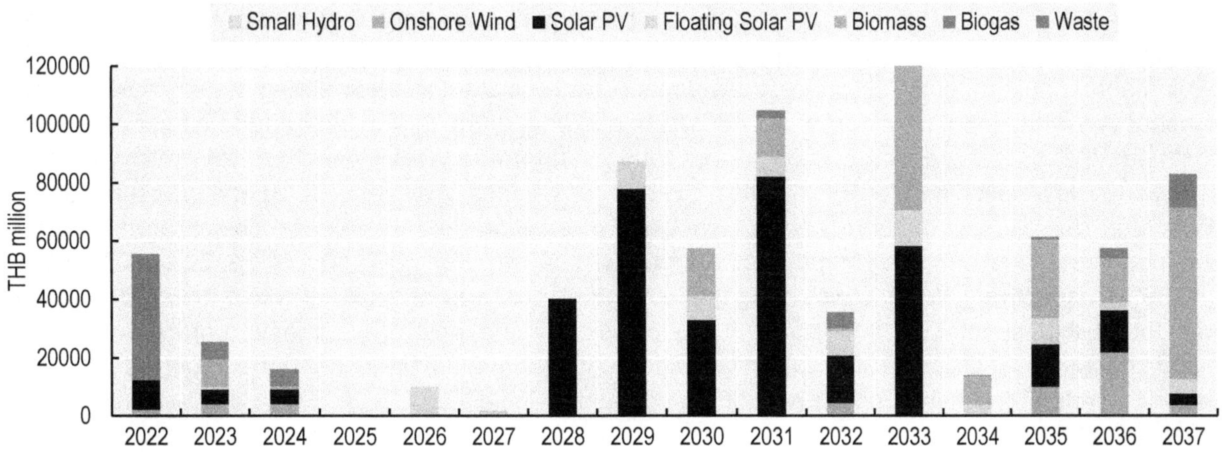


Source: Authors

StatLink https://stat.link/u42thn

**Figure 2.6. Estimates of needed government support, private equity and private debt for investment in new renewable energy installations in the power sector (as per the AEDP 2018)**

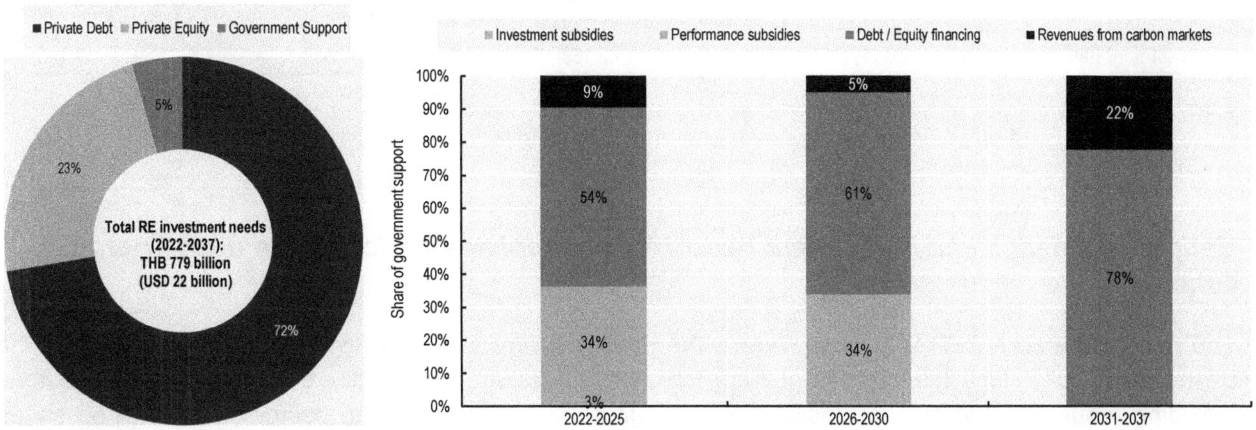


Source: Authors

StatLink https://stat.link/30s6i7

## Box 2.1. Estimated local share of solar PV investment

Under the AEDP plan, an additional analysis has been made for solar PV to assess the distribution of the investment across its supply chain. The supply chain of solar PV consists of two main groups: (i) equipment suppliers and (ii) project developers responsible for engineering, procurement, and construction work. In 2019, Ambition to Action conducted a study that examined the component-level costs and the local share for Solar PV. It was found that for every THB 100 (USD 2.9) of investment, THB 34 would be allocated for PV modules, THB 17 for balance of system (BOS) and grid connection, while the rest is split among inverter, racking, installation and developer costs, and fee and contingencies. Each of these components will have a local share of 10%, 10%, 47%, 32%, 63%, 76%, and 89%, respectively. When considering the total investment size of solar PV within the AEDP plan, it was found that about THB 111 billion (USD 3 billion) represents the domestic portion, while the remaining THB 249 billion (USD 7 billion) would be international, mainly due to the imported solar PV panels, inverters, BOS and grid connection components (Table 2.2).

### Table 2.2. Estimated local share of solar PV investments

| | PV Module | Inverter | Racking | BOS & Grid Connection | Installation | Developer | Fees & Contingencies | Total |
|---|---|---|---|---|---|---|---|---|
| Share | 34% | 6% | 9% | 17% | 12% | 12% | 9% | 100% |
| Local content | 10% | 10% | 47% | 32% | 63% | 76% | 89% | - |
| Investment (THB million) | 122 576 | 22 352 | 33 168 | 62 009 | 43 983 | 43 983 | 32 447 | 360 517 |
| Local investment | 12 258 | 2 235 | 15 589 | 19 843 | 27 709 | 33 427 | 28 877 | 111 061 |
| Investment gap | 110 318 | 20 117 | 17 579 | 42 166 | 16 274 | 10 556 | 3 569 | 249 456 |

Source: Authors

### *Estimated finance and investment needs for the implementation of the draft Energy Efficiency Plan (EEP 2022)*

The goal of the draft EEP 2022 is to reduce the energy intensity (EI) by 36% by 2037, compared to the base year of 2010. To achieve this goal, it is estimated that around 35 497 ktoe of energy from five sectors, including industrial, commercial, residential, agricultural and transportation sectors, needs to be saved from the business as usual (BAU) scenario. However, the modelling work conducted as part of this Roadmap focused on energy efficiency in industrial, commercial, residential, and agricultural sectors. The energy saving target of these four sectors amount to 18 458 ktoe.

Key findings from the model are:

- The total energy efficiency investment required in the four economic sectors between 2022 and 2037 will amount to THB 974 billion (USD 28 billion). The industrial sector needs the largest investment of THB 420 billion (USD 12 billion), or 43% of the total energy efficiency investment (Figure 2.7).
- The extent of government support, private equity and private debt for energy efficiency investment in the four economic sectors during 2022 – 2037 are 9%, 30%, and 61%, respectively. To implement the draft EEP 2022, government support of THB 92 billion (USD 3 billion) is needed. The support could be provided through five financial instruments as shown in Figure 2.8 below.

Box 2.2 below provides an overview of estimates of local investment needed for high-efficiency cooling systems.

**Figure 2.7. Estimates of total energy efficiency investment needs in four economic sectors, as per the draft EEP 2022 (2022 – 2037)**

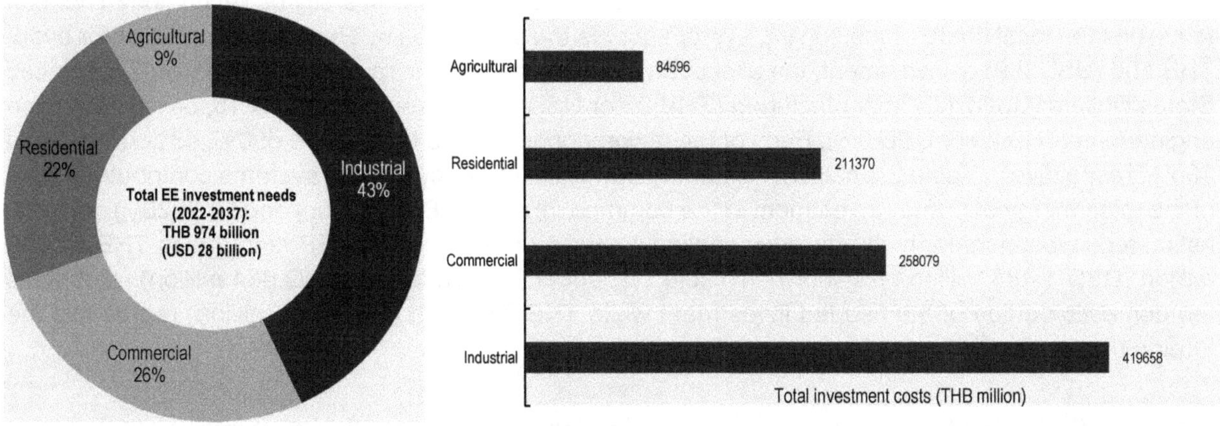


Source: Authors

StatLink https://stat.link/sq89ct

**Figure 2.8. Estimates of needed government support, private equity and private debt for energy efficiency investment, as per the draft EEP 2022 (2022 – 2037)**

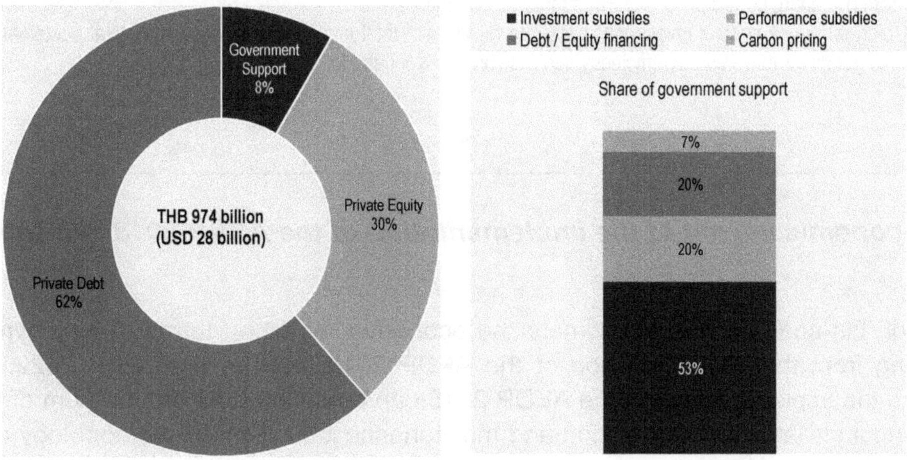


Source: Authors

StatLink https://stat.link/gt80wa

### Box 2.2. Estimated local share of investment in high-efficiency cooling systems

Under the EEP plan, an additional analysis has been made for high efficiency cooling systems to determine how the investment will distribute across the supply chain. The supply chain for cooling systems is composed of four main groups: (i) raw materials; (ii) manufacturing; (iii) assembling; and (iv) engineering. In 2019, a study was conducted by the King Mongkut's University of Technology Thonburi to assess the local share of the cooling system across the supply chain. The study found that for every THB 100 (USD 2.9) of investment, the allocation would be as follows: raw materials (THB 42, or United States Dollars (USD) 1.2), manufacturing (THB 23 or USD 0.6), assembling (THB 15, or USD 0.4) and engineering (THB 20 or USD 0.6). Each of these components has a local share of 0%, 43%, 100%, and 100%, respectively (Table 2.3 below). Assuming that high-efficiency cooling systems contribute to 20% of the total energy efficiency investment in the commercial sector (Brown, Soni and Li, 2020[7]), the total estimated investment for high-efficiency cooling systems under the draft EEP amounts to THB 51 616 million (USD 1 483 million). As shown in Table 2.3, about THB 23 billion (USD 664 million) represents the domestic portion of the needed investment while THB 28 billion (USD 818 million) represents the foreign portion, primarily due to raw material imports.

#### Table 2.3. Estimated local share of investment in high-efficiency cooling systems

| | Raw materials | Manufacturing | Assembling | Engineering | Total |
|---|---|---|---|---|---|
| **Share** | 42% | 23% | 15% | 20% | 100% |
| **Local content** | 0% | 43% | 100% | 100% | - |
| **Investment (THB million)** | 21 808 | 11 743 | 7 742 | 10 323 | 51 616 |
| **Local investment** | 0 | 5 049 | 7 742 | 10 323 | 23 115 |
| **Investment gap** | 21 808 | 6 693 | 0 | 0 | 28 501 |

Notes: * Derived from (Kotanan, Lorterapong and Patoomnakul, 2019[8]).
** Assuming that high-efficiency cooling investment accounts for 20% of total investment in the commercial sector as per the study on Distribution of bills of goods for three energy efficiency sectors (Brown, Soni and Li, 2020[7]).
Source: Authors

### *Estimated economic impact of the implementation of the AEDP 2018 and the draft EEP 2022*

The purpose of this analysis was to estimate the economic impact, in terms of employment and value added, resulting from the implementation of the AEDP 2018 and the draft EEP 2022. The total jobs generated from the implementation of the AEDP 2018 can be estimated from the sum of manufacturing, construction and installation, and operation and maintenance jobs. The full methodology can be found in Annex C.

The estimated impacts of the implementation of the AEDP 2018 include:

- Total investment of renewable energy during 2022-2037 amounting to THB 779 billion (USD 22 billion) is expected to create value added of THB 292 billion on average (USD 8 billion) or about 37.5% of the total investment (Figure 2.9).
- This investment is expected to create 722 thousand jobs on average during the same period, which translates to an average of 45 thousand jobs per year or 2.4 jobs per MW (Figure 2.9).

## Figure 2.9. Estimated value added and employment created as a result of the implementation of the AEDP 2018

Value added created from AEDP 2018 on the left-hand side chart and employment created from AEDP 2018 on the right-hand side chart.

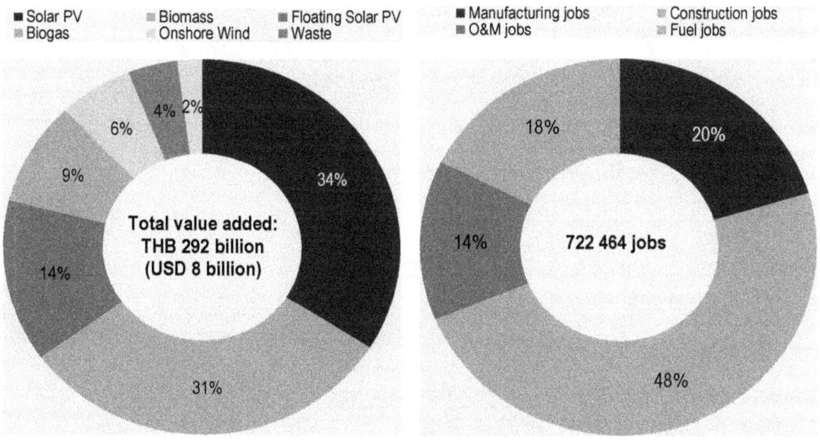


Source: Authors

StatLink https://stat.link/021lq6

The estimated economic impacts of the implementation of the draft EEP are:

- Total investment of energy efficiency during 2022-2037 amounting to THB 974 billion (USD 28 billion) is expected to create value added of THB 187 billion (USD 5 billion) or about 19% (Figure 2.10).
- This investment is expected to create 387 thousand jobs during the same period, out of which on average 119 thousand (31%) are direct jobs and 268 thousand (69%) are indirect jobs (Figure 2.10).

## Figure 2.10. Estimated value added and employment created as a result of the implementation of the draft EEP 2022

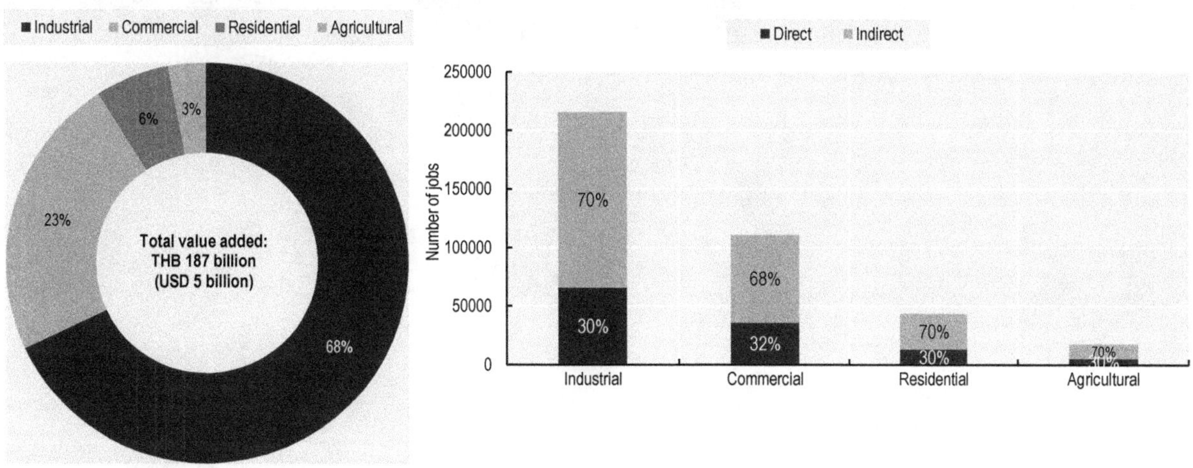


Source: Authors

StatLink https://stat.link/blzikw

## References

Brown, M., A. Soni and Y. Li (2020), "Estimating employment from energy-efficiency investments", *MethodsX*, Vol. 7, p. 100955, https://doi.org/10.1016/j.mex.2020.100955. [7]

CASE for Southeast Asia (2022), *Towards a collective vision of Thai energy transition: National long-term scenarios and socioeconomic implications*, Clean, Affordable and Secure Energy (CASE) for Southeast Asia, https://newclimate.org/sites/default/files/2022-11/2022-11-08_th_ltes_-_full_report.pdf. [6]

DEDE (2023), *Performance on Alternative Energy Policy*, https://www.dede.go.th/articles?id=450&menu_id=1. [2]

DEDE (2023), *Performance on Energy Efficiency Policy*, https://www.dede.go.th/uploads/GDP_EI_4_2566_edit_5a8f948e8c.pdf?updated_at=2024-04-04T03:32:13.061Z. [4]

DEDE (2023), *Thailand's Economy Update*, https://www.apec.org/docs/default-source/Satellite/EGEEC/Files/60/Economy_Updates_-_Thailand.pdf. [3]

DEDE (2018), *Building Energy Code (BEC)*, https://seforallateccj.org/wpdata/wp-content/uploads/ecap17-thailand.pdf. [5]

EPPO (2024), *Electricity*, https://www.eppo.go.th/epposite/index.php/th/energy-information/static-energy/static-electricity?orders[publishUp]=publishUp&issearch=1. [10]

EPPO (2020), *Power Development Plan (PDP) 2018 Revision 1*, https://www.eppo.go.th/images/Infromation_service/public_relations/PDP2018/PDP2018Rev1.pdf. [1]

Kotanan, A., P. Lorterapong and J. Patoomnakul (2019), *Value chain and development of the Thai air conditioning industry*, https://www.thailog.org/wp-content/uploads/2019/01/54-68.pdf. [8]

Office of Natural Resources and Environmental Policy and Planning (2022), *Infographic regarding COP26*, https://www.onep.go.th/infographic-%e0%b8%97%e0%b8%b5%e0%b9%88%e0%b8%99%e0%b9%88%e0%b8%b2%e0%b8%aa%e0%b8%99%e0%b9%83%e0%b8%88%e0%b9%80%e0%b8%81%e0%b8%b5%e0%b9%88%e0%b8%a2%e0%b8%a7%e0%b8%81%e0%b8%b1%e0%b8%9a-cop26/. [9]

## Notes

[1] In the past, the same model has been applied as part of the following studies: (i) Financing Thailand's Climate Actions in NDC and NAP under GIZ's Thai-German Climate Programme (2020), (ii) Ambition to Action's Domestic Expenditure and Employment Impacts of Power Sector Development in Thailand (A2A, 2019), and (iii) Affordable and Secure Energy for Southeast Asia (CASE) on *Towards a collective vision of Thai energy transition: National long-term scenarios and socioeconomic implications* (2022).

[2] In the EEP 2022, energy intensity is measured as final energy consumption divided by GDP (ktoe/billion baht).

# 3 Unlocking finance and investment for small-scale renewable power in Thailand

This chapter provides an overview of policies promoting investment in small-scale renewable power in Thailand. It examines the main financing, policy, regulatory and governance challenges as well as market development barriers. It also presents the main business models for rooftop solar PV that have emerged in Thailand. Based on a set of case studies of financing instruments deployed in other countries, the chapter also presents a series of potential financing models that could be explored in Thailand to de-risk small-scale renewable projects, such as credit guarantee schemes, aggregation and securitisation mechanisms and pay-as-you-go models. To support the Government of Thailand and key Thai stakeholders to promote and de-risk small-scale renewable power investment, the chapter ends with recommendations across three key pillars: (i) financial support; (ii) policy, regulation and governance; and (iii) capacity building, data collection and awareness-raising.

In the last two decades, Thailand achieved significant progress in the development of utility-scale renewable energy projects (APEC, 2012[1]). However, the development of small-scale renewable energy remains a major outstanding challenge for Thailand's achievement of its energy plans. For example, over 90% of solar installations are large-scale solar farms rather than rooftop solar projects (USAID, forthcoming[2]). Deploying small-scale renewable energy in Thailand can provide considerable benefits in terms of development and energy access, especially to rural and remote areas across the country. Small-scale installations bear significant advantages over large-scale projects. For example, rooftop solar projects are simpler to develop, build and operate than ground-mounted PV projects, they use space that would not be used otherwise and often protect roofing material. However, expanding small-scale renewables still faces several market and financing challenges, further outlined below.

## Overview of policies promoting investment in small-scale renewable power

As discussed in Chapter 1, since 2006, Thailand put in place a suite of feed-in-tariff (FiT) schemes to boost the development of renewable energy in Thailand's electricity sector, including that of small-scale sources (see Figure 3.1 below for an overview and timeline of the different FiT schemes for grid-connected renewables).

The first incentive scheme was called the **"adder", a feed-in premium**, implemented by way of an additional compensation, variable by technology and installed capacity, on top of the normal wholesale tariff. The adder rates varied depending on the installed capacity of the SPPs or VSPPs and the type of renewable power plant. For ground-mounted solar (solar farm) projects, the incentive was at around 8 Thai Bht (THB) per kWh in 2007 and it was subsequently revised to 6.5 THB/kWh in 2010.

The adder scheme led to oversubscription with many solar PV systems installed capacities (almost 2 000 MW) and caused stakeholders' concerns on the impacts of this policy support for consumers. As a result, the adder was replaced by a **Feed-in Tariff (FiT)** which is the traditional policy instrument providing a guaranteed purchase rate for each unit of electricity generated from renewable energy resources. The FiT scheme was launched in 2013 to support solar PV rooftops at around 6-7 THB/kWh with a quota of 200 MW. While the quota of commercial and industrial scale (100 MW) was filled quickly, residential-scale projects achieved only around 30 MW in the first round. The FiT scheme was extended to cover ground mounted solar PV systems for government agencies, agricultural co-operatives, and other energy technologies such as for electricity generation from municipal/industrial waste resources. During 2016-2017, a joint "FiT and auction" scheme was introduced for VSPPs (biomass) in three southern border provinces and for SPPs hybrid firms. In 2021, the FiT and auction scheme was extended to support solar community power plants.

In 2022, Thailand introduced a new quota of 5 GW under the FiT scheme for the period covering between 2022 and 2030. This quota is exclusively for ground-mounted solar, wind power, ground-mounted solar and battery storage, and biogas from wastewater and waste (Watson Farley & Williams, 2022[3]).

**Figure 3.1. Adder and Feed-in Tariff systems for grid-connected renewable energy systems**

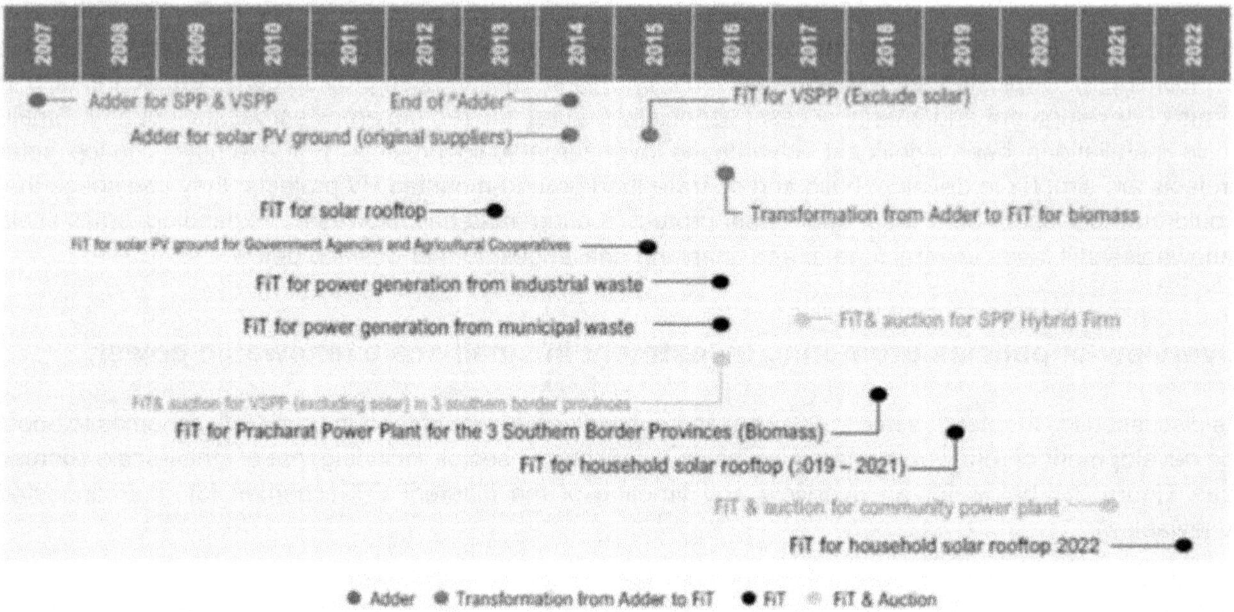


Source: EPPO, 2023

At present, rooftop solar PV installations for self-consumption are permitted for all electricity users. However, any excess electricity generated by the PV systems cannot be fed back into the power grid, with the exception of the residential solar buyback programme (CASE for Southeast Asia, 2022[4]).

Following the FiT scheme, in 2017, a pilot project for self-consumption scheme was launched with a quota of 100 MW of solar rooftop PV. This pilot scheme only encouraged self-consumption, without any incentives to generate and utilise surplus power. This pilot project was unsuccessful, as only around 6 MW was achieved. In 2019, the government started a net billing residential solar programme, allowing households with solar rooftop systems to sell surplus power to the grid, but at a lower price than they buy it for. In the case of Thailand, a rate of around 2 THB/kWh was provided for surplus power which is lower than the previous FiT and Thailand's average wholesale rate. As a result, turnout in installed capacity by residential investors was low. Table 3.1 summarises the suite of solar rooftop PV policies in Thailand (Junlakarn et al., 2021[5]).

**Table 3.1. Timeline of solar rooftop PV policies in Thailand**

| DPV programme | Quota of customer target group | Achieved (MW) | Year implemented (status) |
|---|---|---|---|
| **Feed in Tariff** | Residential: 100 MW<br>Commercial & Industrial: 100 MW | 130 | 2013-2015 (completed) |
| **Self-consumption** only (pilot project) | Residential: 20 MW<br>Commercial & Industrial: 80 MW | 5.63 | 2017 (completed) |
| **Self-consumption** only (no export) | No quota, depending on grid availability | 1 673 | 2018 (ongoing) |
| **Net billing** with buyback rate of 1.68 THB/kWh | Residential (≤ 10 kW) | 5.42 | 2019-2020 (completed) |
| **Net billing** with buyback rate of 2.2 THB/kWh as of January 2021 | Residential (≤ 10 kW) | 25.43 | 2021 – 2022 (ongoing) |

Source: Adapted from Junlakarn et al (2021[5]), A cross-country comparison of compensation mechanisms for distributed photovoltaics in the Philippines, Thailand, and Vietnam, 10.1016/j.rser.2021.110820 and CASE for Southeast Asia (forthcoming[6]), Unlocking Rooftop Solar Investment in Thailand: Facilitating Policy and Financial De-risking Instruments

The Government of Thailand has considered switching from net billing to net metering, which can significantly incentivise the installation of solar rooftop PVs as the household's sell and buy electricity price would be the same. Recently, the government commissioned a study to evaluate the feasibility for net metering, which concluded that the country is not yet ready for it due to technical and regulatory issues related to the fiscal treatment of the scheme and the grid balance. In 2023, the government thus put plans to initiate the net metering scheme on hold (The Nation, 2023[7]).

According to a recent assessment of the Clean, Affordable and Secure Energy (CASE) for Southeast Asia, the levelised cost of electricity (LCOE) of residential, commercial, and industrial rooftop solar PV in Thailand is grid parity as of 2023, ranging between 3.6 and 5 THB/kWh (approximately United States Dollars (USD) 0.10) (CASE for Southeast Asia, forthcoming[6]).

Thailand is also exploring peer-to-peer (P2P) electricity trading, which would enable consumers to trade electricity directly with one another without the state utilities as an intermediary (USAID, 2020[8]). As a first step, in 2022 EGAT introduced a peer-to-peer energy trading platform connecting producers and consumers that have installed solar rooftops for the first time in Thailand (EGAT, 2022[9]).

## Challenges and market development barriers

Unlocking finance and investment for small-scale renewable power in Thailand faces outstanding barriers, linked to:

- financing challenges, including access to financing for Micro, Small and Medium Enterprises (MSMEs), unfavourable conditions for existing renewable loan programmes for MSMEs, limited access to funding and expertise for micro-grids in remote, off-grid island-communities, rising supply chain costs
- policy and regulatory challenges, including cumbersome and costly licensing and permitting procedures, inconsistent and challenging grid codes and regulations, lack of skilled staff and low enrolment in net-billing schemes
- governance challenges, including lack of cross-ministerial co-ordination, overlapping responsibilities, and capacity and information gaps amongst MSMEs.

### *Financing challenges*

#### *MSMEs have limited access to finance for renewable energy*

While large companies can invest in renewable energy projects relatively easily, especially if they are listed companies, it is much more difficult for smaller companies. This is mainly due to their low (perceived) credit worthiness as a result of low or unstable revenue streams. MSMEs also often lack collateral as well as repayment track record. Moreover, unlisted MSMEs and small-scale renewable projects are typically too small to match the ticket size required by institutional investors to invest at scale in debt instruments such as project finance loans or green bonds.

#### *Unfavourable conditions of existing loan programmes for renewable energy*

Current loan programmes for renewable energy available for MSMEs are not easily accessible due to unfavourable conditions, such as short tenor periods, high interest rates and requirements for large amounts of collateral. Moreover, most existing loan programmes in Thailand focus on solar PV and available lending options for other forms of energy remain limited.

#### *Limited access to funding and expertise for micro-grids in remote, off-grid island-communities*

While Thailand achieved full electrification, about 180 islands in the Gulf of Thailand and the Andaman Sea still face limited, intermittent, expensive and environmentally harmful access to electricity (GIZ, 2017[10]). They mainly rely on electricity generated by highly polluting diesel engines, either on household level or supplied by a private operator selling power to the community. Diesel generators typically operate only 4-6 hours a day. The average cost of electricity per unit in these islands is estimated to be six times higher than prices of electricity from the national grid.

Electrification of remote areas and off-grid islands in Thailand was mainly funded by the government, through grants for hybrid micro-grids or for the installation of solar home systems (SHS). However, such projects often failed to achieve scale due to lack of local expertise for repairs and expensive maintenance of equipment and replacements. The sections below discuss the potential of using pay-as-you-go (PAYG) models to make solar home systems and community-owned mini-grids accessible to off-grid communities at an affordable cost, based on two case studies in Jik Island and Bulon Don Island.

#### *Increasing clean energy equipment costs, especially for off-grid solutions and vulnerability to exchange rate fluctuations*

In 2021 and 2022, prices of clean energy equipment rose significantly globally, mainly due to soaring costs of inputs, such as critical minerals, supply shortages, as well as trade and shipment delays. The IEA estimated that prices for solar PV modules were 30% higher in mid-2022 compared to 2020 (IEA, 2023[11]). Off-grid access solutions in developing countries faced even higher price fluctuations, with inflation hitting consumer demand and local currencies depreciating against the dollar. Moreover, since Thailand imports most solar equipment and panels from other countries, it is vulnerable to exchange rate fluctuations.

#### *High cost of debt for rooftop solar and other clean energy projects*

The high cost of debt of clean energy projects in emerging markets and developing economies (EMDEs) is a major barrier to attract investment for the clean energy transition. Results of a survey conducted by the IEA suggest that cost of capital for utility-scale solar photovoltaic (PV) projects in EMDEs is well over twice as high as it is in advanced economies (IEA, 2024[12]). According to CASE for Southeast Asia, the cost of debt associated with rooftop solar PV investment in Thailand, which amounts on average to 5.3%, could be reduced by 1.7% by mitigating power market risk, developer risk and financial risk (forthcoming[6]). Cost of capital and risk perceptions of nascent or unproven clean energy technology (e.g. green hydrogen) is even higher than that of established technologies such as solar PV.

### *Policy and regulatory challenges*

#### *Renewable energy licensing and permitting pose severe burdens to businesses*

Business players are burdened with cumbersome licensing and permitting requirements for renewables projects, which create high transaction costs and are time-consuming. For example, processes for rooftop system owners to request building modification permissions are often lengthy. To overcome this, the ERC office is in the process of developing a digital platform to streamline and expedite permitting process for commercial solar power plants (CASE for Southeast Asia, forthcoming[6]).

#### *Grid codes and regulations remain challenging and inconsistent*

Different electricity authorities in Thailand (namely EGAT, PEA and MEA) have slightly different grid connection codes.[1] For example, different grid codes have different requirements on equipment for solar installation systems.

#### *Solar PV technicians and contractors often lack adequate skills*

The skills of solar PV technicians and contractors vary significantly. Rooftop solar professionals do not have a specific certification to attest their adherence to quality standards for rooftop solar installations (CASE for Southeast Asia, forthcoming[6]). Some companies offer on-the-job training to increase skillsets. Moreover, as supply of solar installations is now increasing and developers are increasingly competing to offer low-cost solar installations, safety issues might be overlooked.

#### *Low enrolment in net-billing schemes*

The existing net-billing scheme for residential rooftop solar PV had relatively low enrolment due to a cap on eligible capacity and a significantly lower net-billing tariff rate for surplus electricity production, compared to residential power prices. Moreover, grid connection fees also hindered take-up.

#### *Lack of cross-ministerial co-ordination*

Roles and responsibilities overlap between different government agencies and ministries, which hinders and slows down processes for licensing and permits.

## Innovative business models and financing opportunities for small-scale renewables

### *Business models for small-scale renewable power*

During the time the feed-in tariff (FiT) was available, four main business models for rooftop solar emerged in Thailand, as discussed in (Tongsopit et al., 2016[13])(Table 3.2 below):

- Solar roof rental
- Solar power purchase agreement (PPA)
- Solar leasing[2]
- Community solar.

Since these business models are still relatively recent and given the discontinued FiT support, it is unclear which models will dominate the solar energy market in Thailand. Some of the business models, such as solar leasing and solar PPA, could further develop even without public support. In contrast, solar roof rental and community solar may require significant public support (such as through a FiT). For the development of the solar leasing market, setting up a dedicated third-party registration system for solar system components (modules and inverters) would be necessary. Such a system would create an active secondary market for solar systems, which is currently missing in Thailand. Figure 3.2 below outlines the different solar PV business models emerging in Thailand and Table 3.2 below summarises the main characteristics, drivers, barriers and risks.

## Figure 3.2. Solar PV business models emerging in Thailand

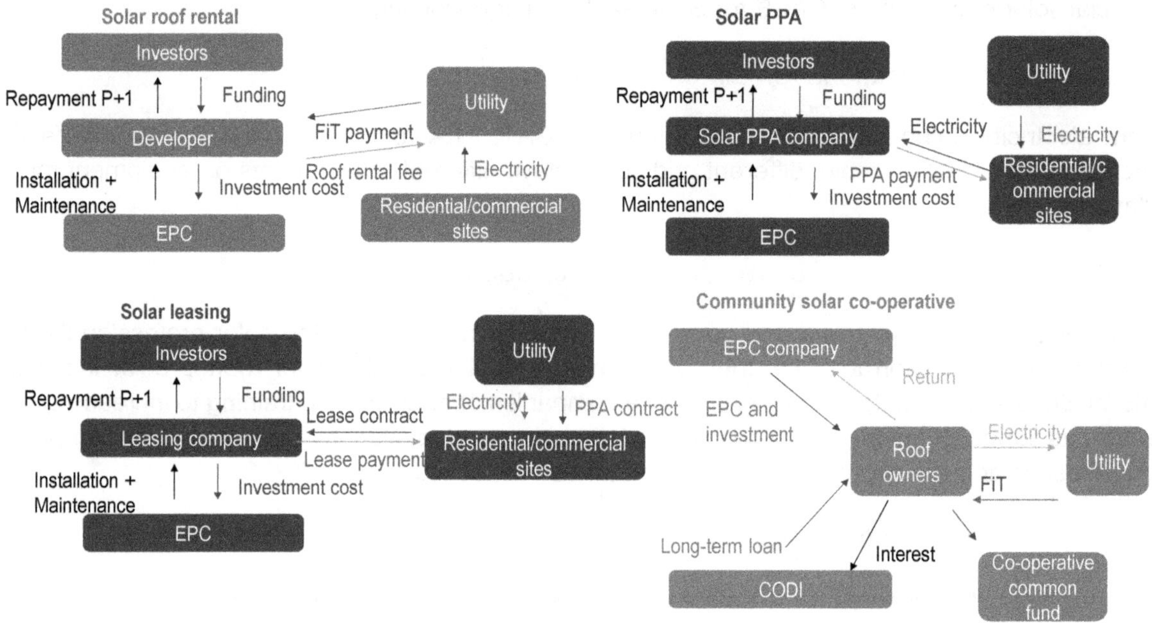


Source: Tongsopit et al (2016[13]), Business models and financing options for a rapid scale-up of rooftop solar power systems in Thailand, https://doi.org/10.1016/j.enpol.2016.01.023.

**Table 3.2. Business models for small-scale solar power in Thailand: drivers, barriers and risks**

| Business model | Business structure | Driver | Barrier | Risk |
|---|---|---|---|---|
| **Solar roof rental** | **Scale**: Commercial<br>**Ownership**: Developer<br>**Customer benefit**: Rental fee<br>**Customer cost**: None | - Roof owners benefit from rental fee and reduced heat absorption, leading to decreased power consumption<br>- Housing developers can increase revenues and value of their houses. | Limited PPA quota programmess from the government. | - Risk of roof damage (for building owners)<br>- Building use changes risks (for developers) |
| **Solar PPA** (or solar shared savings) | **Scale**: Commercial<br>**Ownership**: Developer<br>**Customer benefit**: Bill savings<br>**Customer cost**: PPA electricity price < grid price | - Model shielded from policy support and uncertainty<br>- Economic attractiveness and bill savings from buying solar electricity instead of grid electricity.<br>- The developer would cover O&M costs. | - Limited applicability in residential sector due to high investment costs. | - Risk of increase in electricity price.<br>- Load pattern may change, affecting the amount of PPA electricity needed (risk for building owners) |
| **Solar leasing** | **Scale**: All<br>**Ownership**: Customer<br>**Customer benefit**: Sale of electricity to the grid or bill savings<br>**Customer cost**: Lease payment | - Interest from financial institutions with existing leasing products.<br>- Avoidance of high upfront costs of solar systems for customers. | - Limited feasibility for small-scale systems.<br>- Lack of a third-party registration system for solar system components (modules and inverters). | - Risk of non-payment from the lessee (lessor risk).<br>- Uncertain yield/performance from the solar system (lessee risk) |
| **Community solar** | **Scale**: Residential<br>**Ownership**: Customer<br>**Customer benefit**: Sale of electricity to the grid<br>**Customer cost**: Principal and interest | - Strong neighbor networks.<br>- Peer effects of adopting solar technology. | - Limited financing options for community residential customers. | - FiT sharing agreement deviations.<br>- Unexpected yield/performance from the solar system.<br>- High community co-ordination costs. |

Source: Tongsopit et al (2016[13]), Business models and financing options for a rapid scale-up of rooftop solar power systems in Thailand, https://doi.org/10.1016/j.enpol.2016.01.023.

### *Financing mechanisms for small-scale renewable power*

The following section presents a series of potential financing models that could be explored in Thailand to de-risk small-scale renewable projects and attracting finance and investment towards them:

- credit guarantee schemes targeted at MSMEs and small-scale renewable energy projects
- aggregation and securitisation models for small-scale renewables
- pay-as-you-go and community-owned models to make renewable energy accessible to off-grid islands at affordable costs.

The OECD and the Creagy developed a series of five case studies on financing mechanisms for small-scale renewable power and energy efficiency projects in Thailand. The choice of the case studies was based on consultations and interviews with a wide range of stakeholders on challenges and barriers for attracting financing in the two sectors in Thailand. Further details on each of the five case studies can be found in Annex B.

### *Credit guarantee schemes targeted at MSMEs and small-scale renewable energy projects*

Credit guarantee schemes can help MSMEs access finance by transferring all or part of the borrower's credit and default risks, thus alleviating factors such as limited collateral and track record of MSMEs. Thanks to guarantees, in case of a borrower default, the lender can resort to a full or partial repayment from a third-party guarantor. Guarantees can cover either individual loans of individual borrowers, or a portfolio of loans, for example made by commercial banks to intermediary financial institutions (Alliance for Financial Inclusion, 2022[14]). Green credit guarantee schemes also contribute to improving the ability of banks to price MSME risks and to evaluate green projects.

Governments and public financial institutions can play a key role in de-risking small-scale renewable projects through funding or supporting green guarantee schemes. For example, Malaysia's Green Technology Financing Scheme (GTFS) is a government support programme offering a 2% interest subsidy and a government guarantee covering up to 60% of loans for green projects (Malaysian Sustainable Finance Initiative, 2023[15]) – see Box 3.1 below. Several other emerging markets and developing economies (EMDEs) have sector-neutral credit guarantee schemes (i.e. not specifically targeted at green projects). For example, India's Credit Guarantee Fund Trust for Micro and Small Enterprises (CGTMSE) facilitates access to collateral-free credit for MSMEs by providing a credit guarantee cover of up to 85% on loans up to INR 200 (USD 256 thousand) (OECD, 2022[16]).

#### Box 3.1. Malaysia's Green Technology Financing Scheme (GTFS)

In 2010 the Government of Malaysia established the Green Technology Financing Scheme (GTFS), with initial funding of RM 1.5 billion (USD 470 million). The scheme was extended in the following years and in 2023 the government allocated RB 1 billion to the GTFS, until 2025. The scheme continues to support six sectors, including energy, manufacturing, transport, buildings, waste and water.

The scheme offers a 2% interest subsidy and a government guarantee covering up to 60% of loans for green projects. It targets Malaysian-registered companies with a minimum of 60% Malaysian ownership, focusing on both producers and users of green technologies, including ESCOs. The Malaysian Green Technology and Climate Change Corporation and Credit Guarantee Corporation Malaysia Berhad are the agencies tasked with administering the GTFS. The former is responsible for the promotion, assessment, certification and monitoring of participants, while the latter is responsible for offering and extending guarantees (Figure 3.3 below).

**Figure 3.3. Key players of Malaysia's GTFS**

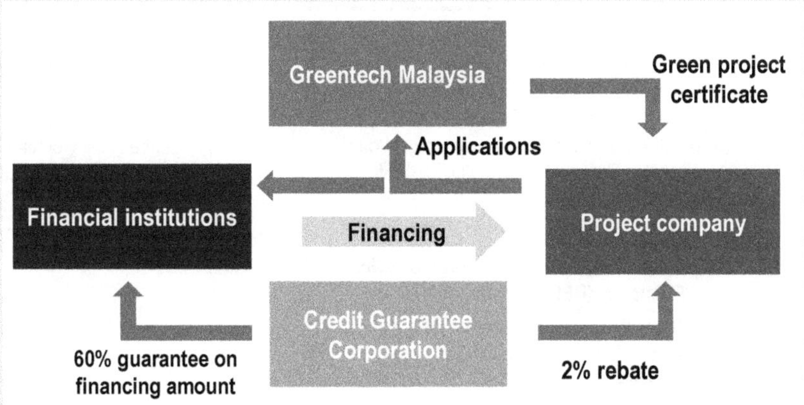


Source: Ministry of Natural Resources and Environment Malaysia (2014[17]), Green Technology Financing Scheme (GTFS), https://unfccc.int/files/focus/mitigation/application/pdf/malaysia_presentation.pdf.

As of 2018, the GTFS resulted in the participation of 28 financial institutions, which extended loans for 319 projects worth approximately USD 875 million (World Bank, 2020[18]). Most of the funding was allocated to solar power projects (Tu, Fan, 2016[19]). A recent study analysing the impact of the GTFS on the business performance of renewable energy producers shows that the scheme improves the financial and non-financial performance of participating companies (Adebiyi et al., 2020[20]).

Annex B provides further information on this scheme.

Extensive stakeholder consultations conducted to develop this Roadmap concluded that Thailand could consider setting up a credit guarantee scheme to reduce risk perceptions of small-scale projects, for both renewable energy and energy efficiency. A potential credit guarantee programme would incentivise small-sized ESCOs and MSMEs with limited track record and collateral to obtain credit to finance their green projects.

Table 3.3 below outlines potential actors involved in the implementation of a risk guarantee scheme in Thailand and the challenges they may encounter. Key actors that would need to be involved in exploring options to pilot a credit guarantee scheme include: the government (especially DEDE and the Ministry of Energy more broadly), the Thai Credit Guarantee Corporation (TCG), the ESCO Association, Thai commercial banks, academic institutions, as well as international partners.

Lack of experience and expertise of credit guarantee institutions and commercial banks in assessing and managing the risks of energy efficiency projects as well as high transaction costs relative to the small ticket size of such projects stand out as key challenges. Moreover, conducting due diligence and processing the guarantee could pose significant administrative burdens, which can be eased using a single digital platform and standardised due diligence checklists. It is also important that the guarantee fees and administrative processes are not prohibitively high for small-sized ESCOs.

**Table 3.3. Key players and potential challenges of implementation of a credit risk guarantee scheme in Thailand**

| Key players | Potential Thai actors | Challenges |
|---|---|---|
| **Funding agencies** | **Domestic public funds:** e.g. the Energy Conservation Promotion Fund (ENCON Fund) & Power Development Fund | • Eligibility criteria of the fund<br>• Political priorities |
| | **Multilateral development banks:** e.g. World Bank, Asian Development Bank (ADB), etc. | • Stringent eligibility criteria<br>• Complex application process<br>• Currency and repayment risks<br>• Competitive funding environment |
| **Technical support agencies** | **Department of Alternative Energy Development and Efficiency (DEDE)**, Ministry of Energy | Limited resources |
| | **Academic and research institutions**, e.g. Joint Graduate School of Energy and Environment, Chulalongkorn University | |
| | **International agencies**, e.g. GIZ, UNDP | |
| **Financial Institutions** | **Commercial banks in Thailand** | • Limited technical capacity to offer financing for small-scale renewable energy projects<br>• Lack of proven track records of MSMEs<br>• Stringent eligibility criteria |
| **Credit guarantee corporations** | **Thai Credit Guarantee Corporation (TCG)** | • Lack of experience and expertise in assessing and managing the risks of energy efficiency projects<br>• High transaction costs and administrative burdens for applying and processing the guarantee<br>• Limited availability and accessibility of donor funds to subsidise the guarantee fee and cover the potential losses<br>• Low awareness and understanding of the benefits and requirements of the guarantee mechanism among potential borrowers and lenders |

Source: Authors

One option for Thailand is to design a green credit guarantee scheme through the Thai Credit Guarantee Corporation (TCG), a state-owned specialised financial institution that already has a legal mandate to be able to extend guarantees. Concessional financing will be required, especially at the onset of the programme, to ensure that the guarantee is accessible by MSMEs, e.g. concessional resources from the government and support by donors and DFIs to fund a reduced uniform guarantee fee for lending for small-scale renewable projects.

Table 3.4 below proposes a roadmap of key activities to be undertaken by responsible organisations and a timeline for implementation for each of the potential responsible agencies. As a first step, a programme feasibility study could be conducted, assessing the market offer and challenges of green financing products for small-scale renewables, readiness of the TCG, potential guarantee take-up challenges faced by ESCOs and MSMEs (e.g. through a market survey) as well as the degree of awareness of financial institutions on the Thai green taxonomy. Since the pre-requisite of providing green credit guarantees is the provision of green loan products, it is important that participating financial institutions have a common understanding on how to apply the recently developed Thai taxonomy, e.g. to assess and classify the "greenness" of activities of their lending portfolios.

The feasibility study could inform decisions on key design elements, namely: (i) the choice between the individual and portfolio guarantee approach; (ii) the coverage ratio (i.e. what portion of a loan can be covered by a guarantee); (iii) the pricing structure for the guarantee fees; (iv) the process for handling defaults and guarantee payouts; and (v) the exit strategy.

The feasibility study could build on the work being conducted by the Carbon Trust on the design of a credit guarantee scheme in Thailand, as part of the ASEAN Low Carbon Energy Programme, which has already developed a financial model to cost the guarantee scheme, quantify the potential lending mobilised and test the sensitivity of market assumptions (e.g. default rates) and design decisions (Carbon Trust, 2023[21]).

It is worth noting that a credit guarantee scheme alone will not be able to bridge the lack of technical capacity of a lender or borrower to assess renewable energy projects, so the guarantee scheme needs to be accompanied by tailored capacity-building programmes, for example on the Thai taxonomy energy criteria and on technical risk assessments for small-scale projects.

#### *Aggregation and securitisation models for small-scale renewables*

Aggregation models can help tackle some of the barriers that small-scale and off-grid renewable projects face. Different types of aggregation exist and can be used to lower transaction costs and risks of projects (IIED, 2017[22]):

- **Financial aggregation**: bundling financial assets or investments into a bigger, individual portfolio or vehicle
- **Demand aggregation**: aggregating demand (e.g. of energy and equipment) of different households or communities
- **Aggregation of companies or projects**: creating a portfolio of companies or projects
- **Information aggregation**: creating platforms to ease and standardise access to information.

Through financial aggregation and securitisation, projects can be bundled to reach a scale and risk profile that is attractive to investors. For example, small loans for renewable energy projects can be pooled and then sold to a separate legal entity, such as special purpose vehicle (SPV), to protect the assets from any insolvency of the sponsoring entity or seller. The SPV can then issue marketable securities, typically in tranches with different risk profiles, to attract different types of investors (Coalition for Green Capital, 2019[23]). Securitisation also allows companies and lenders to recycle capital and free up financial capacity for more business or investment.

As an example, in 2023 Sun King, a Kenyan off-grid solar energy company, closed a securitisation transaction raising USD 130 million from DFIs and commercial investors, backed by future PAYG cash receivables. Earlier in 2022, King Sun also received USD 17 million through the proceeds of two green bonds issued by Symbiotics Investments, an impact asset manager focused on EMDEs. The French DFI Proparco invested in one of the two green bonds for an amount of USD 10 million (see Box 3.2 below).

In addition, the Pro Mini-Grids programme launched in Uganda in 2017 is another example of a pilot aggregation of small-scale renewables. The programme, funded by the Government of Uganda with support from the German Federal Ministry for Cooperation and Economic Development and the European Union, supported the Government of Uganda in bundling multiple mini-grid sites into single tenders to create a larger ticket size for investors to pursue. The bundled tenders were won by an energy developer, Winch Energy, which succeeded in raising approximately USD 20 million from a wide range of investors and DFIs. The OECD Blended Finance Guidance for Clean Energy includes a case study with further information on this programme (OECD, 2022[24]).

**Box 3.2. Sun King: the case of a local currency securitisation and green bonds for off-grid solar projects in Kenya**

In 2023, Sun King, a Kenyan off-grid solar energy company, and Citi established a Kenyan-Shilling-denominated USD 130 million green securitisation transaction. The company's current and future payments from off-grid solar products were securitised and financed by investors. The transaction was arranged by Citi and supported by commercial lenders as well as development finance institutions, including ABSA Kenya, British International Investment, Citi, FMO, Norfund, Standard Bank Kenya and the Trade and Development Bank.

Sun King's customers can purchase products using the company's pay-as-you-go financing service, which splits payments into regular and affordable instalments. These payments can be made via mobile money or cash for as little as USD 0.15 a day. The funds raised through the securitisation will finance further growth and expansion of the company.

In addition, in 2022, Sun King received USD 17 million through the proceeds of two green bonds issued by Symbiotics Investments, an impact asset manager. Symbiotics originates, structures and manages impact investments on behalf of companies in EMDEs. The French DFI Proparco invested in one of the two green bonds for an amount of USD 10 million. The proceeds of the bonds will finance Sun King's activities to ease access to solar energy for off-grid costumers in underserved African markets, mainly though SHS and PAYG. The bonds have been issued by the innovative MSME Bonds SA platform.

A further example of an aggregation model in an emerging market is the Green Receivables Fund in Brazil (Davies and Saygin, 2023[25]). This fund is designed as a securitisation instrument to address the lack of long-term finance for clean energy projects in the Brazilian market, as well as to overcome barriers such as illiquidity of assets. Through a special purpose vehicle (SPV), receivables for contractual debt can be pooled, and financial securities backed by income-generating assets can then be sold to investors.

#### *Pay-as-you-go and community-owned models to make renewable energy accessible to off-grid islands at affordable costs*

Pay-as-you-go (PAYG) models can ease access to clean energy to off-grid communities, using mobile payment technologies to facilitate payment by instalments. PAYG models usually involve home solar systems that customers pay for using mobile payment technologies and mobile phone credit (IRENA, 2020[26]). There are four key players in the PAYG model: an energy service provider, mobile network operators, financiers and end-users. Each player has a unique role to play, as illustrated in Figure 3.4 below.

## Figure 3.4. Key actors in PAYG models

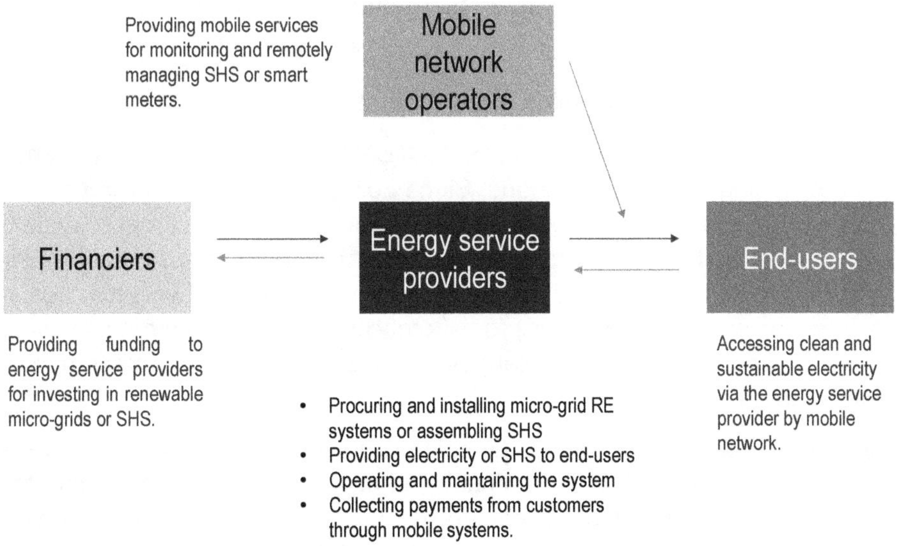


Source: Authors.

PAYG models can be implemented at both household and community level. PAYG systems can also be implemented as a micro-grid solution, where a solar PV system with battery storage is used to provide electricity services to a community (IRENA, 2020[26]). PAYG schemes are often implemented in the context of community-ownership models, which refer to the collective ownership and management of energy-related assets. Through cost-sharing, community-ownership models enable individual participants to own assets with lower levels of investment requirements (IRENA, 2020[27]).

In Thailand, a pilot community-owned PAYG model was launched in 2017 through a collaborative effort between the Ministry of Energy, GIZ Thailand and the social enterprise ReCharge Energy, aiming to develop sustainable electrification using solar home systems (SHS). The targeted areas include two off-grid islands in the Gulf of Thailand and the Andaman Sea, which currently rely on electricity generated by diesel engines: Bulon Don Island and Jik Island.

On the island of Bulon Don, the programme provided three different packages of solar home systems, operationalised and maintained by a local community enterprise through a revolving fund. A PAYG model was set up as a digital pre-payment scheme consisting of monthly instalments. On Jik Island, a private, community-owned hybrid renewable energy mini-grid was upgraded thanks to private equity investments, grants and technical assistance by development partners and the government (International Solar Alliance, 2023[28]). See Box 3.3 below and Annex B for further details on the case studies on the two islands.

In both cases, grant resources and TA provided by the government and development partners have been crucial to the project's kick-off and mobilisation of private investors. This shows that financing at favourable terms from governments or development agencies is often required at the early stage of innovative PAYG models, to cover upfront investment and business planning costs.

## Box 3.3. PAYG and community-owned models in Thailand: The cases of Jik Island and Bulon Don Island

### The Case of Jik Island: microgrid upgrade and prepaid system

Jik Island, located in the Chantaburi province in the Gulf of Thailand, is home to nearly 150 households, mainly dependent on fishing for their livelihoods. Since 2014, Jik Island went through an electrification process mainly funded by the government, which developed a hybrid microgrid system. The system was managed and maintained by the company Koh Jik established by the community itself. Due to the limited capacity of the solar PV system and the expensive maintenance of wind turbines, the community enterprise soon opted to use diesel generators for electrifying the island, incurring substantial expenses. Over time, the ESCO faced increasing challenges in securing funds for replacements of renewable energy equipment such as batteries.

In response, GIZ Thailand, the Ministry of Energy of Thailand and ReCharge Energy, a social enterprise with a mission to develop high impact community energy projects, collaborated to enhance the community's management and technical skills, preparing them to independently own, operate, and maintain the system, thereby attracting private investors. In 2020, a joint venture between private Blue Solar and Symbior Solar provided an equity investment amounting to USD 172 000 for the installation of a 72 kilowatt peak (kWp) solar PV system, batteries with total capacity of 266 kWh and a 60 kW backup diesel generator. A development co-operation agency provided a grant for the installation of 100 smart prepaid meters while Allotrope Partners, which has a network of investors in renewable energy, has entered into a 20-year agreement to purchase Renewable Energy Credits from the Koh Jik renewable electricity project, contributing USD 50 000. This fund has been used to lower the electricity fees charged to the end-users.

### The Case of Bulon Don Island: A digital prepaid method for solar home systems

Bulon Don Island, located in Satun province in the Andaman Sea, is home to 79 households. Bulon Don Island was the first community in Thailand using PAYG for Solar Home Systems (SHS). Until 2019, households on the island had limited access to electricity, mainly provided by central diesel generators. In 2019, ReCharge Energy received a grant from a development co-operation agency to pioneer a sustainable electrification initiative using SHS, in a joint effort with GIZ Thailand, the Ministry of Energy and the island's community enterprise. The SHS offered three different packages for consumers, at different prices depending on the electricity needed. For operation and maintenance, a revolving fund was established and managed by the island's community enterprise. Prepaid fees collected digitally from users are allocated to the fund to cover the operational and maintenance costs of the systems.

Further details on these two case studies, lessons learnt and roadmap for implementation in Thailand are available in Annex B.

The two case studies identified several potential challenges and potential solutions for the implementation of PAYG for renewable energy electrification on other off-grid islands in Thailand:

- **Technical durability**: The coastal environment can hasten the degradation of solar equipment. Frequent maintenance or replacement, particularly of sensitive components like batteries and inverters, is necessary.
- **Financial feasibility**: The substantial upfront investment and ongoing maintenance costs of the microgrid require financial support, often from government or donor resources, to be viable. Public funding could be used effectively to mobilise private investors from the onset of the project.

- **Consumption management**: Controlling the community's electricity usage is a complex task. As electricity becomes more available, consumption typically rises, potentially overwhelming the supply. A prepaid electricity model has been introduced to help manage this.
- **Supply reliability**: Solar energy's intermittent nature poses a challenge for consistent power delivery, especially during periods of reduced sunlight, requiring back-up solutions.
- **Affordability**: The cost of solar systems, both initial and recurring, may be prohibitive for some households, particularly where income is inconsistent due to reliance on seasonal revenues.
- **Service and repairs**: Remote islands often lack skilled maintenance personnel, complicating the prompt repair and servicing of solar systems. Expanding the PAYG model in remote islands would require significant training to ensure the communities have the necessary technical skills.
- **Community engagement**: Effective implementation depends on the community's understanding and engagement with the solar systems. This requires comprehensive awareness-raising.

The primary targets for replicating both models include off-grid communities within national reserve parks, where constructing distribution systems is prohibited, and over 100 islands in the Gulf of Thailand and the Andaman Sea, where extending the grid is not economically viable.

Though initially developed for electrification in off-grid areas, the models are also applicable to on-grid communities seeking low-carbon solutions. By incorporating the PAYG model, on-grid communities can move towards greater energy independence, making them more resilient to grid outages and fluctuations in energy prices and allowing communities to transition towards greener, low-carbon energy sources, thus reducing their environmental impact.

## Recommendations

Meeting Thailand's renewable energy goal will require targeted action and tailored solutions to increase small-scale renewable power, through co-ordinated efforts across a wide range of stakeholders, including MSMEs, industry, the government, financial institutions and international partners. Public-private collaboration can provide solutions to unlock the finance needed to harness small-scale renewable energy potential and scale up decentralised community-based financing solutions.

Innovative business models will be critical to help remote communities access renewable energy at lower costs and achieve the replacement of existing diesel generation. Community-owned renewable energy models can be key enablers of a just energy transition by allowing households to acquire greater control and ownership over their energy resources. They can also be a vehicle to challenge norms and perceptions of gender roles by enabling women to fully benefit from clean energy opportunities and jobs.

To support the Government of Thailand and key Thai stakeholders to promote and de-risk small-scale renewable power investment, the Roadmap proposes recommendations across three key pillars: (i) financial support; (ii) policy, regulation and governance; and (iii) capacity building, data collection and awareness-raising.

### *Financial support*

> *Reviewing and strengthening existing public financial incentives to prioritise the acceleration of small-scale and community-based renewable energy models*

Thailand experienced fast growth of installed capacity of solar PV since the introduction of the FiT policy, especially large, utility-scale projects. However, this has not been the case for small-scale and community-owned or community-led projects, which are instrumental to decentralise energy production and ensure energy supply, provide clean electricity access to off-grid areas and spur local socio-economic development. The Government of Thailand could consider reviewing and strengthening its existing financial incentives to accelerate the installation of small-scale distributed renewable energy projects (e.g. residential rooftop solar PV), which lags behind utility-scale capacity.

Thai energy policymakers and regulators (e.g. the Ministry of Energy and the Energy Regulatory Commission) could regularly monitor the up-take of the ongoing feed-in-tariff scheme, review and adjust FiT tariff rates to encourage small-scale and community-based renewable energy projects if their uptake is low. It is important to ensure that tariffs are calculated to cover investment costs rather than avoided generation cost to kick-start small-scale renewable energy sector. Moreover, the FiT policy can facilitate the development of small-scale solar, for example by developing and disseminating template contracts for solar PPA, solar roof rental and community-ownership models. Such templates could support market players by providing standardised clauses. Furthermore, the FiT policy should also be accompanied by other incentives, such as the ones outlined below, to ease access to finance for small producers, for whom upfront investment costs of solar systems are still significant.

#### *De-risking and improving conditions of green loan programmes for MSMEs*

The government, through the Ministry of Energy and Ministry of Finance, could consider continuing incentives or subsidies to encourage banks to offer green loans to MSMEs at more favourable terms. This could take the form of tax incentives, subsidies for interest rate differentials, or credit guarantees to mitigate banks' risks associated with green lending (see recommendation below on the credit guarantee scheme).

Implementing risk mitigation measures, for example through credit guarantees, can help lower the risk of small-scale projects and MSMEs, increase the confidence of lenders, which can, in turn, improve terms and conditions of existing green loan programmes for small-scale renewable energy projects and MSMEs (e.g. through favourable interest rates, lower collateral requirements, longer tenures and flexible repayment schedules).

Terms and conditions of existing green loan programmes for small-scale renewable energy projects and MSMEs could be improved (e.g. favourable interest rates, lower collateral requirements, longer tenures and flexible repayment schedules). Within the loan origination process, financial institutions could apply adequate and proportionate reporting and verification standards for MSME green loans.

Simplifying and streamlining application and approval processes for green MSME loans could also help to ease MSMEs access to financing for renewable energy projects. Expediting approval timelines and providing online application options can help lower barriers to entry for MSMEs seeking green financing. Access to information and capacity-building activities for both financial institutions and MSMEs could be increased – see a dedicated action plan on this below.

#### *Piloting a green credit guarantee scheme for small-scale RE projects*

The government could consider supporting the pilot of a green credit guarantee scheme to de-risk small-scale renewable projects, designing it to cover grid connected solar rooftops and other renewable energy technologies as well as off-grid renewable energy solutions. A green credit guarantee would incentivise small-sized ESCOs with limited track record and collateral to obtain financing. Such a guarantee scheme could also accelerate the uptake of a net-billing policy offering high enough tariffs.

The Thai Credit Guarantee Corporation (TCG) could act as guarantor, given its mandate and ability to extend and process guarantees. While designing the pilot guarantee scheme, it is important to ensure that guarantee fees and administrative processes do not disproportionately add to the final cost of finance for MSME and ESCO borrowers. Concessional financing from the government and support by donors and DFIs might be required to partially offset guarantee fees and service costs, especially at the onset of the programme, to lower the guarantee fee for MSMEs and small-scale renewable projects as well as to mobilise commercial banks.

As a first step, a programme feasibility study could be conducted, assessing the market offer and challenges of green financing products for small-scale renewables, readiness of the TCG, potential guarantee take-up challenges faced by ESCOs and MSMEs (e.g. through a market survey) as well as the degree of awareness of financial institutions on the Thai green taxonomy. The feasibility study could inform decisions on key design elements, namely: (i) the choice between the individual and portfolio guarantee approach; (ii) the coverage ratio (i.e. what portion of a loan can be covered by a guarantee); (iii) the pricing structure for the guarantee fees; (iv) the process for handling defaults and guarantee payouts; and (v) the exit strategy.

A credit guarantee scheme alone will not be able to bridge the lack of technical capacity of a lender or borrower to assess renewable energy projects, so the guarantee scheme needs to be accompanied by tailored capacity-building programmes, for example on the Thai taxonomy energy criteria and on technical risk assessments for small-scale projects. The full roadmap and timeline for piloting a credit guarantee scheme for small-scale renewable projects in Thailand can be found in Table 3.4 below.

## Table 3.4. Roadmap for a green credit guarantee implementation in Thailand

| Key areas | Activities | Responsible agency | Year 1-2: Preparation | | Year 3-5: Pilot | | | Year 6 onwards: Scale-up |
|---|---|---|---|---|---|---|---|---|
| **Program feasibility** | 1.1. Market and analysis and feasibility study | DEDE | X | | | | | |
| | 1.2. Regulatory review and policy development | DEDE | X | | | | | |
| | 1.3. Financial modelling and risk assessment | DEDE | X | | | | | |
| **Program design** | 2.1. Identify the type and structure of the guarantee scheme that best suits the local context and needs of MSMEs (individual vs portfolio guarantee) | DEDE engaged with all key stakeholders | | X | | | | |
| | 2.2. Design the scheme with appropriate risk sharing, fees, types of loans, defaults and risk management mechanisms to ensure financial sustainability and additionality. | DEDE and TCG | | X | | | | |
| | 2.3. Involve donors, the public sector and the private sector in funding, regulating and operating the scheme, and balance their roles and interests | DEDE, TCG and funding agencies | | X | | | | |
| | 2.4. Create a conducive regulatory and institutional framework that supports the creation and growth of the scheme and promotes its use among the financial sector and the general public | DEDE | | X | | | | |
| **Pilot project** | 3.1. Marketing and outreach | TCG | | | X | X | X | |
| | 3.2. Training and capacity building | Technical support agencies | | | X | X | X | |
| | 3.3. Financing setup | TCG, funding agencies and commercial banks | | | X | | | |
| | 3.4. Installation of clean energy technologies | Project developers | | | | X | X | |
| | 3.5. Monitoring and data collection | TCG and commercial banks | | | | X | X | |
| | 3.6. Evaluation and adjustment | TCG | | | | | X | |
| **Scale-Up** | 4.1. Program revision and finalisation | DEDE and TCG | | | | | | X |
| | 4.2. Capacity building and marketing | DEDE and TCG | | | | | | X |
| | 4.3. Continuous monitoring and evaluation | DEDE and TCG | | | | | | X |

Source: Authors

### *Providing financial support to Pay-As-You-Go (PAYG) models to expand off-grid, community-based RE*

The primary targets for replicating PAYG models include off-grid communities, especially in remote islands, where extending the grid is not economically viable. Financing at favourable terms from the government, donors, multilateral development banks (MDBs) and development finance institutions (DFIs) is necessary at the early stage of innovative PAYG models, to cover upfront investment and business planning costs. Sufficient funding is also necessary for frequent maintenance and/or replacements, particularly of sensitive components like batteries and inverters. Public funding could be used effectively to mobilise private investors from the onset of the project.

Replicating and expanding the PAYG model in remote islands would require significant training to ensure the communities have the necessary technical skills. Effective implementation significantly depends on the community's understanding and engagement with the solar systems. This requires comprehensive awareness raising and capacity-building. The full roadmap and timeline for the PAYG model implementation in Thailand is included in Table 3.5 below.

Though initially developed for clean electrification of off-grid areas, PAYG models are also applicable to on-grid communities seeking clean energy solutions. Through the PAYG model, on-grid communities can move towards greater energy independence, making them more resilient to grid outages and fluctuations in energy prices and allowing communities to transition towards cleaner energy sources.

**Table 3.5. Roadmap for PAYG implementation in Thailand**

| Key areas | Activities | Responsible agency | Year 1: Preparation | Year 2-3: Pilot expansion | Year 4 onwards: Scale-up |
|---|---|---|---|---|---|
| **Stakeholder engagement and policy support** | 1.1 Establish a task force with representatives from the Ministry of Energy, private investors, international aid organisations, and community leaders. | MOEN & ReCharge Energy | X | | |
| | 1.2 Advocate for policy reforms that support microgrid developments in off-grid and on-grid areas. | MOEN & ReCharge Energy | X | | |
| | 1.3 Engage local communities throughout the project development process | Task Force | | X | X |
| | 1.4 Foster public-private partnerships to enhance investment and technology innovation. | Task Force | | X | X |
| **Technical and need assessment** | 2.1 Identify potential off-grid and on-grid communities that can benefit from PAYG. | MOEN & ReCharge Energy | X | | |
| | 2.2 Evaluate current technologies and identify the need for technical upgrades or adaptations to suit local conditions. | MOEN & ReCharge Energy | X | | |
| **Financing** | 3.1 Create a financial strategy suitable for scaling, including identifying sources for funding and investment. | MOEN & ReCharge Energy | X | | |
| | 3.2 Secure financing sources for project investment | Investors, Banks | | X | X |
| **Expansion** | 4.1 Deploy PAYG systems in selected off-grid / on-grid communities. | MOEN & ReCharge Energy | | X | X |
| **Capacity building and training** | 5.1 Develop local capacity in technical, managerial, and financial aspects of PAYG systems. | MOEN & ReCharge Energy | | X | X |
| | 5.2 Implement comprehensive education programs for end-users to ensure proper use and maintenance. | | | X | X |
| **Monitoring and evaluation** | 6.1 Set up systems to monitor usage, payments, and operational metrics. | | X | | |
| | 6.2 Regularly monitor and evaluate projects as per the set-up systems | | | X | X |

Source: Authors

### *Developing aggregation and securitisation models for small-scale renewable energy projects*

Blended finance can be used to support bundling and aggregation of multiple small-scale projects or assets into larger and rateable financial products or vehicles that are more attractive to large institutional investors. With the aggregated portfolio acting as an entry point for investors, transaction costs are reduced as compared to investing in small-scale projects individually. Moreover, financial aggregation and securitisation provide a means of managing portfolio risk as the operational risks of individual assets are diluted within the portfolio.

Through securitisation, projects can be bundled to reach a scale and risk profile that is attractive to investors. For example, small loans for renewable energy projects can be pooled and then sold to a separate legal entity, such as special purpose vehicle (SPV), to protect the assets from any insolvency of the sponsoring entity or seller. The SPV can then issue marketable securities, typically in tranches with different credit risk. Different layers of risk exposure can facilitate the participation of different types of investors and risk-return profiles. Within such structures, donors, DFIs, MDBs and/or the government can provide first loss tranches as credit enhancement to comfort senior tranche investors. Private investors and commercial banks can act either as originators (to reduce credit risks and free up capital for new lending) or as risk buyers (e.g. to get increased exposure in renewable energy portfolios).

This type of financing model has been successfully employed in other emerging and developing economies. Examples include Brazil's Green Receivables Fund, a securitisation instrument to address the lack of long-term finance for clean energy projects, as well as clean energy securitisation transactions in Kenya. Lessons learnt from previous experience with these transactions point to the need for grants and technical assistance to develop large and bankable pipelines of small-scale renewables projects as well as to gather and standardise risk and performance data from small entities. Sharing legal services and technical advice and standardising common documentation can reduce transaction costs associated with structuring, underwriting and due diligence of individual companies or projects.

### *Policy, regulation and governance*

#### *Strengthening policy planning and setting region-specific targets on small-scale renewable energy over the near- and long-term*

To meet distributed renewable ambitions, a clear strategy with near- and long-term targets for small-scale renewable power installed capacity (including a specific target on rooftop solar PV) could help to provide policy direction, clarify long-term opportunities for developers and foster the development of a local industry ecosystem. Such strategy and targets can also help strategically target public and development funds to where they can have the most impact in mobilising private investment to meet sustainable energy needs. While the national energy plan sets out high-level ambitions, developing clear technology- and region-specific targets will be necessary if the aim is to ensure that all communities have access to reliable, clean and affordable electricity.

#### *Encouraging financial institutions to assess and disclose taxonomy alignment of their portfolios*

The first phase of Thailand Taxonomy, launched in 2023 by the Bank of Thailand and the Securities and Exchange Commission, as co-leads of the Thailand Taxonomy Board, was a key step to provide clarity and harmonisation on technical screening criteria and thresholds of green and transition activities in the energy and transport sector. The taxonomy can also stimulate the growth of small-scale renewable energy projects by providing harmonisation of green criteria as well as bring clarity and certainty to investors, who will be able to better assess and compare the environmental benefits of renewable energy projects and thus avoid greenwashing risks.

The next phase of the taxonomy will focus on developing quantitative criteria for additional sectors. Beyond expanding the sectoral coverage of the taxonomy, it is important to encourage and support actual implementation of the taxonomy by financial institutions, for example, by setting requirements for financial institutions to assess and disclose the extent of alignment of their portfolios with the taxonomy. Such regulatory measures shall clarify the taxonomy alignment reporting requirements and timelines for both financial and non-financial entities. Regulatory provisions could also mandate or encourage that the taxonomy is used to identify eligibility criteria of green financial products (e.g. green bonds and loans). On the supply side, developers of small-scale projects would need to incorporate green taxonomy criteria into project design and implementation, which would provide assurance of the mitigation and other environmental benefits, thereby facilitating access to sustainable finance sources. Standardised taxonomy-alignment assessments can also facilitate smaller projects to be pooled together as assets are more readily compared.

Internal capacity of financial institutions to conduct technical assessments of the alignment of financed activities with taxonomy criteria needs to be developed, through appropriate trainings and capacity building. Taxonomy-alignment disclosure requirements to financial institutions and listed companies would indirectly affect their clients and suppliers, regardless of their size. For this reason, it is important to anticipate that MSMEs will need significant support to build the internal capacity and infrastructure to be able to gather climate and environmental risks and performance data, incorporate green criteria and conduct assessments of taxonomy alignment.

#### *Strengthening the regulatory environment for financial securitisation of renewable energy assets*

Developing the green securitisation market in Thailand in a prudent way requires establishing a favourable local regulatory environment by the Thai financial regulator and supervisor (the Bank of Thailand). Such regulation could address the risks inherent to securitisation transactions, for instance by setting strict risk retention requirements, improving transparency and risk management processes, and enhancing underwriting policies (EBA, 2022[29]). Moreover, facilitating the standardisation of contracts and enabling access to issuers' performance data of the underlying assets are key to facilitate due diligence and provide transparency to investors.

The regulatory framework would also clarify eligibility criteria for renewable energy assets to be securitised, e.g. related to the project size, technology type, track record and revenue generation stability. Moreover, the assessment and rating of renewable energy securitisation transactions by independent credit rating agencies would need to be facilitated. To do so, the financial regulator could collaborate with rating agencies and industry associations to develop rigorous methodologies for assessing the creditworthiness of this type of transactions.

Technical assistance and capacity building on securitisation and risk transfer, learning from international experience (e.g. on green securitisation regulation in the United States, European Union and China), can be beneficial for both supervisors and financial institutions.

#### *Simplifying renewable energy licensing and permitting processes and requirements*

Processes and requirements for renewable energy licensing and permitting could be simplified, including building modification permissions for smaller projects. The creation of a single-window service licensing portal (such as an online platform or one-stop service) could significantly reduce administrative barriers and streamline application procedures, especially for small players. To be effective and such one-stop-shop could be adequately staffed and have a digital platform for online monitoring. Such a platform could also provide information about all related regulations, equipment standards as well as available products. Moreover, the governance of the one-stop shop, including management and oversight responsibilities and inter-agency co-ordination for licensing processes, will need to be defined and agreed upon early on to avoid potential operationalisation delays. Additional ways to facilitate small-scale renewable energy development include streamlining permitting requirements for small or community-owned installations (e.g. construction permits, grid connection authorisations, etc.). This can help reduce costs and shorten timelines for obtaining relevant technical and environmental approvals for the project, thereby reducing risks of project development at the pre-feasibility and feasibility stages.

#### *Improving consistency and harmonisation of grid connection codes*

Thailand currently has several different grid connection codes for the power system, defined by the Electricity Generating Authority of Thailand (EGAT) and its two distribution utilities Provincial Electricity Authority (PEA) and Metropolitan Electricity Authority (MEA). For example, EGAT, PEA and MEA have slightly different requirements on equipment for solar systems and this creates complexity and uncertainty.

Grid codes could be harmonised and streamlined across the three agencies, to ensure consistency to accommodate for future increase in variable renewable energy. They could also be reviewed to accommodate for distributed clean energy resources. When revising the codes, it is important to ensure the technical capabilities needed to efficiently operate the system and provide supply security while avoiding excessive requirements that may be a barrier to deployment. Grid codes could be technology neutral to avoid putting up barriers to any new technologies such as distributed resources (IEA, 2023[30]).

The regulator (ERC) can play a key role in improving the consistency of grid codes between EGAT, MEA and PEA and ensuring that stakeholders comply with the grid codes. Effective co-ordination among EGAT, MEA and PEA agencies is necessary to streamline requirements.

### *Capacity building, data collection and awareness*

#### *Building capacity of MSMEs, financial institutions and technicians and developing training programmes*

With grants, technical assistance and support of international development partners, access to information and capacity-building activities for both financial institutions and MSMEs could be increased, in particular by focusing on the following priorities:

- enhancing financial institution capacity on conducting climate-related disclosures, applying green standards for their lending and investment products, assessing portfolio alignment with the Thai taxonomy criteria as well as on assessing small-scale renewable energy business models
- increasing MSMEs awareness and knowledge on the latest renewable energy opportunities as well as to improve their financial literacy
- increasing developers knowledge on designing renewable energy products that are in line with the Thai taxonomy criteria
- developing financial institution and regulators knowledge on securitisation and risk transfer for renewable energy assets, learning from international experience (e.g. on green securitisation regulation in the United States, European Union and China)
- providing adequate training to solar PV technicians and contractors for them to acquire adequate skills and updated knowledge on latest innovations as well as safety standards.

Furthermore, given the rapidly evolving nature of distributed renewable energy technologies, continuous learning and monitoring of technology developments is essential to ensure that technology-selection decisions continue to be well suited to the market's particular stage of development.

#### *Implementing consumer awareness and education campaigns and fostering community engagement*

With support from international development partners, awareness campaigns on small-scale, distributed and off-grid renewable technologies can address different target groups ranging from policy makers, project developers and industry professionals, as well as financial institutions, commercial end-users and civil society. Awareness campaigns could focus not only on spreading knowledge on the latest technologies and regulatory changes and standards, but also on the latest developments in terms of financial instruments, both public and private.

Fostering community engagement and raising community awareness about the benefits of PAYG-enabled renewable energy model are necessary to encourage the up-take of these solutions. Empowering local communities to take ownership of decision-making process, addressing their energy needs and preferences, and demonstrating the socio-economic and environmental benefits of PAYG models can help generate demand and acceptance for these initiatives. Education campaigns on community-based renewable energy models and PAYG solutions in schools can also promote youth engagement.

Furthermore, the local and decentralised nature of community-based renewable energy projects can facilitate the creation of green job opportunities and skill development for women and youth. Community ownership structures can encourage women and youth to participate in decision-making processes, take leadership roles and get involved in project development. Moreover, the provision of cleaner energy opportunities will benefit women who often bear most of the consequences of the use of polluting sources of energy and fuel. Community engagement activities could therefore promote outreach and participation of women and youth.

#### *Fostering data collection on small-scale renewable capacity and financing*

Increasing the availability of data on the expansion of small-scale energy capacity across different types of renewable energy would be beneficial. Financial institutions and investors would benefit from better access to risk and performance data of small-scale renewable projects (e.g. recovery rates, default risks), which would facilitate their aggregation for securitised products as well as more generally increase investors' knowledge and confidence in investing in these models.

## References


Adebiyi, O. et al. (2020), "Impact of Malaysian Green Technology Financial Scheme on Business Performance of Renewable Energy Producers", *Journal of Southwest Jiaotong University*, Vol. 55/6, https://doi.org/10.35741/issn.0258-2724.55.6.19. [20]

Alliance for Financial Inclusion (2022), "Green Credit Guarantee Schemes for MSMEs", https://www.afi-global.org/wp-content/uploads/2022/06/Green-credit-schemes-for-MSMEs_260722.pdf (accessed on 20 December 2023). [14]

APEC (2012), *Peer Review on Low Carbon Energy Policies in Thailand*, https://aperc.or.jp/file/2012/12/28/PRLCE_Phase_1_in_Thailand.pdf. [1]

Carbon Trust (2023), *Designing a credit guarantee scheme to accelerate energy efficiency loans across Thailand*, https://www.carbontrust.com/our-work-and-impact/impact-stories/designing-a-credit-guarantee-scheme-to-accelerate-energy-efficiency-loans-across-thailand. [21]

CASE for Southeast Asia (2022), *Towards a collective vision of Thai energy transition: National long-term scenarios and socioeconomic implications*, Clean, Affordable and Secure Energy (CASE) for Southeast Asia, https://newclimate.org/sites/default/files/2022-11/2022-11-08_th_ltes_-_full_report.pdf. [4]

CASE for Southeast Asia (forthcoming), *Unlocking Rooftop Solar Investment in Thailand: Facilitating Policy and Financial De-risking Instruments*, Clean, Affordable and Secure Energy (CASE) for Southeast Asia. [6]

Coalition for Green Capital (2019), *Aggregation and Securitization*, https://greenbanknetwork.org/wp-content/uploads/2019/04/Green-Bank-Aggregation-and-Securitization-Coalition-for-Green-Capital.pdf. [23]

Davies, L. and D. Saygin (2023), "Distributed renewable energy in Colombia: Unlocking private investment for non-interconnected zones", *OECD Environment Working Papers*, No. 213, OECD Publishing, Paris, https://doi.org/10.1787/deda64ff-en. [25]

EBA (2022), *Developing a framework for sustainable securitisation*, https://www.eba.europa.eu/sites/default/files/document_library/Publications/Reports/2022/1027593/EBA%20report%20on%20sustainable%20securitisation.pdf. [29]

EGAT (2022), *EGAT supports SolarPlus with Peer-to-Peer Energy Trading to connect energy trading among prosumers for the first time in Thailand*, https://www.egat.co.th/home/en/20220816e-02/. [9]

GIZ (2017), *Renewable Energy Hybrid Grid Systems for Thai Islands*, https://www.thai-german-cooperation.info/download/public-report_5s.pdf (accessed on 20 December 2023). [10]

IEA (2024), *Reducing the Cost of Capital: Strategies to unlock clean energy investment in emerging and developing economies*, https://iea.blob.core.windows.net/assets/227da10f-c527-406d-b94f-dbaa38ae9abb/ReducingtheCostofCapital.pdf. [12]

IEA (2023), *A new tool to track transitions: the IEA clean energy equipment price index*, https://www.iea.org/commentaries/a-new-tool-to-track-transitions-the-iea-clean-energy-equipment-price-index. [11]

IEA (2023), *Thailand's Clean Electricity Transition*, https://iea.blob.core.windows.net/assets/dd5b10b2-b655-4c7d-8c09-d3d7efe6bd50/ThailandsCleanElectricityTransition.pdf. [30]

IIED (2017), *Turning up the volume: Financial aggregation for off-grid energy*, https://www.iied.org/sites/default/files/pdfs/migrate/16636IIED.pdf. [22]

International Solar Alliance (2023), *Roadmap of Solar Energy for Universal Energy Access*, https://isolaralliance.org/uploads/docs/540dc1da191598c88320bf07b42e8d.pdf. [28]

IRENA (2020), *Community-ownership models: Innovation Landscape Brief*, https://www.irena.org/-/media/Files/IRENA/Agency/Publication/2020/Jul/IRENA_Community_ownership_2020.pdf. [27]

IRENA (2020), *Pay-as-you-go Models: Innovation Landscape Brief*, https://www.irena.org/-/media/Files/IRENA/Agency/Publication/2020/Jul/IRENA_Pay-as-you-go_models_2020.pdf. [26]

Junlakarn, S. et al. (2021), "A cross-country comparison of compensation mechanisms for distributed photovoltaics in the Philippines, Thailand, and Vietnam", *Renewable and Sustainable Energy Reviews*, Vol. 145, p. 110820, https://doi.org/10.1016/j.rser.2021.110820. [5]

Malaysian Sustainable Finance Initiative (2023), *Green Technology Financing Scheme (GTFS)*, https://www.msfi.com.my/incentives-green-technology-financing-scheme-gtfs/. [15]

Ministry of Natural Resources and Environment Malaysia (2014), *Green Technology Financing Scheme (GTFS)*, https://unfccc.int/files/focus/mitigation/application/pdf/malaysia_presentation.pdf. [17]

OECD (2022), *Clean Energy Finance and Investment Roadmap of India: Opportunities to Unlock Finance and Scale up Capital*, Green Finance and Investment, OECD Publishing, Paris, https://doi.org/10.1787/21b6e411-en. [16]

OECD (2022), "OECD blended finance guidance for clean energy", *OECD Environment Policy Papers*, No. 31, OECD Publishing, Paris, https://doi.org/10.1787/596e2436-en. [24]

OECD/IEA (2018), *Thailand Renewable Grid Integration Assessment*, https://iea.blob.core.windows.net/assets/c41cd30d-5f69-4b12-9502-3e7caaca294e/Partner_Country_Series_Thailand_Grid_Renewable_Integration_Assessement.pdf. [31]

The Nation (2023), *Household 'net energy metering' plan put on hold*, https://www.nationthailand.com/thailand/general/40029286. [7]

Tongsopit, S. et al. (2016), "Business models and financing options for a rapid scale-up of rooftop solar power systems in Thailand", *Energy Policy*, Vol. 95, pp. 447-457, https://doi.org/10.1016/j.enpol.2016.01.023. [13]

Tu, Fan (2016), *Promoting urban sustainability through green technology in Malaysia*, https://scienceimpact.mit.edu/sites/default/files/documents/Tu.pdf. [19]

USAID (2020), *Distributed Photovoltaics: Trends and Policies in Southeast Asia*, https://pdf.usaid.gov/pdf_docs/PA00WKS8.pdf. [8]

USAID (forthcoming), *Strategies for Expansion of Rooftop Solar PV*, USAID Southeast Asia's Smart Power Programme. [2]

Watson Farley & Williams (2022), *THAILAND'S 5 GW RENEWABLE PPA FIT SCHEME: 2022-203*, https://www.wfw.com/articles/thailands-5-gw-renewable-ppa-fit-scheme-2022-2030/. [3]

World Bank (2020), *Green loans: Financing the transition to a low-carbon economy*, https://blogs.worldbank.org/climatechange/green-loans-financing-transition-low-carbon-economy. [18]

## Notes

[1] These grid codes can be categorised according to transmission and distribution levels and by the types of generators (IPP, SPP and VSPP) as follows: EGAT (connection and operation codes for IPP, EGAT power plants, SPP, IPS, MEA and PEA; service code); MEA (VSPP connection code, VSPP operation code, VSPP service code); and PEA (VSPP connection code, VSPP operation code, VSPP service code) (OECD/IEA, 2018[31]).

[2] Solar leasing is considered both a business and a financing model. It can be considered a business model as it is structured to enable enterprise and customer value creation, but it is also a financing model, as it provides the capital needed for consumers to own a solar system (Tongsopit et al., 2016[13]).

# 4 Unlocking finance and investment for energy efficient cooling and buildings

This chapter presents current trends in energy efficiency in Thailand's building and cooling sectors and examines the policy and regulatory framework and targets for energy efficiency in buildings and cooling appliances. It also provides an overview of the key business models for energy efficiency projects in Thailand, as well as an analysis of the main financing barriers and regulatory challenges. Based on a set of case studies of financing instruments deployed in other countries, the chapter also presents a series of potential financing models that could be explored in Thailand to mobilise financing and investment for energy efficiency buildings and cooling systems, such as energy savings insurance, green bonds, on-bill financing, bulk procurement and green mortgages. The chapter ends with recommendations for the Government of Thailand and key Thai stakeholders across three key pillars: (i) financial support; (ii) policy, regulation and governance; and (iii) capacity building, data collection and awareness-raising.

The buildings sector has a critical role to play in meeting global decarbonisation ambitions. The IEA estimates that energy consumption in buildings accounted for 30% of global final energy demand in 2022 and 26% of emissions (including 8% of direct emissions, such as from gas heating and cooking, and 18% of indirect emissions from consumption of electricity) (IEA, 2023[1]). Space cooling, particularly the use of air conditioners (ACs), is showing the fastest growth in final energy consumption among building end-uses. Emerging markets and developing economies (EMDEs) are experiencing the most significant increase as the stock of ACs is set to double by 2030 due to rising incomes and cooling needs in EMDEs.

In the Association of Southeast Asian Nations (ASEAN) region, where nearly a quarter of final energy consumption is dedicated to buildings, cooling demand is increasing rapidly. Between 1990 and 2020, electricity for space cooling in buildings multiplied by seven, reaching 80 TWh. Efficient cooling measures could help cut electricity demand in ASEAN by over a third by 2040 (IEA, 2022[2]).

Improved building design can reduce the need for cooling through natural ventilation, nature-based solutions and superior air sealing and insulation, which, coupled with efficient fans and smart devices, can already combat much of Thailand's cooling needs. At the same time, where space cooling is used, increasing the efficiency of ACs, or developing district cooling solutions for groups of buildings or big commercial premises, such as office complexes, shopping malls, hotels, and hospitals, can moderate the pace at which energy demand and related GHG emissions increase. On-site consumption of distributed renewable energy such as rooftop solar photovoltaic (PV) systems can also help meet increasing demand. Several features such as battery storage, demand response ready equipment, and smart devices can also help to reduce peak demand from space cooling.

## Current trends in energy efficiency for cooling in Thailand's building sector

### *Demand for cooling in Thailand is increasing*

Thailand has a warm and humid climate, averaging around 28 degrees Celsius and 75% humidity throughout the year. The climate is marked by three broad seasons, including a summer season from mid-February to mid-May, a rainy season until mid-October, and a winter season from mid-October to mid-February. The rainy season is influenced by a south-west monsoon wind, bringing warm, moist air from the Indian Ocean to Thailand, causing abundant rain. In the winter season, relative humidity drops to its lowest levels (70%) under a north-east wind bringing cold and dry air from the Chinese mainland (World Data, 2024[3]). Cooling demand is greatest in the summer months, where high levels of humidity amplify Thailand's cooling needs. Mean maximum temperatures in Thailand have been rising steadily over the last decades, which suggests that rising temperatures will continue to drive increasing cooling needs (Figure 4.1) (Government of Thailand, 2021[4]).

### Figure 4.1. Annual mean maximum temperatures in Thailand

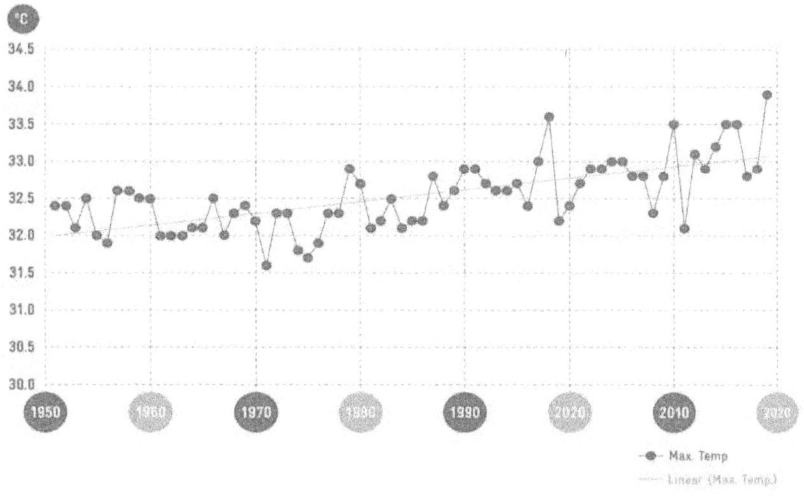


Source: Ministry of Natural Resources and Environment (2022[5]), Thailand's long-term low greenhouse gas emission development strategy (revised version), https://unfccc.int/sites/default/files/resource/Thailand%20LT-LEDS%20%28Revised%20Version%29_08Nov2022.pdf

While there is increasing interest in efficient cooling strategies through green building design and district cooling, refrigerant-based AC systems remain the most accessible option to achieve thermal comfort in buildings. The summer months are marked a sharp peak in electricity consumption reflecting unbridled use of cooling systems, increasing year-on-year (Figure 4.2) (EPPO, 2022[6]).

### Figure 4.2. Monthly electricity consumption in Thailand (2020-2023)

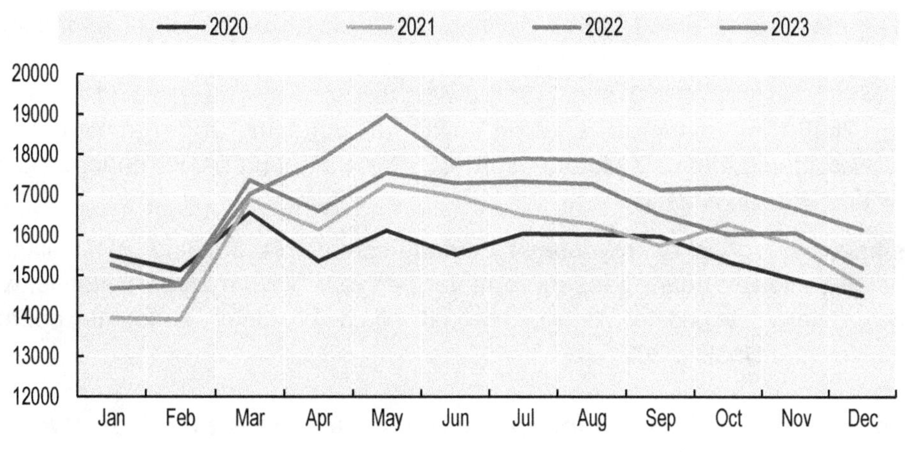


Source: EPPO (2022[6]), Energy Statistics, http://www.eppo.go.th/index.php/en/

StatLink https://stat.link/urb67e

Thailand is seeing increasing cooling demand as incomes are increasing, tourism is booming and temperatures are rising. Already in 2019, the share of households using ACs was around one third, but this is much lower than in other Southeast Asian countries such as Malaysia and Singapore, which have similar cooling needs, measured in cooling degree days. In these countries in 2017, 80% of households used AC units, as opposed to roughly 30% in Thailand, pointing to increasing levels of AC ownership in the years to come as incomes continues to rise in Thailand (IEA, 2019[7]) (Figure 4.3).

**Figure 4.3. Cooling degree days and share of households using air conditioning systems by country (2017)**

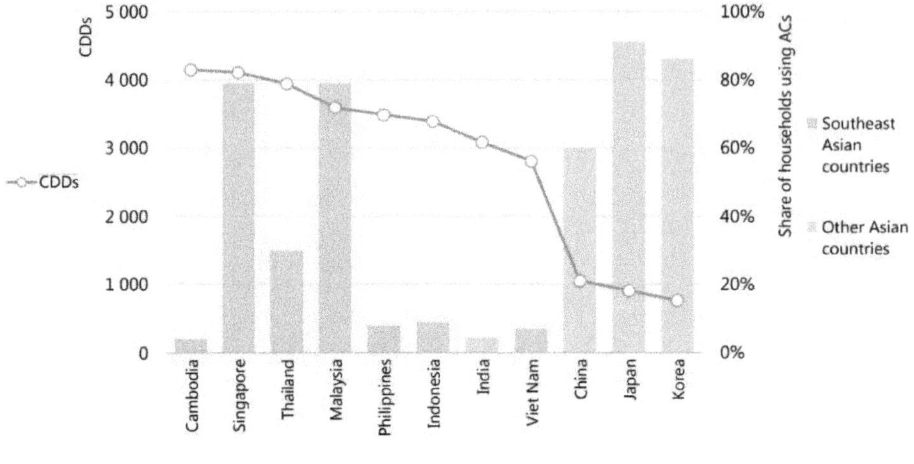


Note: CDD = cooling degree days.
Source: IEA (2019[7]), The Future of Cooling in Southeast Asia, https://iea.blob.core.windows.net/assets/dcadf8ee-c43d-400e-9112-533516662e3e/The_Future_of_Cooling_in_Southeast_Asia.pdf.

### *Commercial and public buildings are seeing increasing electricity demand*

The buildings sector represented on average approximately 25% of the total electricity consumed in Thailand in 2019 (EPPO, 2024[8]). Electricity consumption of the building sector has grown from roughly 27 855 GWh in 2009, to 49 128 in 2019, with an annual increase of 5.91% and has been the most rapidly increasing sector in terms of electricity consumption growth (Seeley and Dhakal, 2021[9]).

In 2018, shopping malls represented the single largest electricity consumed at approximately at 5 235 GWh, equivalent to 8% of the total electricity consumption of the building sector. Hotels and commercial office buildings were next with 4 363 and 2 966 GWh, respectively (Seeley and Dhakal, 2021[9]). It is projected that by 2036 the commercial building sector will consume approximately 175 000 GWh of electricity, with an estimated 425 649 kilotonnes of $CO_2$ equivalent (kt $CO_2e$) under a business-as-usual scenario (Seeley and Dhakal, 2021[9]).

Shopping malls have the highest energy intensity among commercial buildings in Thailand, estimated to consume roughly 295 kilowatt hours per square meter per year (kWh/m2/year). Hotels, which consume 255 kWh/m2/year, were second, while commercial office buildings consume approximately 225 kWh/m2/year (Seeley and Dhakal, 2021[9]).

### *Building design for many commercial and public buildings is ill-adapted to Thailand's climate*

Rapid urbanisation in Thailand drew from ideas and building materials from Europe and America, which can be ill-suited for the Thai climate. For example, many buildings did not feature overhangs or other features to provide shading, resulting in easy penetration of solar radiation. This is particularly problematic for office buildings that favour glass facades. Other types of building materials used for building envelopes typically include concrete and brick, which have a high thermal mass. This means that a large amount of heat is stored during the day, transferring heat both day and night (Tantasavasdi, Srebric and Chen, 2001[10]).

A recent study by JLL – a real estate investment consulting firm – measured the total stock of office space in Bangkok at 9.97 million square metres, of which nearly 70% represents buildings aged over 20 years

(JLL, 2022[11]). This means that more than two-thirds of Bangkok's office stock is classified as ageing, with a significant portion of these buildings poorly maintained compared to newer stock. This is causing challenges for building owners in post-COVID-19 times, as tenants tend to prefer premium office buildings due requirements for new hybrid working models and high maintenance costs for older buildings. Between 2022 and 2026, the Bangkok office market will see an additional 2.2 million sqm of new space. Of this, more than 1.7 million sqm or 81% will consist of prime grade developments (JLL, 2022[12]).

Good building design is a fundamental component to enabling thermal comfort for building occupants, for example through natural ventilation, thermal insulation and shading from direct sunlight to moderate temperature and humidity in interior spaces. Other approaches for large buildings include ground floor openings for cross ventilation and use the Box-in-Box concept that includes interior and exterior shell, where the zone between two facades can also act as a buffer area to cool down the air before entering to the building. These features are an important consideration for new constructions to avoid the same challenges of those built over the last decades. Retrofits provide significant opportunities to improve energy efficiency and reduce cooling needs, particularly via increasing thermal insulation of building envelopes.

In a study of 42 commercial building retrofits undertaken between 2011 and 2020 (mainly for heating ventilation and air conditioning), it was found that energy savings ranged from 6% to 31%. Hotels had the highest average energy reduction at just under 19%, with retail having a slightly lower average at 18%, and commercial office buildings at just above 15% (Seeley and Dhakal, 2021[13]). Other research in Thailand on office buildings in three cities in hot and humid summer zones found that natural ventilation was able to provide up to 30% energy savings. High-performance windows and installation of wall insulation were also seen to have created energy saving for cooling of an average of 12.4–15.1%. Other approaches such as horizontal shading devices could slightly save the cooling energy by approximately 2.7% (Lohwanitchai and Jareemit, 2021[14]).

Yet, as the main driver of electricity consumption in commercial and public buildings, besides building efficiency improvements the importance of high-performance ACs could not be underestimated. Building retrofits with high-performance ACs were seen to deliver total estimated electricity savings ranging from 38% for hotels to up to 58% for retail buildings (Seeley and Dhakal, 2021[13]).

### *Increasing sales of air conditioners in Thailand*

There is a wide range of air conditioners (ACs) available on the market which vary enormously in scale and cost, from small (sometimes portable) devices designed to cool a single room to large-scale systems for entire buildings. Products include Split, variable refrigerant flow, Window, Chillers and others (Business Wire, 2022[15]).

There are two main types of ACs used in in large buildings in Thailand. A central cooling system through water chiller can produce cold water that is distributed to parts of the building. Heat from rooms is transferred to the cold water, which is returned to the water chiller for heat removal. Air temperature and humidity of each room are adjusted or set from a single control location. Some large buildings with several tenants also use split-type ACs, which provide total control on how to condition the air inside each room.

The split-type AC are most common in small buildings and consequently dominate AC market sales in Thailand. These include both wall-mounted split units and concealed split units. At larger capacities, standing, cassette and floor/ceiling units are more common. The figures below represent models available on the market. Cooling capacities are between 11 000 British thermal unit per hour (Btu/h) and 15 000 Btu/h are the most popular, with ACs under 15 000 Btu/h accounting for most of the sales, even though they represent only approximately 30% of the models available on the market (CLASP, 2019[16]).

For commercial buildings, the choice of AC unit depends on several factors, including the cost of system, ease of maintenance and size of project. For energy conscious developers requiring large systems this tends to be chiller systems, for medium this could be variable refrigerant flow, or else it could be many small-scale split systems. Only governmental and prestige projects are exploring water cooled, oil free systems which have the highest efficiency but are the most expensive.

Thailand has a large air conditioning manufacturing industry with a deep local supply chain (CLASP, 2019[16]). Systems with Seasonal Energy Efficiency Rating of up to around 4 W/W are widely available and are often locally manufactured. More efficient systems are also available (up to 6 W/W) but are not widely used. Thailand's air conditioner (AC) industry is heavily export-driven. Almost 10% of the ACs manufactured worldwide come from Thailand, and the country is the second-largest producer of air conditioners after China, thanks to its strategic location coupled with its manufacturing competency. In 2021, Thailand's air conditioning industry was valued at Thai Baht (THB) 39 billion (USD 1.2 billion) almost on a par with 2020, compared with THB 36-37 billion (USD 0.99-1.07 billion) in 2019 (Jitpleecheep, 2022[17]).

Several international multinational companies have chosen Thailand to be their production site both to tap into the Thai market and to respond quickly to the demand for residential and commercial ACs from Asian markets. Manufacturers are also looking at energy efficiency as a strategy to increase market shares, with manufacturers working towards providing Wi-Fi enabled, higher efficiency inverter-based ACs, to fulfil the need for energy and cost-saving (Business Wire, 2022[15]).

### *Solar Photovoltaics (PV) can contribute to meet the rising electricity demand for cooling*

Commercial buildings and factories in Thailand are increasing using solar PV for self-consumption, given the falling cost of solar PV systems, emergence of innovative financing options and the potential to reduce electricity bills using solar power, as shown in Chapter 3. Solar PV can contribute to meeting rising energy demand for cooling with clean energy produced on-site as well as to achieving zero-energy building goals (Suntorachai, 2020[18]). However, it would be difficult to achieve zero-energy buildings relying primarily on PV in the rainy season, where the PV production capacity is relatively low under cloudy sky conditions and not matching evening load peaks, so other energy efficiency measures will be needed (Lohwanitchai and Jareemit, 2021[14]).

Solar PV for self-consumption in commercial buildings faces several other challenges, including limited space on rooftops. Furthermore, the timing of PV energy production (which spans from November to March) does not match AC cooling peaks (April to October) (Lohwanitchai and Jareemit, 2021[14]).

### *District cooling is becoming more commonplace in Thailand*

District cooling, which is the distribution of cooling from one or more sources to multiple buildings, can be a cost-effective alternative to conventional AC systems as it leverages a centrally located chilled water plant to serve a cluster of buildings through a network of pipes. By aggregating the customers' energy loads, the overall installed capacity can be lower than if each building used a separate cooling unit. The Thai district cooling market is dominated by absorption cooling and electric chillers. In 2021, absorption cooling, which uses heat waste rather than electricity (electric chillers) as the primary energy source, dominated the market. This further results in reduced cost of heating and cooling for facilities and increased energy saving during peak demand. An alternative means of district cooling is free cooling, using which uses external ambient temperature to reject heat (Data Bridge, 2021[19]).

District cooling projects have been developed in Thailand, mainly as government-funded projects or as prestige projects in the private sectors. For the private sector, projects have typically been developed by the land or building owner, an equity investor and a project developer. A number of district cooling projects are in operation in Thailand in governmental buildings, commercial building, industrial, hospital, airports, data centers and others (Table 4.1) (Vorasayan, 2021[20]).

The earliest project dates back to a government project in 2006 and according to the DEDE, district cooling is currently under development in most large business districts and mixed-use complexes. The commercial buildings sector is experiencing the largest growth due to ongoing district cooling projects in commercial buildings, including malls and corporate offices, greater focus on energy efficiency, and increasing expectations for better thermal comfort. The district cooling market is expected to grow to a United States Dollars (USD) 202 million market by 2028 (Data Bridge, 2021[19]).

### Table 4.1. District cooling projects in Bangkok

| Project | Owner | Description | Technology | Cooling capacity | Year |
|---|---|---|---|---|---|
| District Cooling System and Power Plant | Electricity Generating Authority of Thailand (EGAT), Metropolitan Electricity Authority (MEA) and PTT Public Company Limited (PTT) | Supply Electricity, Chilled Water and Steam to Suvarnabhumi International Airport | 110 MW combined cycle power plant using 2 sets of gas turbine generators for cooling and electricity generation. Cooling through electric Chillers and cooling towers. | 13 748 RT | 2006, upgraded in 2018 |
| Chaengwattanna, Bangkok | Government Complex | Multiple Office Buildings, Convention Center | Electricity used as primary energy source. Electrical Chiller, cooling tower, condenser water pump and chilled water pump. | GFA 975,200 sqm 12 000 RT | 2009, 2013 |
| Siriraj towards Medical Excellence in Southeast Asia | State facility Siriraj Piyamahajkarun Hospital | Multi Buildings Hospital Campus | Chilled Water & Electricity | GFA 238,000 sqm, 6,000 RT | 2012 |
| Kasikornbank – Head Office Ratburana Office | Kasikornbank | Office Building | Chilled Water & Electricity | GFA 163,000 sqm 4,000 RT | In operation |
| The Forestias | Magnolia Quality Development Corporation Limited | Mixed Use Complex (e.g. hotels, offices, hospitals, retail) | 115 kV MEA electrical substation compressors | GFA 750,000 sqm 10,000 RT | Design Development / Construction 2024+ |
| One Bangkok | TCC Group | Mixed Use Complex | Chilled Water & Electricity | GFA 1,830,000 sqm 38,000 RT | Design Development / Construction |
| CU Smart City | Property Management of Chulalongkorn University (PMCU) | Mixed Use Complex | Chilled Water & Electricity | GFA 842,000 sqm 18,000 RT | Concept Development |

Note: Refrigeration ton (RT), Square meters (sqm), Mega Watts (MW)
Source: Vorasayan (2021[20]), Energy Efficiency and District Cooling in Thailand

There is growing interest in district cooling as a cost-efficient means of cooling commercial and public buildings. However, project development costs for district cooling are still relatively high.

## Governance and planning of energy efficiency policies for buildings and cooling

### *The building sector's contribution to Thailand's draft Energy Efficiency Plan (EEP)*

The Government of Thailand set a 20-year Energy Efficiency Plan (EEP) which aims to reduce energy intensity by 30% by 2037, compared to 2010 levels. Within the EEP, commercial buildings are expected to conserve 21,167 ktoe, by 2037 (Ministry of Natural Resources and Environment, 2022[5]). The commercial sector is expected to account for the largest share of energy efficiency improvements (41%).

Policy measures contained in the EEP include minimum energy performance standards (MEPS), energy efficiency resource standards (EERS) and energy management systems in buildings.

Thailand aims to reach Zero Energy Buildings in 2036, a type of building whose external energy supply is near-zero thanks to low energy demand on-site energy generation from renewable sources. In this scenario, office buildings are consuming around 57 kWh/m$^2$ per year from a business-as-usual energy consumption of 219 kWh/m$^2$ per year. Thailand also aims to implement High Energy Performance Standards (HEPS) by 2025, where office buildings consume 141 kWh/m$^2$ per year via high efficiency standards of existing technology and systems, and to reach the Economic Buildings (ECON) category by 2031, where technologies and systems are developed to be more energy efficient (82 kWh/m$^2$ energy consumption a year) but still cost effective (Figure 4.4) (Lohwanitchai and Jareemit, 2020[21]). The estimated energy saving of HEPS-type buildings amounts to 30-35% whereas for ECON it is 60-65% (Thailand's Ministry of Energy, 2020[22]). Concrete actions on how to implement the next steps of the roadmaps have not yet been determined.

**Figure 4.4. Building Energy Code (BEC) Roadmap**

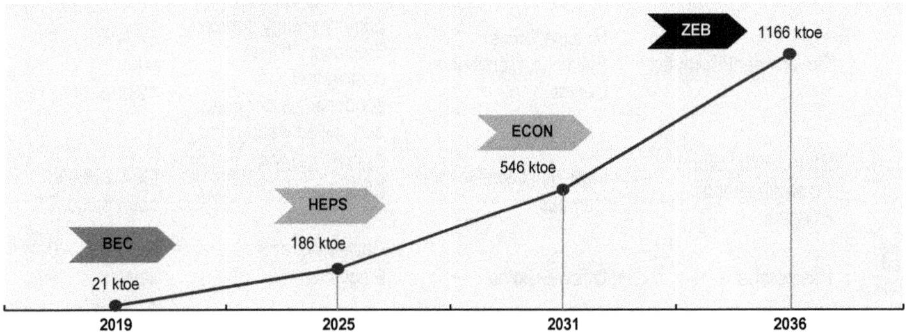


Source: DEDE (2018[23]), Building Energy Code, https://seforallateccj.org/wpdata/wp-content/uploads/ecap17-thailand.pdf.

### *Institutional co-ordination and governance*

The Department of Alternative Energy Development and Efficiency (DEDE)'s duties include energy efficiency promotion and energy conservation regulation. DEDE is responsible for developing Minimum Energy Performance Standards (MEPS) and high efficiency performance standards (HEPS), which designate the top performing products in the market. Although DEDE develops MEPS, the Thai Industrial Standards Institute (TISI), under the Ministry of Industry, is responsible for regulating MEPS. On the other hand, DEDE alone responsible for regulating HEPS.

The Department of Alternative Energy Development is also responsible for determining standards for the building energy code (BEC) but implementation of the BEC is under the Ministry of Interior, who oversees land management and public works. Review of permits for building construction therefore falls under the purview of the Ministry of Interior. Moreover, implementation of the BEC requires significant levels of co-ordination with local authorities across Thailand's 76 provinces and one special administrative areas. Co-ordination between these agencies has led to some delays in the implementation of the BEC.

## Energy efficiency policies for buildings

The Energy Conservation Promotion (ECP) Act B.E. 25351 of 1992 (amended in 2007) is the cornerstone of energy efficiency and cooling regulation in Thailand. It covers energy conservation in factories, buildings, machinery, equipment and materials, and listed AC as one of the specific methods of building energy efficiency. The ECP Act requires "designated" factories and buildings to conduct an energy audit. The ECP contains legal requirements for designated buildings to appoint a "person responsible for energy", who is in charge of maintaining and monitoring efficiency of machines, improving energy use and helping to conduct energy management, amongst other duties (Thailand's Ministry of Energy, 2017[24]).

### *Minimum energy performance standards and labelling of cooling appliances*

The Electricity Generating Authority of Thailand (EGAT) has had a pivotal role in the labelling programme for energy efficient products, with initial support from the World Bank and other donors. EGAT is responsible for developing monitoring and enforcing the voluntary labelling programme.[1]

Minimum Energy Performance Standards (MEPS) for room ACs were developed in 2002 and became compulsory standards in 2005. In 2009, HEPS for eight products, including water heaters, window glass, chillers, electric kettles, refrigerators, ACs, fans and rice cookers, were created. While MEPS focus on removing the least energy efficient products from the market, High Energy Performance Standards (HEPS) intend to stimulate the development and demand of higher energy performance products (Table 4.2). The Electrical and Electronics Institute of Thailand, an autonomous institution under the supervision of the Thai Ministry of Industry, which possesses three AC test chambers, conducts AC testing for the MEPS and labelling program (CLASP, 2019[25]).

ASEAN member states have explored options for harmonisation of MEPS while strengthening the existing ASEAN Roadmap Towards Sustainable and Energy-Efficient Space Cooling (ASEAN, 2023[26]; IEA, 2022[27]). Harmonisation of MEPS throughout the region could allow deeper integration of the air conditioning market and reduce barriers to trade including tariffs and inconsistent labelling and enable energy efficiency improvements in the buildings sector. As incomes grow throughout the region and appliance penetration grows, consumers and manufacturers alike will benefit from this (E3G, 2020[28]).

**Table 4.2. Thai Minimum energy performance standards for air conditioners**

| Type | Capacity | EER |
|---|---|---|
| Window type | ≤8 000 W | ≥ 9.6 (Btu/hr/W)<br>≥ 2.82 (W/W) |
| | ≥ 8 000 W ≤ 12 000 W | ≥ 8.6 (Btu/hr/W)<br>≥ 2.53 (W/W) |
| Split type | ≤ 8 000 W | ≥ 9.6 (Btu/hr/W)<br>≥ 2.82 (W/W) |
| | ≥ 8 000 W ≤ 12 000 W | ≥ 9.6 (Btu/hr/W)<br>≥ 2.82 (W/W) |

Source: TISI (2011[29]), Thai Minimum energy performance standards for air conditioners, https://service.tisi.go.th/fulltext/2134_2553.pdf.

Labelling in Thailand is now well established depending on energy-saving performance, products are classified into five levels, with level 5 products having the highest level of energy efficiency. The EGAT level 5 label displays the product's energy rating, estimated electricity bill cost (in THB per year), electricity consumption (in kWh per year), seasonal energy efficiency ratio, brand, model and capacity. However, there are different label requirements for inverter and fixed speed models. In 2019, EGAT updated the label to include 3 stars that go beyond the level 5 (Table 4.3).

The most efficient level 5 products are generally in line with HEPS which are established by DEDE. Though there is currently no HEPS for AC. Labelling also only covers units up to 12kW which leaves a gap in regulation of large units.

Refrigerants used in AC are not currently indicated by labelling (GIZ, 2021[30]). Thailand ratified the Montreal Protocol in 1989, aiming to phasing out the production and consumption of ozone-depleting substances. Thailand had yet to ratify the Kigali Amendment to the Montreal Protocol.

### Table 4.3. EGAT No 5 labelling

| Type | Capacity | No Star | One Star | Two Stars | Three Stars | Four Stars | Five Stars |
|---|---|---|---|---|---|---|---|
| Fixed speed | ≤ 8 000 W | 13.17 – 13.70 | 13.71 – 14.23 | 14.24 – 14.77 | 14.78 – 15.30 | 15.31 – 15.84 | ≥ 15.85 |
| | > 8 000 W – 12 000 W | 12.56 – 13.12 | 13.13 – 13.69 | 13.70 – 14.25 | 14.26 – 14.82 | 14.83 – 15.39 | ≥ 15.40 |
| | > 12 000 W – 18 000 W | 10.00 – 10.59 | 10.60 – 11.19 | 11.20 – 11.79 | 11.80 – 12.39 | 12.40 – 12.99 | ≥ 13.00 |
| Variable speed / inverter | ≤ 8 000 W | 17.06 – 18.55 | 18.56 – 20.05 | 20.06 – 21.55 | 21.56 – 23.05 | 23.06 – 24.55 | ≥ 24.56 |
| | > 8 000 W – 12 000 W | 16.04 – 17.15 | 17.16 – 18.27 | 18.28 – 19.38 | 19.39 – 20.50 | 20.51 – 21.62 | ≥ 21.63 |
| | > 12 000 W – 18 000 W | 14.00 – 15.49 | 15.50 – 16.99 | 17.00 – 18.49 | 18.50 – 19.99 | 20.00 – 21.49 | ≥ 21.50 |
| Variable Refrigerant Flow (VRF) | ≤10 000 BTU/hr | 14.00 – 15.49 | 15.50 – 16.99 | 17.00 – 18.49 | 18.50 – 19.99 | 20.00 – 21.49 | ≥ 21.50 |

Source: EGAT (2024[31]), Energy Efficiency Criteria
https://www.eppo.go.th/images/Infromation_service/public_relations/PDP2018/PDP2018Rev1.pdf.

### *Building energy code*

While Thailand has building energy codes in place since 2009, only from 2021 did building energy codes become binding on state agency buildings. Over the past decade, the Building Energy Code (BEC) was revised to strengthen the code requirements (see Table 4.4 below) and the last updates strengthens enforcement on new and retrofitted buildings with floor areas equivalent to or exceeding 2 000 square meters. The Thai BEC is the key tool to ensure that buildings are designed to conserve energy, increase energy efficiency and reduce energy consumption and greenhouse gas emissions. The latest BEC prescribes better building practices for greener and more efficient buildings and has a greater focus on enforcement of BEC standards, with priority given to building capacity for auditing.

**Table 4.4. Thailand's Building Code revisions**

| Year | Regulation | Title | Overview |
|---|---|---|---|
| 1992 | B.E. 2535 Amended | Energy Conservation Promotion Act | Annual report regarding the energy usage and a plan concerning energy policy, energy training etc. to be submitted to the Department of Alternative Energy Development and Efficiency |
| 1995 | B.E. 2538 | Royal Decree on designated buildings | Definition of designated buildings |
| 2007 | B.E. 2550 | Energy Conservation Promotion Act (No.2) | |
| 2009 | B.E. 2552 Repealed by B.E. 2563 | Ministerial Regulation Prescribing the Type and Size of Buildings and Standards, Rules, and Procedures for Designing Energy Conservation Buildings | Standards on building envelope, HVAC, lighting, water heating for construction or modification of buildings with the total area in all stories of 2 000 sq square meters or more |
| 2020 | B.E. 2563 | Ministerial Regulation Prescribing Type or Size of Building and Standard, Criteria and Procedures in Designing Building for Energy Conservation (Umeyama, 2020[32]). | Standards on building envelope, electric lighting, air conditioning, water heating, whole building energy, and renewable energy system. |
| 2021 | B.E 2564 | Ministry of Energy's Notification Prescribing Standard Values in Designing Building for Energy Conservation B.E. 2564 Ministry of Energy's Notification on Criteria, Calculation Methods and Certification in Designing Building for Energy Conservation of Various Systems, an Overall Energy Consumption of Buildings and a Use of Renewable Energy Systems. | Prescribes energy performance standards for different types of buildings as well as related technical standards. |

Source: Authors

From 2023 onwards, new buildings larger than 2000 $m^2$ are required to achieve the BEC energy standard as a minimum requirement in the approval process. The BEC targets nine types of buildings, including exhibition buildings, hotels, entertainment services, hospitals, schools, offices, department stores, condominiums and theatres. Buildings can meet the standard by either passing energy performance standards for all four systems, which includes the building envelope, lighting system, air conditioning system and hot water generating system, or by passing the whole building energy performance and hot water generating system. If a building uses renewable energy, this is taken into consideration when calculating the energy performance of the building. Annex D provides further details on BEC standards and specifications.

### *Green building certification scheme*

Green buildings are usually certified on the basis of voluntary green building certification programmes. The term "green building" refers to environment-friendly and eco-efficient planning, constructing, operating, renovating and demolition of buildings, with a view to energy saving, water efficiency, reduction of waste, reduction of carbon dioxide and pollution control. The voluntary green building certifications that are mostly used in Thailand are (Lorenz & Partners, 2020[33]):

- Leadership in Energy and Environmental Design (LEED): it was developed by the U.S. Green Building Council and is used worldwide.
- Thailand Rating Energy & Environment System: it was developed on the basis of the LEED and tailored to fit Thailand's needs and circumstances.

Green buildings in Thailand mostly concern government projects or private sectors prestige projects. This is notably due to the higher construction and renovation costs for these buildings and low recognition of the resulting cost savings. Construction costs of green buildings exceed those of a standard building by approximately 20% (Lorenz & Partners, 2020[33]). Renovating a standard building into a certified green building would also exceed the simple renovation costs by roughly 30%. These costs can significantly dissuade building developers, despite the potential for long-term savings of 20-30% on electricity and water supply expenses compared to a standard building, which will benefit building owners in the long run.

### *The regulatory framework for district cooling*

There is no specific regulatory framework for district cooling (DC) in Thailand. Lack of awareness and knowledge also emerges as a barrier hindering the development of DC projects (APUEA, 2022[34]). Thailand's DC market is dominated by absorption cooling and electric chillers, which are not governed by MEPS when over 12 kW. Guidance could be strengthened for DC to ensure that those systems are green and energy efficient as well as cost effective.

As an example, in 2023, the Bureau of Energy Efficiency of India, with support of development partners and research centres, developed District Cooling Guidelines, to provide guidance on planning, construction and business models for DC in India and identify roles of different stakeholders involved in decision-making processes of DC projects (GIZ, 2023[35]).

## Business models for energy efficiency projects in Thailand

There are two key business models for energy efficiency (Figure 4.5 below):

- **Self-financing model**: Under the self-financing model, businesses finance energy efficiency projects through the savings generated by those projects. With this form of on-balance-sheet financing, the building owner typically borrows money from a bank and/or uses its own equity to buy and install the energy efficiency device. The energy savings resulting from energy efficiency measures are used to pay for their costs, making the projects self-sustaining over time. The business can be financed by a third party (e.g. shareholders, commercial banks or the government) but the financing obtained would be booked on the corporate's balance sheet (on-balance-sheet model).
- **Third-party financing model**: Under the third-party financing model (or off-balance sheet financing model), businesses can finance energy efficiency projects through a third-party, such as energy service companies (ESCOs). The third-party financing entity provides upfront capital to finance the project and the client/business will then share some or all monetary savings generated by the project with the ESCO as a repayment for the delivered services over a defined period of time.

**Figure 4.5. Business models for energy efficiency**

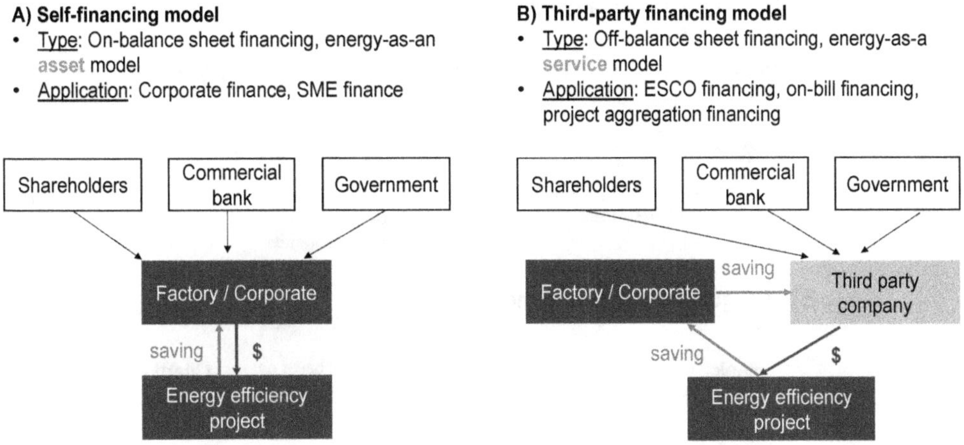


Source: Authors

Energy Performance Contracts (EPCs) are often used to finance energy efficiency projects. EPCs are contracts in which the ESCO is paid based on the realisation of energy or cost savings and transfers certain risks away from the customer. Two common types of EPC models include (IEA, 2018[36]) (see Figure 4.6):

- The **EPC shared savings model** – an off-balance-sheet model whereby the ESCO provides the financing as well as project development and implementation services and agrees with the client on sharing the realised energy savings over a defined period of time. Under this model, the ESCO is taking on technical, financial and credit risks, which can be valuable to the client as it avoids the need for upfront capital costs, with ongoing payments to the ESCO based on the savings obtained.
- The **EPC guaranteed savings model** – an on-balance-sheet contractual agreement whereby the ESCO guarantees a certain savings on the client's energy bill. The client obtains third-party capital, e.g. a bank loan, or uses their own equity, to pay contractually determined fees to the ESCO and the bank, and keeps the difference. Under this model, the ESCO does not provide finance to the client and only bears the technical (energy performance) risk.

On-bill financing (OBF) is also an effective instrument to incentivise energy efficiency investments. OBF is a mechanism in which the financing entity, typically a utility or financial institution, provides upfront capital to fund energy efficiency measures. The business repays the financing over time through a surcharge on its utility bill.

ESCOs are key players in Thailand's energy efficiency financing landscape and Thailand's ESCO market is dynamic and fast-growing. In 2012, the Thai ESCO Association was founded, tasked with establishing an accreditation process for registered ESCOs and fostering ESCO activities across Thailand, such as training, capacity building and other initiatives to increase the development of the overall Thai ESCO market. As of October 2023, there are 27 ESCOs registered as members with Thai ESCO Association.

The dominant ESCO business model in Thailand is the EPC guaranteed savings model (Ablaza, Liu and Llado, 2020[37]). Thailand is one of the countries with the highest presence of private companies among ESCOs' client base, as nearly all Thai ESCOs generate their revenues from private clients (UNDP, 2023[38]).

**Figure 4.6. Types of Energy Performance Contract (EPC) models**

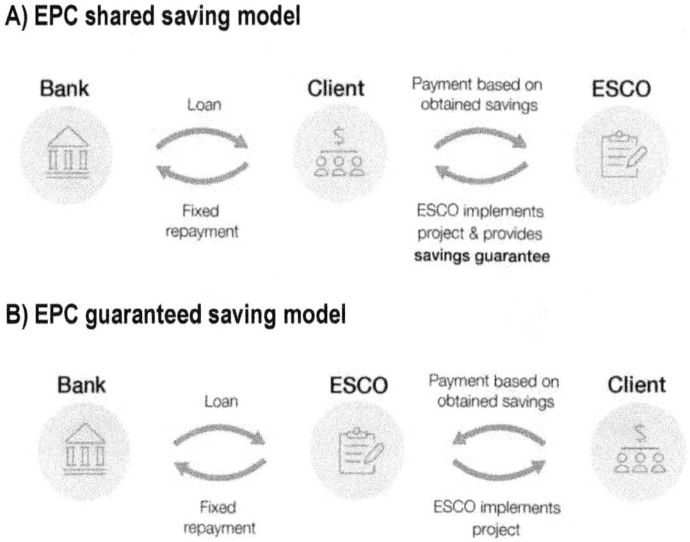


Source: IEA (2018[36]), ESCO contracts, https://www.iea.org/reports/energy-service-companies-escos-2/esco-contracts.

## Financing barriers and regulatory challenges

### *Finance*

*ESCOs face challenges in accessing finance for energy efficiency projects*

Most ESCOs in Thailand are of small size. Currently ESCOs mainly operate within a business model where the customer finances the energy efficiency investment directly (guaranteed savings) and so far the shared savings model has been rarely applied in Thailand (Seeley and Dhakal, 2021[9]). Interviews conducted for this report revealed that this is mainly due to the fact that ESCOs still face severe barriers in accessing affordable financing for energy efficiency projects, which are often perceived as too risky by commercial banks. Many ESCOs in Thailand also have low capitalisation and can thus offer low collateral to banks. In addition, many commercial banks are not familiar with energy efficiency technologies and ESCO's business model as energy efficiency projects involve uncertain revenue streams, making traditional financing evaluation methods inadequate. Therefore, banks often find it challenging to evaluate revenue streams or cash flows derived from energy savings. Moreover, demand for ESCO services is still relatively low due to limited understanding of the ESCO business model by the private sector (Ablaza, Liu and Llado, 2020[37]).

*Thailand's efforts to boost energy efficiency financing through national initiatives have spurred commercial banks to introduce products for both energy efficiency and renewable energy projects, yet limited access persists for MSMEs due to creditworthiness constraints.*

As mentioned in Chapter 1, the Department of Alternative Energy Development and Efficiency (DEDE) under the financial support from Energy Conservation Promotion Fund (ENCON Fund), established the ESCO and the Energy Efficiency Revolving Fund to encourage private investments in renewable energy and energy efficiency projects which are viable, but lack project finance.

The EERF and ESCO revolving funds have been hailed as effective tools for bolstering commercial lending, especially at their inception when commercial banks were unfamiliar with energy efficiency (EE) and renewable energy (RE) projects. The EERF succeeded in stimulating the appetite of commercial banks in energy efficiency financing and creating connections between private financiers and ESCOs (Frankfurt School - UNEP Collaborating Centre for Climate & Sustainable Energy Finance, 2012[39]). The ESCO revolving fund notably played a pivotal role in financing Thailand's first commercial solar farm. Government support for these funds extends beyond financial aid, encompassing valuable technical assistance.

As the fund periods draw to a close, commercial banks have responded by introducing a range of products aimed at promoting energy efficiency and renewable energy initiatives. This proactive approach has significantly increased accessibility to financing for energy efficiency and renewable energy projects, particularly among large companies. However, most of the projects financed under the EERF tended to be large projects and many small and medium-sized enterprises (MSMEs) still face challenges accessing financing due to issues related to creditworthiness. Moreover, these funds were channelled mainly through few large Thai commercial banks, whereas uptake from other banks outside of the programme was limited. Most banks suspended the loan product during the gap in the concessional funding that occurred between different phases of the Funds. Moreover, the EERF received limited marketing and promotion, and frequent staff changes within banks increased communication costs (ACE and GIZ, 2019[40]).

The ESCO Fund also had low up take. Requirements on equity were stringent, which maxed out ESCO borrowing capacity very quickly. ESCOs were not financially strong enough to raise equity portion which was around 25%. ESCO lending was also limited due to high collateral requirements.

### *The economics of energy efficient building retrofits in Thailand are positive but widespread adoption is still limited*

In Thailand, over the last decade various retrofitting initiatives and case studies of implemented projects demonstrate that in commercial buildings energy consumption is typically reduced by approximately 15 to 20% by energy efficient retrofits. Improving the efficiency of the Heating Ventilation and Air Conditioning (HVAC) system alone can often deliver savings of between 10-15%of a commercial building's total energy consumption. These projects had an average payback period ranging between 4 to 5 years. However, although these findings demonstrate the positive economics of retrofits and could be sufficient to instigate widespread adoption, this has not yet taken place (Seeley and Dhakal, 2021[13]). This points to the need for stronger policy to drive investment in retrofits.

Recent concern over office vacancy during the COVID-19 period has had positive impacts on retrofits, which are seen as means of increasing the competitiveness of buildings on the market. The current market is showing that retrofits have the potential to maintain occupancy rates above 80% and generate rental increases of up to 20% compared to pre-enhancement. The costs of retrofits typically range between USD 850 000 and 5.8 million (THB 30 million to 200 million), while redevelopment typically costs up USD 28 million (THB one billion). LEED-certified standard, which requires higher investment, is also being targeted by some investors as these are more attractive to major multinational corporations and will have higher energy savings (JLL, 2022[12]).

### *Misaligned incentives of market participants deter investment in green buildings*

High upfront costs, a mismatch between the life of the asset and its holding period in a portfolio, and misplaced incentives of market participants can deter investment in green buildings (ADB, 2020[41]). While owners and occupants directly benefit from the cost savings associated with energy efficiency measures, developers are hesitant to bear large upfront costs of construction. Landlords have low incentives to invest energy-efficiency measures as long as the tenant is paying the utility bill.

*Mismatch between the longevity of buildings and the time horizon of real estate investment portfolios*

Another reason for the financing gap for green buildings is the mismatch between the longevity of buildings and the relatively short holding periods for real estate assets in investment portfolios (ADB, 2020[41]). For instance, while the lifespan of a building is 70 to 100 years, financiers hold real estate assets mostly for 7 to 10 years while building owners hold them for 10 to 15 years. Moreover, the buildings sector is also subject to high and unpredictable climate risks and hazards.

### *Regulation and implementation*

The AC labelling system only goes up to 12 kW AC units, whereas commercial AC unites are as large as 16 to 18kW. Labelling does not extend to large commercial systems. There is a need to expand labelling for commercial projects to use higher efficiency systems. Without adequate requirements, project developers will pick the lowest cost system, as they are not responsible for consumption costs.

One regulatory tool to promote and facilitate investment in energy efficient cooling appliances would be to develop a high-performing Energy Efficient Technology List (EETL), with appliances and solution providers that have been pre-approved as eligible for financing from partnering financial institutions. The pre-approved equipment would meet defined minimum energy performance requirements as well as safety standards and surpass prevailing market practices to ensure the desired outcomes in terms of energy savings and co-benefits achieved. Performance requirements for technologies are regularly updated to reflect market developments. This tool could be made available through an online platform such as the European Bank for Reconstruction and Development (EBRD)'s Green Technology Selector, which offers a shopping-style platform that connects vendors of best-in-class green technologies with businesses and homeowners (EBRD, 2024[42]).

Partnerships with international and local financial institutions can ensure that financing with favourable conditions or tax incentives are made available to businesses and homeowners that want to invest in pre-approved equipment already contained in the EETL. Even without direct collaboration with financial institutions, lists of energy efficient technologies can be used as effective information and procurement tools. An example for such an EETL was published by the Indian Bureau of Energy Efficiency in 2023, containing information on energy efficient technologies with their sectoral applicability, savings potential, estimated investment costs as well as typical payback times, annual monetary savings potential and typical equipment capacity (Bureau of Energy Efficiency of India, 2023[43]).

### *Governance*

Institutional co-ordination remains a challenge for effectively enforcing and promoting energy efficient cooling standards in Thailand. Implementation of the Building Energy Code (BEC) falls under both DEDE and the Ministry of Public Works. There has been a lengthy delay in enforcement of BEC between 2009 and 2017 due to co-ordination challenges.

The implementation plan towards Net Zero Building is not yet in place. There is no clear plan to incrementally increase stringency of MEPS on space cooling and other standards in building codes. Clearer milestones would help to build momentum. A cooling action plan is needed to establish a systemic approach with clear milestones and priorities for the building envelope, AC standards and district cooling.

## Financing models for mobilising finance and investment for energy efficient buildings and cooling systems

Blended finance mechanisms including technical assistance can de-risk energy efficiency projects and thus mobilise commercial finance and investment. Blended finance instruments can take the form of first loss or non-payment guarantees as well as project preparation support to improve the capacity of project developers and financial institutions to improve access to both domestic and international debt finance.

Based on stakeholder consultations, the Roadmap focuses on a set of potential financial instruments that were highlighted as having a high potential to mobilise private investment for energy efficient buildings and cooling systems, notably: energy savings insurance (ESI), green bonds for buildings, on-bill financing (OBF), bulk procurement for energy-efficient appliances and green mortgages. Several of these financing mechanisms are applicable to both energy efficient buildings and energy efficient appliances, which go hand-in-hand as enhancing building efficiency would reduce active energy needs (including for cooling).

Some of these mechanisms (namely, ESI, OBF and bulk procurement) were developed as fully-fledged and detailed case studies in Annex B. The choice of the case studies was based on consultations and interviews with a wide range of stakeholders on challenges and barriers for attracting financing in the two sectors in Thailand.

### *Energy savings insurance (ESI) model*

One of the barriers to implementing energy efficiency projects in Thailand is the uncertainty about their performance. An energy savings insurance (ESI) model directly addresses this challenge by insuring the projected savings. With such an insurance product, ESCOs can back their contractual guarantees for the performance of their products and clients can be assured of compensation in case the projected energy savings are not realised. In addition to addressing scepticism regarding technology providers' claims, the ESI model alleviates the challenge of accessing financing for energy projects. Implementation of the ESI model could significantly ease barriers to investment in energy efficiency for Thai firms.

The ESI model was first developed by the Inter-American Development Bank (IDB) in Colombia in 2014, with the support of Basel Agency for Sustainable Energy (BASE), as a mechanism to build investor confidence and improve access to low-cost finance for energy efficiency projects. Since its conceptualisation, the ESI model has been replicated in many other countries worldwide, usually in co-operation with National Development Banks. See Annex B below and (OECD, 2023[44]) for an overview of previous and ongoing ESI programmes in other countries.

ESI is a de-risking package which combines four financial and non-financial elements to support the identification and structuring of technically robust and bankable projects: a standard performance contract, a technical validation, an energy savings insurance product, and concessional financing. Table 4.5 below summarises the main function of each of these four products.

## Table 4.5. Financial and non-financial elements of ESI: functions and benefits

| Element | Functions | Benefits |
|---|---|---|
| **Standard performance contract** | • establishing the responsibilities of the supplier in terms of supply and installation of equipment, corresponding guarantees and the promised energy savings relative to a benchmark;<br>• committing the customer to timely payments, access to facilities, and adequate maintenance of the equipment. | • boost the confidence of the firms, insurance providers, and financial institutions in the technology provider's products<br>• lowers transaction costs |
| **Technical validation** | • evaluating the project's technical potential to achieve the promised savings;<br>• verifying that the project has been built according to agreed specifications;<br>• determining which party is entitled to compensation in case of disagreements. | • boost the confidence of the firms, insurance providers, and financial institutions in the technology provider's products<br>• lowers transaction costs |
| **Energy savings insurance** | • partially covering the energy savings commitment made by the technology supplier under the performance contract for a specific period of time. | • allows technology providers to back the performance of their products and distinguish themselves from lowerquality providers;<br>• improves firms' trust and boosts their sales. |
| **Concessional financing** | • Financing insured projects with funding from international donor agencies and/or multilateral development banks (MDBs), with concessional elements such as such as lower interest rates, longer loan terms or grace periods. | • reduces the cost of capital<br>• improves access to finance |

Source: OECD (2023[44]), Energy Savings Insurance: International Focus Group Discussion, https://www.oecd.org/environment/cc/cefim/cross-cutting-analysis/Discussion-paper-first-energy-savings-insurance-international-focus-group-discussion.pdf.

A conceptual visualisation of the ESI model is shown in Figure 4.7 below, while key players and potential challenges of implementation of an ESI in Thailand are presented in Table 4.6 below. Key challenges with the implementation of ESI in Thailand include the limited technical capacity to assess risks of energy efficiency projects by Thai financial institutions as well as potential lack of confidence in and familiarity with ESI models. Moreover, accurately assessing energy savings and determining insurance premiums would necessitate reliable data on energy consumption as well as on performance factors, which is challenging to obtain from diverse businesses in different sectors.

## Figure 4.7. ESI implementation: institutional arrangement

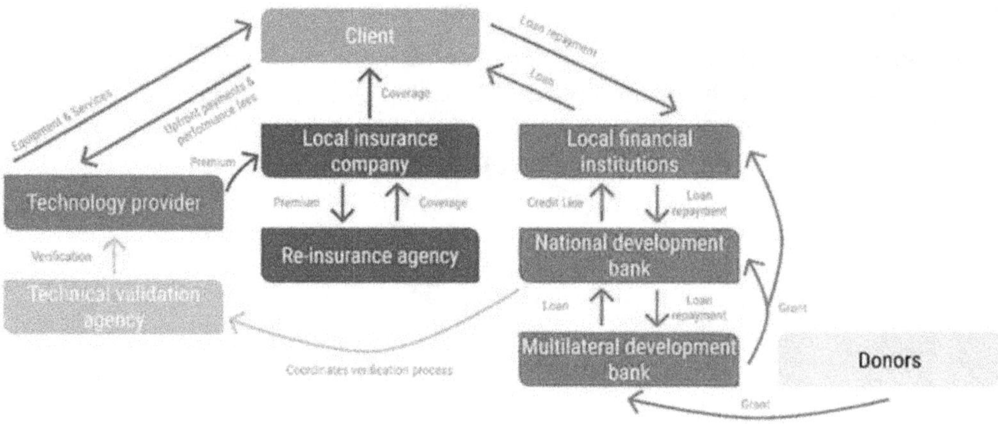


Source: Authors based on OECD (2023[44]), Energy Savings Insurance: International Focus Group Discussion, https://www.oecd.org/environment/cc/cefim/cross-cutting-analysis/Discussion-paper-first-energy-savings-insurance-international-focus-group-discussion.pdf.

**Table 4.6. Key players and potential challenges of implementation of an ESI in Thailand**

| Key players | Potential Thai actors | Challenges |
|---|---|---|
| **Donor** | **Domestic public funding:** Energy Conservation Promotion Fund (ENCON Fund) | • Eligibility criteria of the fund<br>• Political priorities |
| | **Multilateral development Banks:** World Bank, ADB, etc. | • Stringent eligibility criteria<br>• Complex application process<br>• Currency and repayment risks<br>• Competitive funding environment |
| **Financial institutions** | Local commercial banks | • Limited technical capacity to offer energy efficiency financing<br>• Lack of confidence in the new business model<br>• Stringent eligibility criteria |
| **Insurance regulator** | Office of Insurance Commission | • Lack of understanding on EE |
| **Insurance company** | Local insurance companies | |
| **Re-insurance agency** | e.g. Thai Reinsurance Public Co., Ltd. | |
| **Technology provider** | ESCOs<br>RE & energy efficiency equipment supplier | • Difficult access to market |
| **Technical validation agency** | **Academic and research institutions,** e.g. Joint Graduate School of Energy and Environment, Chulalongkorn University | • Limited resources |
| | **International agencies,** e.g. GIZ, UNDP | |

Source: Authors

Experience with ESI in other countries provides insights that could be useful for the design and implementation of an ESI scheme in Thailand (OECD, 2023[44]). In particular, the experience of Colombia provides a proof of concept for other countries to replicate. For example, several countries benefited from the availability of templates, methodologies for standard performance contracts, project investment analysis and validation and verification tools developed by predecessors like Colombia. The availability of standard documents can reduce complexity and transaction costs. Moreover, one lesson learnt from previous programmes is that concessionality was often incorporated into their ESI credit lines, thanks to the concessional financing and non-reimbursable grants extended by international donors. These concessional elements allowed to offer preferential terms to MSMEs at suitably long payback periods than available in the commercial market.

Experience from other countries also highlight the importance of having existing acceptance and up-take of insurance products in the market, an enabling insurance regulatory environment as well as a holistic demand creation strategy. Several approaches to demand creation exist, such as marketing and information dissemination campaigns, targeting specific clients based on market research, or establishing ESI as a pre-requisite for accessing concessional credit lines. Choosing the most effective mix of approaches entails undertaking a detailed market assessment, including consultations with key stakeholders, to understand the specific barriers to demand and identify the right solutions. Finally, training and capacity building efforts are also a critical success factor of ESI programmes. Stakeholder consultations and market research will be needed to assess the training needs of each of the different actors involved.

### *Green bonds for green buildings*

As discussed in Chapter 1, in Thailand the green bond market is emerging as an important source of financing for projects or assets with positive environmental or climate benefits. In ASEAN countries, green buildings are one of the main uses of green bonds' proceeds. Green buildings accounted for just 20% of green bond issuance proceeds in ASEAN+3 (USD 52.9 billion) and approximately the same share of local currency bond issuance in ASEAN+3 (USD 34.5 billion) as of 2021 (ADB, 2022[45]).

Green bonds appear to be a viable and important financing mechanism for green building projects in ASEAN and they hold large potential for growth (ADB, 2020[41]). However, in Thailand the vast majority of green bond proceeds are used to finance renewable energy generation projects and they are underutilised in the buildings sector (CBI, 2019[46]).

Examples of green bond proceeds used to finance green buildings in ASEAN states include Merdeka Ventures Sdn. Bhd.'s green sukuk in Malaysia and Arthaland Corp.'s green bond in the Philippines.

In 2017, Merdeka Ventures Sdn. Bhd issued a MYR 690 million green sukuk (USD 170 million), aligned with ASEAN Green Bond Standards and used to finance its Merdeka PNB Tower, the tallest building in Malaysia, with triple-platinum ratings using the international LEED, Malaysia's Green Building Index, amongst others (Malaysian Sustainable Finance Initiative, 2017[47]). In the Philippines, Arthaland Corp. issued a first tranche of USD-equivalent 59 million ASEAN green bond in 2020 to finance its real estate portfolio certified by multiple national and international green building standards, followed by a second tranche of the same amount in 2023 (Arthaland, 2023[48]).

Certification schemes for green buildings increase the credibility of green building projects and information availability within bond market players, thus improving the attractiveness of green bonds issued for green building projects (ADB, 2020[41]).

### *On-bill financing (OBF)*

On-bill financing (OBF) is a financing mechanism whereby utilities or private lenders provide customers with capital for energy-efficient, renewable, or other power-related projects, with repayment being made through the customer's regular utility bill payments. On-bill financing programmes rely on the willingness of the utility to invest and/or collect repayments from their customers via the monthly utility bills. On-bill programmes may require customers to select technologies and/or suppliers from a pre-approved list, and can be combined with government rebate programmes for high-efficiency appliances or equipment. OBF financing is typically applied for smaller scale energy efficiency projects.

Typical on-bill financing or repayment structure comprises investors, utilities, contractors or ESCOs, and customers as shown in Figure 4.8 below.

**Figure 4.8. On-bill financing structure**

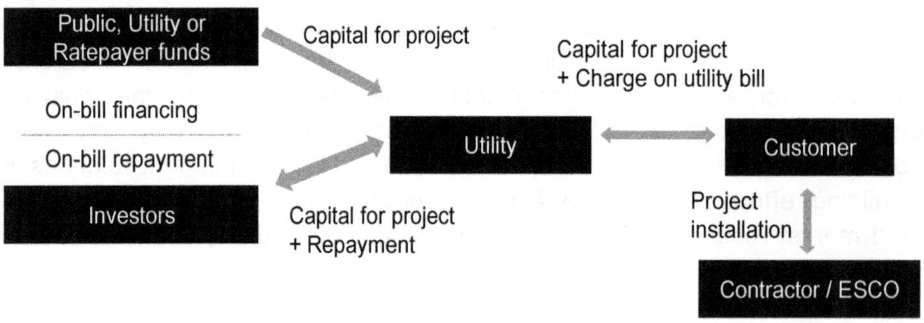


Source: US Department of Energy (2023[49]), On-Bill Financing / Repayment, https://betterbuildingssolutioncenter.energy.gov/financing-navigator/option/bill-financingrepayment#case-studies.

The OBF model has multiple advantages:

- **Improved energy efficiency:** OBF programs help customers invest in energy efficiency improvements, such as upgrading to a high-efficiency air conditioner or adding insulation, yielding mutual advantages like lowered energy bills, enhanced property values, amongst others.
- **Convenient repayment and simple structure:** Regular monthly loan payments are collected by the utility on the utility bill until the loan is repaid. This makes it easier for customers to repay the loan and helps ensure that the loan is repaid on time. OBF agreements are typically simple, thereby creating confidence for customers, utilities and possible investors.
- **Reduced risk of loan default risk:** OBF schemes authorise utilities to discontinue services for non-payment, thereby reducing the risk of loan defaults and assuring repayment. The customer's repayment obligation can also be collateralised by the installed equipment.
- **Bill neutrality**: Energy efficiency improvements financed through OBF can be structured to match or exceed loan payments, ensuring that the customer's utility bill remains neutral or decreases post-upgrade.
- **Wider adoption of energy efficiency measures:** The unique characteristics of on-bill loans, particularly their tie to utility services and the assurance of bill neutrality, provide tangible benefits that can encourage more customers to invest in energy efficiency upgrades.

The past decade saw the introduction of several on-bill programs, notably in the United States' residential sector and later in Europe. In the US, OBF programmes have been used to finance energy efficiency improvements in the residential, commercial and industrial sectors, as well as for universities, schools and hospitals, but not typically in government facilities (US Department of Energy, 2023[49]). A notable OBF example is that of Southern California Edison (SCE), which offered qualified non-residential customers 0% financing from USD 5 000 to USD 1 000 000 per Service Account for a wide variety of efficiency improvement projects. The monthly loan payments are added directly to the customer's bill over a period of up to five years. Monthly energy savings help to offset the monthly loan charges. The program was delivered by a dedicated third-party contractor, who provided energy audits, technical assistance, and project implementation to customers. After pilot tests in 2007 – 2008, the program was launched in 2010, The execution of the program during 2010 – 2012 resulted in the issuance of over USD 10 million in loans and had commitments in place for another USD 20.4 million. The loans issued supported energy efficiency projects with ex ante savings of 17 GWh and 2.8 MW (US Department of Energy, 2024[50]). The program has been continued and expanded by the California Public Utilities Commission (CPUC) due to high demand and success. See Table 4.7 below for further details on the SCE case, including challenges encountered throughout the programme. Annex B includes an overview of the actors, timeframe and potential challenges of OBF implementation in Thailand.

## Table 4.7. Southern California Edison's OBF programme

| | Key characteristics |
|---|---|
| **Terms and conditions** | • **No-interest, no-fee loan**: A loan that is repaid on the utility bill or in full by the borrower, with no interest or fees charged to the customer.<br>• **Site meter attachment**: A feature that attaches the financing obligation to the site meter rather than the customer, allowing the charge to transfer to the next service account holder automatically.<br>• **Customer eligibility**: A criterion that is based on the customer's payment history and standing with SCE and does not require credit or income qualification. |
| **Implementation dates** | 2007 – ongoing |
| **Outcomes** | • 2010 – 2012 resulted in the issuance of over USD 10 million in loans and had commitments in place for another USD 20.4 million. The loans issued supported energy efficiency projects with ex ante savings of 17 GWh and 2.8 MW.<br>• Till 2023, over 2 400 loans were issued, worth USD 99 million, with a 99.3% collection rate. |
| **Financed activities** | 2007 – 2022: Energy efficiency measures such as insulation upgrades, HVAC system replacements, or purchasing energy-efficient appliances<br>2003: Expansion to finance clean energy projects beyond energy efficiency measures |
| **Targeted sectors** | 2007 – 2022: Non-residential sectors<br>2023: Expansion to both non-residential and residential sectors |
| **Stakeholders involved** | • **Southern California Edison Company (SCE):** SCE is the primary stakeholder and the proposer of the OBF program to the California Public Utilities Commission (CPUC).<br>• **California Public Utilities Commission (CPUC):** CPUC is the regulatory agency that oversees the OBF program and approves the program design, funding, and implementation.<br>• **Non-residential customers:** Non-residential customers are eligible to participate in SCE's OBF program and can use it to finance energy efficiency and renewable energy projects.<br>• **Residential customers:** Residential customers are expected to be eligible for SCE's OBF program in the future, once the program is developed and approved by the CPUC.<br>• **Third-party lenders:** Third-party lenders can partner with SCE to provide financing for the OBF program and receive a return on investment.<br>• **Energy service companies (ESCOs):** ESCOs can partner with SCE to provide energy efficiency and renewable energy services to customers and receive payments through the OBF program.<br>• **Other Investor-owned Utilities in California:** Under the CPUC's leadership, SCE has partnered with other utilities to develop a statewide model for OBF in California. |
| **Challenges** | • **Limited customer awareness:** Many customers are not aware of the programme or its benefits.<br>• **Lack of contractors' skills:** The programme requires customers to choose and retain a licensed contractor to install measures, but many contractors are not familiar with the programme or do not have the necessary qualifications or experience to participate.<br>• **Limited funding:** The programme has limited funding and loan capacity, which restricts the number and size of projects that can be financed and the customer segments that can be served.<br>• **Complex design:** The programme design and delivery have been criticised for being too complex, bureaucratic, and inflexible, which discourages customer participation and satisfaction.<br>• **Lack of evaluation:** The programme lacks a comprehensive and transparent evaluation framework that can measure the programme's effectiveness, efficiency, equity, and environmental impact, and provide feedback for improvement. |

Source: US Department of Energy (2024[50]), Southern California Edison: On-Bill Financing for Energy Efficiency Projects, https://betterbuildingssolutioncenter.energy.gov/implementation-models/southern-california-edison-bill-financing-energy-efficiency-projects.

### *Bulk procurement and demand aggregation for energy-efficient appliances*

As mentioned in Chapter 2, aggregation models can help tackle some of the barriers that clean energy projects face, and lower transaction costs and risks. Bulk procurement models can significantly boost the deployment of energy efficiency technologies. By aggregating demand, bulk procurement harnesses economies of scale, achieves cost savings and operational efficiency and manages repayment risks while encouraging manufacturers to innovate and produce more competitive and efficient products.

In a bulk procurement model, key players include (see Figure 4.9 below):

- the aggregator: an entity responsible for aggregating demand and co-ordinating the procurement process (e.g. a government agency or an ESCO)
- suppliers: manufacturers or distributors of energy-efficient technologies and equipment
- end-users: businesses, government agencies, households, or other entities looking to improve energy efficiency
- financial institutions: banks or lending institutions that provide financing options (loans, grants, etc.) or incentives to help end users acquire energy-efficient products.

#### Figure 4.9. Bulk procurement structure

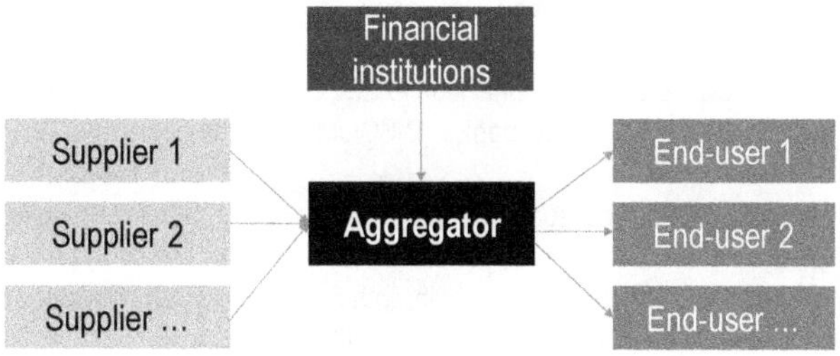


Source: Authors

A notable example of a subsidy-free bulk procurement model that delivered significant efficiency improvements in an emerging economy is India's UJALA programme. The Government of India launched the UJALA light-emitting diode (LED) scheme in 2015 to help households save money on their electricity bills through efficient lighting while enhancing Light Emitting Diode (LED) affordability (OECD, 2022[51]).

By January 2022, more than 367 million LED bulbs were distributed, saving an estimated 47.78 billion kWh energy per year, with an avoided peak demand of 9567 MW and estimated GHG emission reduction of 38.70 million tonnes $CO_2$ (Energy Efficiency Services Limited, 2022[52]). UJALA also distributed over seven million LED tube lights and over two million energy efficient fans. By aggregating demand, procuring appliances and equipment in bulk as well as providing innovative up-front payment options to consumers, UJALA managed to reduce the retail price of LEDs price from USD 3.60 – 4.20 in 2014 to USD 0.84 – 0.96 in 2017, or by almost 80%. Concessional financing covered all initial costs for the bulk procurement of LED bulbs. The programme also incorporated quality control measures (such as a less than 0.3% failure rate and mandatory three-year warranty for LED bulbs) and comprehensive measuring, reporting and verification procedures to create trust in the initiative and ensure its effectiveness and impact. The massive scale of the programme and the Government of India's financial incentives in support of UJALA contributed to boosting the local manufacturing capacity. Table 4.8 below and Annex B provides further details on the UJALA scheme.

## Table 4.8. Bulk procurement of efficient lighting: India's UJALA scheme

| | Key characteristics |
|---|---|
| **Implementation dates** | 2015 – 2021 |
| **Lead implementer** | Energy Efficiency Services Limited (EESL), a super energy service company (ESCO), promoted by the Ministry of Power, Government of India, as a Joint Venture company of four Central Public Sector Undertakings. |
| **Financiers** | • Equity capital from its four promoters<br>• Proceeds from domestic bond issuances within 2016-2018<br>• Financial support from multilateral and bilateral donors<br>• Lines of credit with commercial banks to finance its working capital needs |
| **Outcomes** | • over 367 million LED bulbs distributed, with an estimated energy savings of 47.78 billion kWh per year and GHG emission reduction of 38.70 million tonnes $CO_2$ per year;<br>• seven million LED tubes distributed, with an estimated energy savings of 316.17 million kWh per year and GHG emission reduction of 259.26 kilotonnes $CO_2$ per year;<br>• 2 million energy-efficient fans distributed, with an estimated energy savings of 219.40 million kWh per year and GHG emission reduction of 179.91 kilotonnes $CO_2$ per year. |
| **Financed activities** | • 7 W and 12 W LED light bulb<br>• 20 W LED light tube<br>• Energy efficient fans with a BEE 5-star rating |
| **Targeted sectors** | Residential sector |
| **Stakeholders involved** | • The Ministry of Power is the nodal ministry that plans and coordinates India's energy efficiency efforts;<br>• the Bureau of Energy Efficiency (BEE) is the nodal agency for implementing the national energy efficiency plan;<br>• the EESL is the implementer of the UJALA scheme;<br>• the World Bank provided a concessional loan to EESL under the India Energy Efficiency Scale-up Program;<br>• the State Electricity Distribution Companies (DISCOMS) are the partners of EESL for implementing UJALA in each state. |
| **Financing model** | The UJALA scheme provides consumers with two payment options for purchasing LED bulbs:<br>• full payment upfront at 40% of market price;<br>• initial payment of USD 0.15 (Rs. 10) per bulb, with the remaining amount recuperated in monthly installments of USD 0.15 (Rs. 10) added to the electricity bill (on-bill financing).<br>Customers can purchase a maximum of eight LED bulbs per electricity bill under this program. |

Source: Authors based on (Energy Efficiency Services Limited, 2022[52]; India Brand Equity Foundation, 2021[53]; Partnership on Transparency in the Paris Agreement, 2018[54]), https://eeslindia.org/wp-content/uploads/2022/09/Annual-Report-FY-2021-22.pdf, https://www.ibef.org/government-schemes/ujala-yojna, https://api.knack.com/v1/applications/5b23f04fd240aa37e01fa362/download/asset/5c94a552be4c1909acfe389b/190318_gpd_parisabkommen_india_rz.pdf.

The success of the UJALA program underscores several key lessons to promote energy efficiency at scale, which could be useful for Thailand to consider for setting up a bulk procurement scheme for energy efficiency appliances. Firstly, the robust business model of a super ESCO, taking on the upfront investment risk for bulk procurement of energy-efficient appliances, is instrumental in creating a conducive environment for market growth. By demonstrating tangible benefits and significantly lowering retail prices through volume discounts, the super ESCO can stimulate demand and foster widespread adoption of energy-efficient technologies among consumers. Moreover, comprehensive policy support from the government, electricity distribution companies and multilateral development banks can lend credibility and legitimacy, crucial for securing buy-in from various stakeholders and ensuring sustained momentum.

Secondly, evidence from the UJALA programme suggest the need for building awareness and trust in energy-efficient products, by effectively communicating about the results and impacts of the programme. To enhance customer trust in a relatively pricey and unfamiliar technology, an on-bill financing option was added at the onset of the programme, so that customers would not have to bear the upfront investment costs but instead paid for their LED bulbs through monthly instalments on their electricity bills. In addition, stringent quality specifications and robust after-sales services bolstered consumer trust in the reliability and durability of energy-efficient appliances, further enhancing adoption rates. The programme was combined with a large-scale consumer awareness and education programme as well as a national UJALA dashboard, tracking and updating LED deployment in real time and providing essential performance data.

More recently, examples of private sector initiatives taking the role of the aggregator entities have also emerged, namely in the Philippines. The OECD Clean Energy Finance and Investment Roadmap of the Philippines showcases the example of Climargy, a private company that serves as a commercial ESCO aggregator of energy efficiency project assets, fully funded with private capital (OECD, 2024[55]). Climargy is also tapping into grant funding through a partnership with the United Nations Office for Project Services Southeast Asia Energy Transition Partnership. The company is planning to use these grants to subsidise and de-risk the upfront development costs of energy audits for energy efficiency projects in commercial and industrial entities.

The USAID Southeast Asia's Smart Power Program is currently working with partners in the region, including Thailand, to support the bulk procurement of energy efficiency technologies, with an initial focus on cooling and lighting technologies (USAID, 2022[56]).

### *Green mortgages*

Through green mortgages, banks or mortgage lenders can offer home buyers preferential access to finance, such as discounted interest rates or higher loan amounts for building construction or building renovations meeting efficiency criteria (IEA, 2023[57]). Green mortgages have been offered by financial institutions in several countries, with the United Kingdom and United States leading the way, with around 60 green mortgage products available in the United Kingdom alone (IEA, 2023[58]). Evidence from the EU suggests that green buildings represent lower risk investments for banks because i) their operating costs are lower, thereby putting the borrower in a better position to repay the mortgage with a lower probability of default; and ii) they have higher value compared to so-called "brown discount" in markets where inefficient or unsustainable buildings become less attractive (World Green Building Council, 2024[59]). Green mortgages are also a type of financial product that can be easily securitised and tranched, allowing banks to transfer their credit risks and free up their lending capacity.

In Thailand, the green mortgage market is nascent, but some banks have recently started to develop and offer green mortgages schemes. In 2022, the Thai bank Kasikornbank Pcl and the Thai leading property developer SC Asset partnered to offer green home loans to buyers of energy-efficiency homes. The loan program offers interest rates starting at 2.5% per annum during the first three years with loan amount granted at up to 100% and loan term up to 30 years, with no appraisal fee (KBank, 2022[60]).

In 2023, UOB, a leading bank headquartered in Singapore and active in Asia, launched "U-Green" home loan campaign, offering green home loan solutions for customers seeking to make energy efficiency improvements in their houses in Thailand. The campaign includes financing options for home renovation and refurbishment, solar panel and electric vehicle charger installation, in line with the UOB's recent partnership with the Provincial Electricity Authority (PEA). Offered products under this campaign include loans with an average interest rate of 3.49% per year during the first three years, a credit line of up to 100% of the appraised value and a maximum loan tenor of 30 years (UOB, 2023[61]).

## Recommendations

The Government of Thailand is committed to accelerate finance and investment in energy efficiency projects in the Thai building sector and has put in place several supportive policies comprising government regulations, financial incentives and awareness-raising initiatives. Based on extensive desk research and a series of in-country stakeholder consultations, this Roadmap provides a set of recommendations to further support Thailand's efforts to mobilise financing for energy efficient buildings and cooling. It should be noted that several of the following recommendations can also be applied to promote energy efficiency across sectors. Key recommendations for unlocking financing for energy efficiency buildings and cooling in Thailand addresses three main areas summarised below:

- *Financial support*, including: maintaining consistent public support to promote the ESCO market; conducting ex-post evaluations of the Energy Efficiency Revolving Fund and the ESCO Fund; establishing a bulk procurement model for energy-efficient cooling appliances; implementing the energy savings insurance (ESI) model in Thailand; creating an on-bill financing programme for energy-efficient cooling appliances; and fostering issuances of green bonds in the building sector.
- *Policy, regulation and governance,* including: incrementally increasing stringency of minimum energy performance standards and expanding air conditioners' labelling to large commercial buildings; setting up an institutional co-ordination scheme and revising roles and responsibilities of implementing agencies; strengthening the policy framework for district cooling; developing an Energy Efficient Technology List (EETL) and collaborating with financial institutions to provide financial incentives to the listed technologies.
- *Capacity building, data collection and awareness-raising*, including: establishing capacity building and training programmes for financial institutions and ESCOs; implementing consumer awareness and education campaigns for efficient buildings and cooling; and fostering data collection on energy savings of energy-efficient buildings and cooling systems.

## ***Financial support***

### *Maintaining consistent public support to promote the ESCO market*

Further promoting the ESCO market requires (i) ensuring that market regulations and accounting rules enable ESCO operations; and (ii) setting financing incentives, training programmes, accreditation and certification schemes for qualified ESCOs to raise confidence in ESCO market. Thailand has a relatively developed and vibrant ESCO market, which has successfully implemented numerous energy efficiency projects but has not yet achieved the desired scale. The government can first ensure that market regulations and accounting rules allow for ESCO operations in-country and particularly with regards to their service offerings in the commercial and public buildings sector. In addition, the operation of ESCOs can be encouraged with dedicated financial incentives, training programmes as well as accreditation and certification of qualified ESCOs to enhance trust in the quality of energy service provision. Favourable financing conditions or de-risking instruments like energy savings insurance models or credit guarantees for ESCOs can help improve access to financing, including for the implementation of energy efficiency measures and small-scale renewable power in large-scale commercial and public buildings.

To further promote the ESCO market development, the government could also evaluate the possibility of establishing an aggregator entity for energy efficiency projects, such as a Super ESCO, which can help to stimulate the market for energy efficient appliances and equipment and create economies of scale (additional information on benefits and risks of super ESCOs are detailed on the next page).

### *Conducting ex-post evaluations of the Energy Efficiency Revolving Fund and the ESCO Fund*

The Energy Efficiency Revolving Fund (EERF) and the ESCO Revolving Fund terminated various rounds of implementation in 2019 and 2020 respectively. Currently, their focus is on managing existing investments, monitoring project performance and collecting repayments. While both funds were critical to help financial institutions familiarise with energy efficiency projects, evidence on the results of the two funds is mixed and ex-post evaluations would be beneficial to assess whether the funds shall be recapitalised.

Conducting ex-post evaluations would allow the government to properly assess the results achieved through these funds over the years of implementation and gather knowledge on their relevance, coherence, effectiveness, efficiency, impact and sustainability (i.e. the main international criteria for evaluations). The evidence produced by such evaluations could then be used to inform decision-making on the need for future public funding and interventions in the clean energy domain.

Conducting ex-post evaluations of the Energy Efficiency Revolving Fund (EERF) and the ESCO Fund would also help to identify the strengths and weaknesses of these mechanisms, the achieved impact on Thailand's energy efficiency market and remaining gaps and needs in improving energy efficiency to inform the design of any potential follow-up mechanisms.

#### *Establishing a bulk procurement model for energy-efficient cooling appliances*

The implementation of bulk procurement in Thailand presents a significant opportunity to streamline energy efficiency across various sectors. Thailand already has a favourable regulatory environment for promoting the ESCO market. Building on this, the government could consider the possibility of establishing an aggregator entity for public energy efficiency projects, similarly to the super ESCO model that has been adopted in India and many other countries, which contributed to the success of kickstarting local energy efficiency markets.

The government could consider establishing a bulk procurement scheme for energy-efficient cooling appliances. Concessional financing from the government and international development finance providers could cover the upfront costs of the scheme.

Building on the existing but still nascent ESCO market in Thailand, a public-private aggregator or Super ESCO with a robust business model could be established to take on the upfront investment risks and costs for bulk procurement. A super ESCO can help with the creation of a robust and fair tendering process and development of pipelines of projects that can be implemented through private ESCOs – which can be accredited with the Super ESCO based on a predefined set of eligibility criteria. A Super ESCO can stimulate demand and strengthen confidence amend-users and financiers dealing with ESCOs, thereby fostering widespread adoption of energy-efficient technologies among consumers. A Super ESCO can also standardise technical specifications and transaction templates (e.g. measurement and verification (M&V) protocols) and make them available to private ESCOs, thereby decreasing transaction costs. International experience shows that for super ESCOs to work effectively, there is a need for supporting legislation mandating government entities to work with them for public buildings retrofits.

Public Super ESCOs often face severe budget constraints and administrative backlogs, therefore consideration on setting up a Super ESCO would require a careful ex-ante impact assessment and cost-benefit analysis, to better understand and quantify budget, institutional capacity and governance implications. Consultations conducted for this Roadmap revealed that a public-private Super ESCO model could be more suitable for Thailand. This model could build on the experience of Climargy, a private company that serves as a commercial ESCO aggregator of energy efficiency project assets in the Philippines, fully funded with private capital (see the OECD Clean Energy Finance and Investment Roadmap of the Philippines (OECD, 2024[55]) for further details).

Table 4.9 illustrates the roadmap for the implementation of the bulk procurement model in Thailand, identifying key activities, responsible agencies and an indicative timeline.

## Table 4.9. Roadmap for bulk procurement implementation in Thailand

| Key areas | Activities | Responsible agency | Year 1-2: Preparation | Year 3-5: Pilot | Year 6 onwards: Scale-up |
|---|---|---|---|---|---|
| **1. Idea generation** | 1.1 Prioritisation of energy efficiency actions as per national or provincial plan | DEDE and provincial authorities as an aggregator | X | | |
| | 1.2 Provide guidance on best practices | DEDE, academic institutions, research institutes, or international agencies like USAID and GIZ | | | |
| | 1.3 Connect to partners, networks, sources | Provincial authorities as an aggregator | X | | |
| | 1.4 Assess in ideas scoping | | X | | |
| **2. Technical and financial evaluation** | 2.1 Prepare standard template for project ideas | DEDE, provincial authorities as an aggregator with technical support | X | | |
| | 2.2 Conduct the feasibility assessment | | X | | |
| **3. Business modelling and financing** | 3.1 Select the most suitable business model and financing scheme for the energy efficiency project bundle, based on the technical and economic assessment and the local context | Provincial authorities as an aggregator with technical support | X | | |
| | 3.2 Design the right financing solution for each municipal energy efficiency project bundle, based on a decision tree and a checklist tool | | X | | |
| | 3.3 Develop project proposal in a standardized format | | X | | |
| **4. Strategic procurement** | 4.1 Develop a procurement strategy | Provincial authorities as an aggregator with technical support | | X | |
| | 4.2 Prepare the tender process including process of identifying and selecting contractors | | | X | |
| | 4.3 Organize the tender process | | | X | |
| **5. Investing in infrastructure** | 5.1 Oversee the installation process, ensuring adherence to performance standards | Provincial authorities as an aggregator with technical support | | X | |
| | 5.2 Facilitate the disbursement of funds to the individual projects within the aggregation | | | X | |
| | 5.3 Maintain customer satisfaction through the project lifecycle | | | X | |
| **6. Performance and impact assessment** | 6.1 Establish a system for measuring, reporting, and verifying (MRV) the effectiveness and benefits of the energy efficiency project aggregation | Provincial authorities as an aggregator with technical support | | X | |
| | 6.2 Track performance metrics and evaluate the overall impact of the aggregation initiative | | | X | |
| **7. Scale-up** | 7.1 Program revision and finalisation | DEDE and provincial authorities as an aggregator | | | X |
| | 7.2 Capacity building and marketing | | | | X |
| | 7.3 Continuous monitoring and evaluation | | | | X |

Source: Authors

### *Implementing the energy savings insurance (ESI) model in Thailand*

The government could consider promoting the energy efficiency market and unlock Thai ESCOs' potential by piloting an Energy Savings Insurance (ESI) model. When piloting ESIs, Thailand could benefit from the availability of templates, methodologies for standard performance contracts, project investment analysis and verification tools developed in other markets, which could be adapted to Thailand's specific country context. Concessionality could be incorporated into ESI credit lines, thanks to concessional financing and grants extended by multilateral development banks and donors. These concessional elements enable commercial financial institutions to offer preferential financing terms to MSMEs or ESCOs at either longer payback periods or lower rates than available in the commercial market.

An enabling insurance regulatory environment as well as a holistic demand creation strategy are necessary for the take-up of ESI. Choosing the most effective mix of approaches entails undertaking a detailed market assessment, including consultations with key stakeholders, to understand the specific barriers to demand and identify the right solutions. Finally, repeated training, outreach and capacity building efforts are also a critical success factor of ESI programmes. Stakeholder consultations and market research will be needed to assess the training needs of each of the different actors involved.

The optimal sectoral applicability of ESIs in Thailand will depend on the market needs and demand, which could be carefully assessed through sectoral market research. ESIs usually target MSMEs and aim to help them invest in small-scale energy efficiency projects. For example, ESIs in Thailand could incentivise MSME investment in acquiring energy-efficient appliances such as lighting, HVAC systems, refrigerators as compressed air systems in industrial processes, which appear to be the energy-efficient appliances in most demand by MSMEs in Thailand according to available studies (NEDO, 2023[62]; Prukvilailert and Wangskarn, 2011[63]).

The Government of Thailand (DEDE) could also consider setting up a digital, publicly-accessible financing platform (e.g. based on the U-Energy platform) to exchange information and documents between the stakeholders for an ESI implementation, and to publish anonymised information about already implemented energy efficiency projects and their performance (e.g. median payback times per measure or building type, avoidance cost per building type, default rates, energy efficiency technology lists etc.). This would contribute to improve data availability on the performance of energy efficiency measures, reduce risk perception of financial institutions, project developers and building owners, and help reduce costs of financing.

Table 4.10 illustrates the roadmap for the implementation of an ESI mode in Thailand, identifying key activities, responsible agencies and an indicative timeline.

## Table 4.10. Roadmap for ESI implementation in Thailand

| Key areas | Activities | Responsible agency | Year 1-2: Preparation | Year 3-5: Pilot | Year 6 onwards: Scale-up |
|---|---|---|---|---|---|
| **Market assessment, and feasibility study** | | DEDE | X | | |
| **Financing structure** | 1. Design financing model | DEDE , donors, FIs, insurance companies | X | | |
| | 2. Secure funding | | | X | X |
| **Regulatory framework** | 3. Explore existing laws to provide a legal basis for ESI operations | DEDE, insurance regulator | X | | |
| **Standard performance contract & Energy savings insurance** | 4. Create standardised energy performance contracts to be used by businesses, specifying (i) the basic responsibilities of all parties, (ii) monitoring and reporting procedures, (iii) dispute resolution mechanism, and (iv) internal risk mitigation structures | DEDE, technical validation agency, technology providers and insurance regulator | X | | |
| | 5. Determine the appropriate structure for an ESI product | | X | | |
| | 6. Identify insurance and reinsurance companies willing to participate in the programme | | X | | |
| | 7. Develop a risk coverage structure and pricing methodology | DEDE, insurance regulator, insurance and reinsurance companies | X | | |
| **Validation & verification procedure** | 8. Define appropriate validation and verification procedures | All key stakeholders | X | | |
| **Marketing and communication plan** | 9. Conduct market research and develop a targeted strategy to inform potential clients about the ESI pilot programme and build their confidence in its ability to deliver results | DEDE | X | X | X |
| **Capacity building** | 10. Equip key stakeholders (technology providers, insurance providers, financial institutions) with the necessary tools and training to participate in the ESI programme | DEDE | X | X | X |

Source: Authors

### *Creating an on-bill financing programme for energy-efficient cooling appliances*

The government (DEDE) and the main utility (EGAT) could contribute to expanding the uptake of energy efficient cooling appliances and equipment in the building sector by creating an on-bill financing (OBF) programme. The OBF model enables utility customers to acquire energy efficient equipment, such as air conditioning and lighting systems, and to pay for it over time through their monthly utility bills. In many cases, on-bill financing programmes are designed to deliver overall cost savings from the onset, thus ensuring bill neutrality for the consumer. Based on existing experience, for the OBF programme to be successful, adequate investments in consumer awareness shall be planned. Moreover, to ensure that households of all income levels can access OBF loans, financial incentives might be required, such as preferential interest rates for low-income households. The roadmap for the implementation of OBF in Thailand is shown in Table 4.11 below, identifying key activities, responsible agencies and an indicative timeline.

**Table 4.11. Implementation Roadmap for on-bill financing in Thailand**

| Key areas | Activities | Responsible agency | Year 1-2: Preparation | Year 3-5: Pilot | Year 6 onwards: Scale-up |
|---|---|---|---|---|---|
| **1. Program feasibility** | 1.1 Market analysis and feasibility study | DEDE | X | | |
| | 1.2 Regulatory review and policy development | DEDE | X | | |
| | 1.3 Financial modelling and risk assessment | DEDE | X | | |
| **2. Program design** | 2.1 Secure funding for the program | Utilities | X | | |
| | 2.2 Engage all key stakeholders | Utilities | X | | |
| | 2.3 Design of program structure and key elements | DEDE and utilities | X | | |
| | 2.4 Development of standardised contracts and agreement for customers, contractors, and utilities | DEDE and utilities | X | | |
| | 2.5 Readiness assessments of key stakeholders | DEDE and utilities | X | | |
| **3. Pilot project** | 3.1 Marketing and outreach | Utilities | | X | |
| | 3.2 Training and capacity building | DEDE, utilities and think tanks | | X | |
| | 3.3 Financing setup | Utilities and investors | | X | |
| | 3.4 Installation of clean energy technologies | ESCO | | X | |
| | 3.5 Monitoring and data collection | ESCO and customers | | X | |
| | 3.6 Evaluation and adjustment | DEDE and utilities | | X | |
| **4. Scale up** | 4.1 Program revision and finalisation | DEDE and utilities | | | X |
| | 4.2 Capacity building and marketing | DEDE and utilities | | | X |
| | 4.3 Continuous monitoring and evaluation | DEDE and utilities | | | X |

Source: Authors

*Fostering green bonds' issuances in the building sector*

The green bond market in Thailand is already well-established and liquid but it is under utilised for the building sector. Government incentives for green bond issuance, such as financial support for green building certification and green bond verification costs, can encourage the up-take of this instrument, especially for MSMEs that might not have sufficient resources to pay for certification and verification services.

Clear criteria on which types of buildings are eligible to be financed through proceeds of green bonds, in line with green building standards, will facilitate issuance in this sector. Eligibility criteria of projects to be finance through green bond proceeds could be anchored to the Thai taxonomy criteria. Taxonomy criteria for the construction and real estate sectors are currently under development and they will provide a useful basis to issue green bonds or extend green loans for buildings. In addition, as identified by the latest green bond market survey for Thailand conducted by ADB, capacity building for both investors and financial officers of companies is required to increase their familiarity with green bond criteria (ADB, 2022[64]).

## *Policy, regulation and governance*

*Incrementally increasing stringency of minimum energy performance standards and expanding AC labelling to large commercial buildings.*

Recent updates to Building Energy Codes (BEC) take a first step on this path by enforcing BEC standards which apply minimum energy consumptions standards on certain types of new buildings and aim to reduce the average energy consumption of office buildings. DEDE, the Ministry of Interior and TISI could consider gradually and periodically increasing the scope and stringency of minimum energy performance standards for buildings as well as for appliances (such as air conditioners), to reflect technological advancements and best practices in energy efficiency. Green building certifications could also be regularly updated to reflect the latest performance standards.

Furthermore, the AC labelling system only goes up to 12 kW AC units, whereas commercial AC unites are as large as 16 to 18 kW. AC labelling currently does not extend to large commercial systems. AC labelling could be expanded to cover commercial projects to use higher efficiency systems and labelling implementation could be encouraged.

*Setting up an institutional co-ordination scheme and revising roles and responsibilities of implementing agencies*

Improving co-ordination between DEDE, the Ministry of Industry, Ministry of Interior and local administrative authorities can help streamline efficiency performance standards and accelerate their implementation and enforcement across the public and private sector. An inter-agency task force could be established to co-ordinate the different responsible agencies and oversee application of energy efficiency standards.

*Strengthening the policy framework for district cooling*

Currently, there is no specific regulatory framework for district cooling in Thailand. As demand for district cooling projects is expected to increase, regulatory expectations could be established and clearly communicated and disseminated. Moreover, integrating stringent energy efficiency standards and encouraging the utilisation of renewable energy sources, such as heat pumps, could be encouraged to enhance the overall sustainability and performance of the systems.

The Government of Thailand, represented by DEDE, could consider developing District Cooling Guidelines as an informative guidebook for national, province and district development authorities, developers and investors. Based on successful case study examples, such guidelines could outline key technical components and stakeholders to consider, project evaluation criteria as well as information on typical project cycles, economics and selection processes, while proposing specific implementation actions for province and district-level stakeholders.

*Developing an Energy Efficient Technology List (EETL) and collaborating with financial institutions to provide financial incentives to the listed technologies*

The government (e.g. through DEDE) could consider developing a high-performing Energy Efficient Technology List (EETL), with appliances that have been pre-approved as eligible for financing from partnering financial institutions. The pre-approved equipment would meet defined minimum energy performance requirements and surpass prevailing market practices to ensure the desired outcomes in terms of energy savings and co-benefits achieved. Performance requirements for technologies, as well as the reference baseline are regularly updated to reflect technology market developments, changes in the maturity of market supply, as well as market penetration rates and technology costs. The EETL would also contain information on the sectoral applicability, savings potential, estimated investment costs as well as typical payback times, annual monetary savings potential and typical equipment capacity of the energy efficient technologies. For the first phase of the EETL, cooling appliances could be prioritised. Partnerships with international and local financial institutions can ensure that financing with favourable conditions or tax incentives are made available to businesses and homeowners that want to invest in pre-approved equipment already contained in the EETL.

This tool could be made available through an online platform such as the EBRD's Green Technology Selector, which offers a shopping-style platform that connects vendors of best-in-class green technologies with businesses and homeowners. Performance requirements for technologies and vendors would be based and assessed against the EETL (EBRD, 2024[42]). Sufficient budget shall be foreseen for dedicated staff to monitor and manage such a platform, assess technology against performance standards as well as to revise the EETL based on market developments.

### *Capacity building, data collection and awareness-raising*

#### *Establishing capacity building and training programmes for financial institutions and ESCOs*

With support of international development partners, tailored capacity building programmes could be established to enhance the technical capacity and skills of financial institutions, ESCOs, building developers alike. Targeted capacity building support could aim to achieve the following priorities:

- training engineers and architects with latest green building design techniques and standards, including by upgrading university curricula
- training monitoring and verification professionals (e.g. energy auditors);
- educating and training financial institutions to increase their knowledge and familiarity with energy efficiency projects
- strengthening measurement and verification (M&V) skills to assess energy savings.
- enhancing institutional capability of agencies responsible for the design, implementation and monitoring of energy efficiency policies.

#### *Implementing consumer awareness and education campaigns for efficient buildings and cooling*

With support from international development partners, awareness campaigns on energy-efficient buildings and cooling can address different target groups ranging from policy makers, project developers and industry professionals, as well as financial institutions, commercial end-users and civil society. Awareness campaigns could focus not only on spreading knowledge on the latest technologies and regulatory changes and standards, but also on the latest developments in terms of financial instruments, both public and private.

#### *Fostering data collection on energy savings of energy-efficient buildings and cooling systems*

More and better data on the performance, cost and energy savings of energy efficient buildings and cooling appliances can help inform financing and investment decisions as well as policy design. The government could continue collecting data and information on government facilities' energy profile and could further encourage private entities to provide similar data. Collecting and publishing data in aggregated form in publicly available dashboards, for instance, integrated in UOB's U-Energy platform or DEDE's website, can help to gather knowledge and thus strengthen market confidence in energy efficiency projects.

## References


Ablaza, A., Y. Liu and M. Llado (2020), *Off-Balance-Sheet Equity: The Engine for Energy Efficiency Capital Mobilization*, Asian Development Bank Institute, https://www.adb.org/sites/default/files/publication/636646/adbi-wp1183.pdf. [37]

ACE and GIZ (2019), *Energy Efficiency Financing Guideline in Thailand*, https://agep.aseanenergy.org/wp-content/uploads/2019/05/EEF-Guideline-in-Thailand.pdf. [40]

ADB (2022), *Green Bond Market Survey for Thailand*, https://www.adb.org/sites/default/files/publication/801601/green-bond-market-survey-thailand.pdf. [64]

ADB (2022), *Promoting Local Currency Sustainable Finance in ASEAN+3*, https://www.climatebonds.net/files/reports/asean3_report.pdf. [45]

ADB (2020), *The viability of green bonds as a financing mechanism for green buildings in ASEAN*, https://www.adb.org/sites/default/files/publication/636661/adbi-wp1186.pdf. [41]

APUEA (2022), *Accelerating District Cooling Developments in Thailand*, https://www.asew-expo.com/2023/download/webinar/webinar9/presentation_APUEA.pdf. [34]

Arthaland (2023), *Arthaland offers second tranche of up to P3 Billion ASEAN green bonds*, https://arthaland.com/news/arthaland-offers-second-tranche-of-up-to-p3-billion-asean-green-bonds. [48]

ASEAN (2023), *ASEAN's Future Cooling Potential: Addressing Energy Efficiency in Indonesia's Air Conditioning Market*, https://aseanenergy.org/aseans-future-cooling-potential-addressing-energy-efficiency-in-indonesias-air-conditioning-market/. [26]

Bureau of Energy Efficiency of India (2023), *List of Energy Efficient Technologies*, https://www.adeetie.beeindia.gov.in/list-of-energy-efficient-technologies. [43]

Business Wire (2022), *Thailand Air Conditioner Market Report 2022: Increasing Online Presence & Rising Technological Innovations Fuel Growth*, Research and Markets, https://www.businesswire.com/news/home/20220907005888/en/Thailand-Air-Conditioner-Market-Report-2022-Increasing-Online-Presence-Rising-Technological-Innovations-Fuel-Growth---ResearchAndMarkets.com (accessed on 10 November 2022). [15]

CBI (2019), *ASEAN Green Finance State of the Market 2019*, https://www.climatebonds.net/files/reports/cbi_asean_sotm_2019_final.pdf. [46]

CLASP (2019), *Thailand Room Air Conditioner Market Assessment and Policy Options Analysis*, CLASP, https://www.clasp.ngo/research/all/thailand-rac-market-assessment-and-policy-options-analysis-2019/ (accessed on 15 December 2022). [16]

CLASP (2019), *Thailand Room Air Conditioner Market Assessment and Policy Options Analysis*, https://www.clasp.ngo/research/all/thailand-rac-market-assessment-and-policy-options-analysis-2019/. [25]

Data Bridge (2021), *Thailand District Cooling Market Report – Industry Trends and Forecast to 2028*, Market Research, https://www.databridgemarketresearch.com/reports/thailand-district-cooling-market (accessed on 15 December 2022). [19]

DEDE (2018), *Building Energy Code (BEC)*, https://seforallateccj.org/wpdata/wp-content/uploads/ecap17-thailand.pdf. [23]

E3G (2020), *Spotlight on cooling in Southeast Asia: A risk for energy security*, https://www.e3g.org/news/spotlight-on-cooling-in-southeast-asia-a-risk-for-energy-security/. [28]

EBRD (2024), *Green Technology Selector*, https://techselector.com/ts-en/. [42]

EGAT (2024), *Energy Efficiency Criteria*, https://labelno5.egat.co.th/home/%E0%B9%80%E0%B8%81%E0%B8%93%E0%B8%91%E0%B9%8C%E0%B8%9B%E0%B8%A3%E0%B8%B0%E0%B8%AA%E0%B8%B4%E0%B8%97%E0%B8%98%E0%B8%B4%E0%B8%A0%E0%B8%B2%E0%B8%9E%E0%B8%9E%E0%B8%A5%E0%B8%B1%E0%B8%87%E0%B8%87%E0%B8%B2/. [31]

Energy Efficiency Services Limited (2022), *Notice of 13th Annual General Meeting*, https://eeslindia.org/wp-content/uploads/2022/09/Annual-Report-FY-2021-22.pdf. [52]

EPPO (2024), *Energy overview*, https://www.eppo.go.th/epposite/index.php/th/energy-information/static-energy/summery-energy. [8]

EPPO (2022), *Energy Statistics*, Energy Policy and Planning Office (EPPO), Ministry of Energy, http://www.eppo.go.th/index.php/en/ (accessed on 10 November 2022). [6]

Frankfurt School - UNEP Collaborating Centre for Climate & Sustainable Energy Finance (2012), *Case Study: The Energy Efficiency Revolving Fund*, https://unfccc.int/files/cooperation_and_support/financial_mechanism/standing_committee/application/pdf/fs-unep_thai_eerf_final_2012.pdf. [39]

GIZ (2023), *District Cooling Guidelines, India*, https://www.energyforum.in/fileadmin/user_upload/india/media_elements/publications/20230725_District_Cooling_Guidelines/20230722_mn_DC_Guidelines.pdf. [35]

GIZ (2021), *RAC NAMA successfully transforms the Thai cooling sector, pushing it towards more climate-friendly and energy-efficient technologies*, https://www.thai-german-cooperation.info/en_US/rac-nama-successfully-transforms-the-thai-cooling-sector-pushing-it-towards-more-climate-friendly-and-energy-efficient-technologies/. [30]

Government of Thailand (2021), *Mid-century, Long-term Low Greenhouse Gas Emission Development Strategy*, Government of Thailand, Bangkok. [4]

IEA (2023), *Buildings*, https://www.iea.org/energy-system/buildings. [57]

IEA (2023), *Energy Efficiency 2023*, https://iea.blob.core.windows.net/assets/dfd9134f-12eb-4045-9789-9d6ab8d9fbf4/EnergyEfficiency2023.pdf. [1]

IEA (2023), *World Energy Investment 2023*, https://iea.blob.core.windows.net/assets/8834d3af-af60-4df0-9643-72e2684f7221/WorldEnergyInvestment2023.pdf. [58]

IEA (2022), *Roadmap Towards Sustainable and Energy-Efficient Space Cooling in ASEAN*, https://aseanenergy.org/roadmap-towards-sustainable-and-energy-efficient-space-cooling-in-asean/. [27]

IEA (2022), *Roadmap towards Sustainable and Energy-Efficient Space Cooling in the Association of Southeast Asian Nations*, Analysis, https://www.iea.org/reports/roadmap-towards-sustainable-and-energy-efficient-space-cooling-in-the-association-of-southeast-asian-nations (accessed on 14 December 2022). [2]

IEA (2019), *The Future of Cooling in Southeast Asia*, IEA, Paris, https://iea.blob.core.windows.net/assets/dcadf8ee-c43d-400e-9112-533516662e3e/The_Future_of_Cooling_in_Southeast_Asia.pdf (accessed on 15 December 2022). [7]

IEA (2018), *ESCO contracts*, https://www.iea.org/reports/energy-service-companies-escos-2/esco-contracts. [36]

India Brand Equity Foundation (2021), *UJALA Yojana*, https://www.ibef.org/government-schemes/ujala-yojna. [53]

Jitpleecheep, P. (2022), *Air conditioner market forecast to shrink*, Bangkok Post, https://www.bangkokpost.com/business/2427945/air-conditioner-market-forecast-to-shrink (accessed on 10 November 2022). [17]

JLL (2022), "Bangkok's ageing offices: asset enhancement", *JLL Commentary - Bangkok's ageing offices: asset enhancement*, https://www.jll.co.in/en/trends-and-insights/research/bangkoks-ageing-offices-asset-enhancement (accessed on 10 November 2022). [12]

JLL (2022), *Revitalising aged office buildings in Bangkok's city centre*, https://www.jll.com.au/en/trends-and-insights/research/revitalising-aged-office-buildings-in-bangkoks-city-centre. [11]

KBank (2022), *KBank and SC Asset unveils Green Home Loan*, https://www.kasikornbank.com/en/news/pages/kbank-sc-asset_go-green.aspx. [60]

Lohwanitchai, K. and D. Jareemit (2021), "Modeling Energy Efficiency Performance and Cost-Benefit Analysis Achieving Net-Zero Energy Building Design: Case Studies of Three Representative Offices in Thailand", *Sustainability*, Vol. 13(9), 5201. [14]

Lohwanitchai, K. and D. Jareemit (2020), *Analysis in Integrated Design Potentials Achieving Nearly Zero Energy in Office Buildings in Bangkok Neighborhood*, https://iopscience.iop.org/article/10.1088/1757-899X/910/1/012016/pdf. [21]

Lorenz & Partners (2020), *Green Building in Thailand*, https://www.lorenz-partners.com/wp-content/uploads/2020/02/NL208E-Green-Building-in-Thailand-Feb20.pdf. [33]

Malaysian Sustainable Finance Initiative (2017), *PNB Merdeka Ventures Sdn Berhad – Green Sukuk*, https://www.msfi.com.my/pnb-merdeka-ventures-sdn-berhad-green-sukuk/. [47]

Ministry of Natural Resources and Environment (2022), *THAILAND'S LONG-TERM LOW GREENHOUSE GAS EMISSION DEVELOPMENT STRATEGY (REVISED VERSION)*, https://unfccc.int/sites/default/files/resource/Thailand%20LT-LEDS%20%28Revised%20Version%29_08Nov2022.pdf. [5]

NEDO (2023), *Current Situation of Energy Consumption of SMEs in Manufacturing Sector in Thailand*, https://www.nedo.go.jp/content/100959495.pdf. [62]

OECD (2024), *Clean Energy Finance and Investment Roadmap of the Philippines*, Green Finance and Investment, OECD Publishing, Paris, https://doi.org/10.1787/7a13719d-en. [55]

OECD (2023), *Energy Savings Insurance: International Focus Group Discussion*, https://www.oecd.org/environment/cc/cefim/cross-cutting-analysis/Discussion-paper-first-energy-savings-insurance-international-focus-group-discussion.pdf. [44]

OECD (2022), *Clean Energy Finance and Investment Roadmap of India: Opportunities to Unlock Finance and Scale up Capital*, Green Finance and Investment, OECD Publishing, Paris, https://doi.org/10.1787/21b6e411-en. [51]

Partnership on Transparency in the Paris Agreement (2018), *MARKET-MAKING FOR LOW-CARBON ENERGY TECHNOLOGIES: THE UJALA SCHEME IN INDIA*, https://api.knack.com/v1/applications/5b23f04fd240aa37e01fa362/download/asset/5c94a552be4c1909acfe389b/190318_gpd_parisabkommen_india_rz.pdf. [54]

Prukvilailert, M. and P. Wangskarn (2011), "Energy Conservation Potential in SMEs of Thailand", *Energy Procedia*, Vol. 12, pp. 143-148, https://doi.org/10.1016/j.egypro.2011.10.020. [63]

Rogat, J. et al. (2020), *Upscaling Energy-effi ciency in Municipalities: Sourcebook on Project Bundling*, Copenhagen Centre on Energy Effi ciency, UNEP DTU Partnership, https://c2e2.unepccc.org/wp-content/uploads/sites/3/2020/10/upscaling-energy-efficiency-in-municipalities-sourcebook-on-project-bundling.pdf. [65]

Seeley, C. and S. Dhakal (2021), "Energy Efficiency Retrofits in Commercial Buildings: An Environmental, Financial, and Technical Analysis of Case Studies in Thailand", *Energies 2021, Vol. 14, Page 2571*, Vol. 14/9, p. 2571, https://doi.org/10.3390/EN14092571. [9]

Seeley, C. and S. Dhakal (2021), "Energy Efficiency Retrofits in Commercial Buildings: An Environmental, Financial, and Technical Analysis of Case Studies in Thailand", *Energies*, Vol. 14(9), 2571, https://doi.org/10.3390/en14092571. [13]

Suntorachai, N. (2020), *Bangkok Residential Project : A Contemporary of Passive Cooling*, https://www.iaacblog.com/programs/bangkok-resedential-studio-project/. [18]

Tantasavasdi, C., J. Srebric and Q. Chen (2001), "Natural Ventilation Design for Houses in Thailand", *Energy and Buildings*, Vol. 33(8) 815-824. [10]

Thailand's Ministry of Energy (2020), *Current Situation of ZEB in Thailand*, https://www.aots.jp/application/files/8615/7017/2439/File_03.pdf. [22]

Thailand's Ministry of Energy (2017), *Existing Legislation in Thailand and its relevance to development of ETS*, https://ghgreduction.tgo.or.th/th/pmr-news-and-activities/download/1582/1039/17.html. [24]

TISI (2011), *Thai Minimum energy performance standards for air conditioners*, https://service.tisi.go.th/fulltext/2134_2553.pdf. [29]

Umeyama, K. (2020), *Thailand announces a new building energy code*, https://enviliance.com/regions/southeast-asia/th/report_1359. [32]

UNDP (2023), *An Overview of the Best Practices of ESCO Market Design and Recommendations for Ukraine*, https://www.undp.org/sites/g/files/zskgke326/files/2023-05/english.pdf. [38]

UOB (2023), *UOB Thailand launches "U-Green" home loan campaign to support eco-friendly home renovations*, https://www.uob.co.th/investor-en/news/press-news/2023/news-26jun2023.page. [61]

US Department of Energy (2024), *SOUTHERN CALIFORNIA EDISON: ON-BILL FINANCING FOR ENERGY EFFICIENCY PROJECTS*, https://betterbuildingssolutioncenter.energy.gov/implementation-models/southern-california-edison-bill-financing-energy-efficiency-projects. [50]

US Department of Energy (2023), *On-Bill Financing / Repayment*, https://betterbuildingssolutioncenter.energy.gov/financing-navigator/option/bill-financingrepayment#case-studies. [49]

USAID (2022), *USAID Southeast Asia's Smart Power Program (SPP) - Year 1 Annual Work Plan*, https://pdf.usaid.gov/pdf_docs/PA00ZDK4.pdf. [56]

Vorasayan, P. (2021), *Energy Regulation and Conservation Division Department of Alternative Energy Development and Efficiency Thailand Energy Efficiency and District Cooling in Thailand*, Energy Regulation and Conservation Division, Department of Alternative Energy Development and Efficiency, https://www.google.com/url?sa=t&rct=j&q=&esrc=s&source=web&cd=&cad=rja&uact=8&ved=2ahUKEwjaseGu27eGAxWKVqQEHUHICQIQFnoECBQQAQ&url=https%3A%2F%2Fasew-expo.com%2F2024%2Fdownload%2Fwebinars%2Fwebinar7%2Fpresentation_IntroductionDistrictCooling.pdf&usg=AOvVaw (accessed on 15 December 2022). [20]

World Data (2024), *The climate in Thailand*, https://www.worlddata.info/asia/thailand/climate.php. [3]

World Green Building Council (2024), *What are green mortgages & how will they revolutionise home energy efficiency?*, https://worldgbc.org/article/what-are-green-mortgages-how-will-they-revolutionise-home-energy-efficiency/. [59]

## Note

[1] This refers to the ratio of the total cooling output to the total energy consumption for cooling over the year.

# Annex A. Process of developing the Roadmap and key stakeholders

The process for preparing the Roadmap included two in-person workshops held in Bangkok on 28 April and 24 November 2023, to consult local stakeholders and discuss barriers possible solutions.[1] Thanks to the fruitful discussions in these workshops, key financing solutions were identified, roadmap findings were discussed, and consensus was reached on the roadmap actions and areas of recommendation. These have also been supported with desktop research and analysis, case studies and interviews with Thai, regional and international experts. The Roadmap will be supplemented with support activities intended to create an impactful collaboration across relevant domestic and international stakeholders.

The local and international organisations that have been involved and consulted throughout the development of the Roadmap, either through stakeholder consultation workshops or interviews, include (but are not limited to) the following:

- Department of Alternative Energy Development and Efficiency (DEDE), Ministry of Energy, Government of Thailand
- Energy Policy and Planning Office (EPPO), Ministry of Energy, Government of Thailand
- Provincial Energy Promotion and Development Division, Office of the Permanent Secretary, Ministry of Energy, Government of Thailand
- Office of the Permanent Secretary, Ministry of Energy, Government of Thailand
- Fiscal Policy Office, Ministry of Finance, Government of Thailand
- Office of Natural Resources and Environmental Policy and Planning (ONEP), Ministry of Natural Resources and Environment (MNRE), Government of Thailand
- Office of the National Economic and Social Development Council (NESDC), Government of Thailand
- Department of Industrial Promotion, Ministry of Industry, Government of Thailand
- National Science and Technology Development Agency (NSTDA)
- National Energy Technology Center (ENTEC)
- Office of SME Promotion
- Thailand Board of Investment (BOI)
- The Securities and Exchange Commission (SEC), Thailand
- Electricity Generating Authority of Thailand (EGAT)
- Metropolitan Electricity Authority (MEA)
- Provincial Electricity Authority (PEA)
- Embassy of Denmark in Thailand
- GIZ
- UNDP
- USAID SEA Smart Power Program
- Asian Development Bank (ADB)

- World Bank
- International Finance Corporation (IFC)
- Bangkok Bank
- Kasikornbank
- Export-Import Bank of Thailand
- Thai ESCO Association
- The Thai Bankers' Association (TBA)
- The Thai Bond Market Association
- International Institute for Energy Conservation (IIEC)
- Thailand Development Research Institute
- Asia Clean Energy Partners
- Greenergy Thailand
- B.Grimm Power Public Company Limited
- SCG Power Public Company Limited
- Sena Solar Energy Company Limited
- EGS-plan (Bangkok) Company Limited
- Enapter
- Siam Commercial Bank Public Company Limited
- Asia Pacific Urban Energy Association (APUEA)
- The Joint Graduate School of Energy and Environment, King Mongkut's University of Technology Thonburi
- Energy Research Institute, Chulalongkorn University
- Agora Energiewende.

The process of developing the Clean Energy Finance and Investment Roadmap for Thailand was divided into two main parts, as illustrated in Figure A A.1 below. Part 1, covering steps 1 to 3, focuses on analysing the investments necessary for Thailand to meet its renewable energy (RE) and energy efficiency (EE) targets. Part 2, covering steps 4 to 6, concentrates on devising a strategy to efficiently access, mobilise and expand financing to support the achievement of the national renewable energy and energy efficiency objectives.

**Figure A A.1. Development process of the Clean Energy Finance and Investment Roadmap of Thailand**

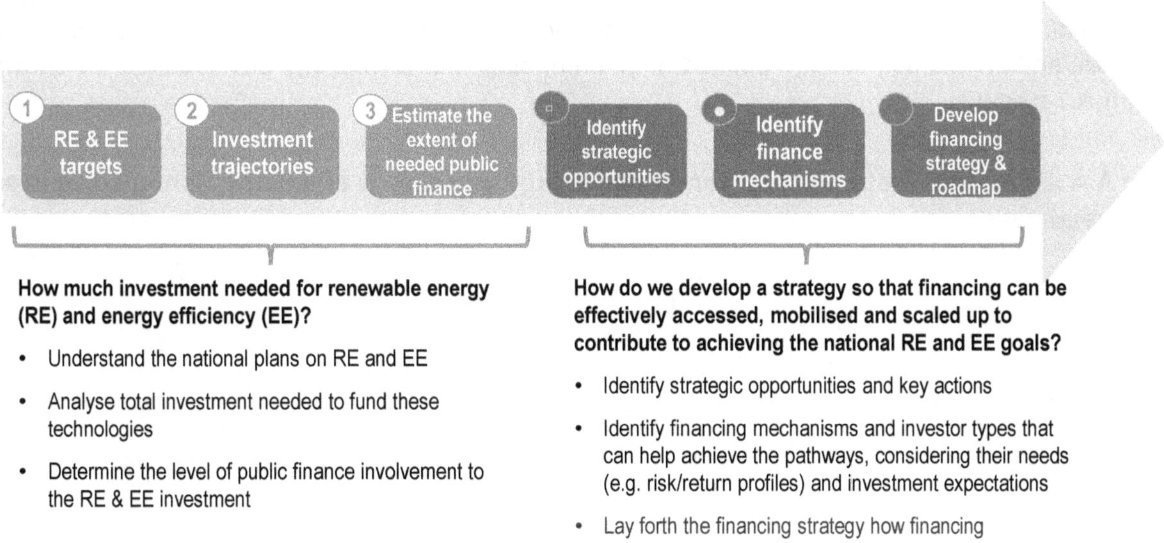


Source: Authors

A detailed description of each step is provided below:

**Step 1: Understand the national targets for renewable energy and EE.**

The first step involves thoroughly examining Thailand's existing national plans and policies related to renewable energy and EE. The Ministry of Energy intended to integrate all energy plans into a national energy plan starting in 2021, but an official version has not yet been launched. However, two recent plans related to renewable energy and energy efficiency have been released: the Alternative Energy Development Plan 2018 (AEDP 2018) and the draft version for a public hearing of the Energy Efficiency Plan 2022 (EEP 2022). These two plans served as the basis for analysing the investments required to achieve Thailand's renewable energy and energy efficiency targets.

**Step 2: Analyse the total investment needed to fund these technologies.**

In this step, a comprehensive analysis was conducted to calculate the total investment needed to facilitate the implementation of renewable energy and energy efficiency technologies in Thailand. This analysis encompassed the assessment of both capital expenses (CAPEX) and operational expenses (OPEX) associated with various clean energy projects. Information regarding CAPEX and OPEX for these technologies was sourced from multiple references, including IRENA's Renewable Power Generation Costs in 2022 (August, 2023), Ambition to Action's Domestic Expenditure and Employment Impacts of Power Sector Development in Thailand (November, 2019), A2A (2019), and Clean, Affordable and Secure Energy for Southeast Asia (CASE)'s study on Towards a collective vision of Thai energy transition: National long-term scenarios and socioeconomic implications (November, 2022).

**Step 3: Determine the level or degree of public finance involvement in renewable energy and energy efficiency investments.**

This step involves assessing the role of government funding, subsidies, incentives and grants in supporting clean energy initiatives. It helps in understanding the government's commitment to driving clean energy adoption and identifying areas where public financing can be optimised. In order to determine the level of public finance involvement in renewable energy and energy efficiency investments, the readiness level of each technology was assessed. At different levels of technology readiness, the degree of public finance involvement was adjusted.

Technology readiness is categorised into six levels, including pre-feasibility study, research and development, demonstration/pilot, deployment, diffusion, and commercial maturity. Financial instruments from public and private sources are applied at different stages of technology development, as shown in Figure A A.2 below.

### Figure A A.2. Financial instrument for renewable energy and energy efficiency technologies at each level of readiness

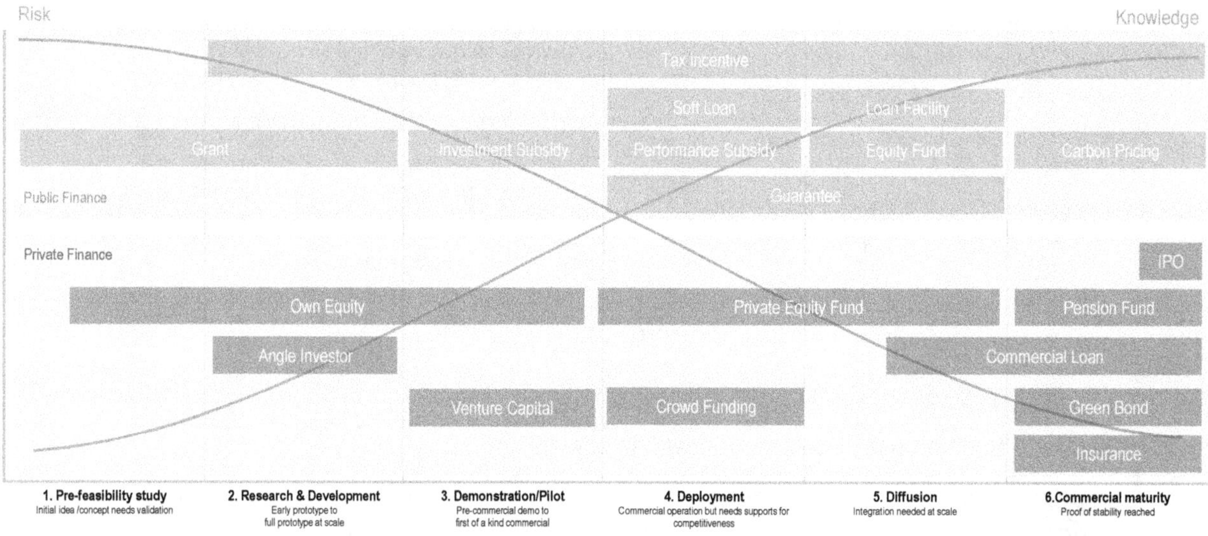


Source: Authors (The Creagy)

To identify the employment opportunities and the value added generated from the implementation of AEDP and EEP, an economic impact analysis of the AEDP and EEP was conducted. In addition, a supply chain analysis of potential technologies for clean energy deployment, including solar PV rooftop and high-efficiency cooling systems for buildings was conducted.

**Step 4: Identify strategic opportunities and key actions, including potential initiatives/pilots as actionable items.**

In the fourth step, the focus is on identifying strategic opportunities and key actions to accelerate progress towards clean energy objectives. As a result of the consultation with the Department of Alternative Energy Development and Efficiency (DEDE), two potential technologies for clean energy deployment were selected: solar PV rooftops and high-efficiency cooling systems for buildings. To kickstart progress, actionable initiatives and pilot projects were recommended.

**Step 5: Identify finance mechanisms and investor types that can help achieve the pathways, considering their needs (e.g. risk/return profiles) and investment expectations.**

This step involves identifying the different finance mechanisms and investor categories that can contribute to achieving Thailand's clean energy goals. It includes assessing the risk and return profiles of various investors, such as private sector entities, financial institutions and international organisations. Understanding these factors helps tailor financing strategies to attract diverse sources of funding.

**Step 6: Lay out the strategy for how financing could be scaled up and by whom and define which financing mechanisms are to be developed and used where for which technology.**

The final step involves formulating a comprehensive strategy for scaling up clean energy financing. This includes defining how financing could be expanded and by whom. It also outlined which financing mechanisms could be developed and applied for two specific technologies. The strategy will provide a clear roadmap for mobilising and allocating resources effectively to meet Thailand's renewable energy and energy efficiency targets.

## Note

[1] Further details about the stakeholder consultation workshops can be found at Clean energy finance and investment roadmap - OECD

# Annex B. Case Studies

The OECD and the Creagy developed a series of five case studies on financing mechanisms for small-scale renewable power and energy efficiency projects in Thailand (Table A B.1 below). The choice of the case studies was based on consultations and interviews with a wide range of stakeholders on challenges and barriers for attracting financing in the two sectors in Thailand.

### Table A B.1. Overview of case studies

| Financing instrument | Countries | Focus area | Source(s) of finance |
|---|---|---|---|
| **Risk guarantee** | Malaysia | Small-scale clean energy | Government funding and commercial finance |
| **Pay-as-you-go (PAYG)** | Thailand | Off-grid small-scale renewable power | Government funding, development finance and private impact investment |
| **Energy savings insurance (ESI)** | Colombia, El Salvador, Mongolia | Energy efficiency | International development partners (e.g. multilateral development banks), local financial institutions, government funding |
| **On-bill financing** | United States | Energy efficiency | Private investors, utilities and ESCOs |
| **Bulk procurement and demand aggregation** | India | Small-scale renewables and energy efficiency | Government funding, international development partners, commercial actors |

Source: Authors

Each case study includes:

- an overview of the financing model
- examples from other countries (including key stakeholders, outcomes and lessons learnt)
- an explanation of how the financing mechanism could address specific challenges and barriers in Thailand
- a recommended roadmap and timeline for implementation of the financing mechanism in Thailand.

The case studies pertain to emerging and developing countries wherever possible, to show how the specific challenges in these countries can be overcome. Some examples may refer to developed economies, where the key learnings provide insights to replicate a similar scheme in Thailand. One case study presents a financing model (PAYG) that has already been tested in Thailand and could be further expanded. Desk research and interviews were the main sources of information for the development of the case studies.

## Case study 1: Credit risk guarantee: Malaysia's Green Technology Financing Scheme (GTFS)

Credit guarantee schemes can help MSMEs access finance by transferring all of part of the borrower's credit and default risk, thus alleviating factors such as limited collateral and track record. Thanks to guarantees, in case of a borrower default, a lender can resort to a full or partial repayment from a third-party guarantor. Guarantees can cover either individual loans of individual borrowers, or a portfolio of loans, for example made by commercial banks to intermediary financial institutions (Alliance for Financial Inclusion, 2022[1]).

Governments and public financial institutions can play a key role in de-risking small-scale renewable projects through funding or supporting guarantee schemes. For example, in 2010 the Government of Malaysia established the Green Technology Financing Scheme (GTFS), with initial funding of RM 1.5 billion (USD 470 million). The scheme offers guarantees to participating financial institutions, with the aim of easing green companies' access to private commercial finance. Malaysia's Green Technology Financing Scheme (GTFS) is a government support programme offering a 2% interest subsidy and a government guarantee covering up to 60% of loans for green projects (Malaysian Sustainable Finance Initiative, 2023[2]). The sections below explore Malaysia's GTFS in greater detail and provide a roadmap on how a similar scheme could be implemented in Thailand.

### *Financing model*

Malaysia's GTFS scheme offers a 2% interest subsidy and a government guarantee covering up to 60% of green loan portfolios of participating financial institutions. It targets Malaysian-registered companies with a minimum of 60% Malaysian ownership, focusing on both producers and users of green technologies, including ESCOs.

The Government of Malaysia allocated an initial funding of RM 1.5 billion (USD 470 million) in 2010 and received an additional RM 2 billion (USD 630 million) in 2013 and extended the funding period until 2017. The GTFS 2.0 was earmarked with RM 5.0 billion in 2018, and later the allocation was reduced to RM 3.0 billion in 2019, with the funding period extending until 2020. In 2023, the government continued to support the development of green businesses with the reinstatement of the GTFS 4.0 up to RM 1.0 billion (USD 208.4 million) for the period until 31 December 2025.

In 2023, GTFS' financed activities include: producers of green technologies, users of green technologies, Energy Services Companies (ESCOs), housing developers and low carbon mobility infrastructure. Targeted sectors include: energy, manufacturing, transport, building, waste and water.

### *Key stakeholders*

Key stakeholders of the GTFS include (Figure A B.1 below):

- The **Government of Malaysia** is the main driver of the scheme, responsible for allocating funds and formulating policies for the scheme.
- The **Malaysian Green Technology and Climate Change Corporation** is the key implementer of GTFS and it is responsible for the promotion, assessment, certification and monitoring of participants.
- The **Credit Guarantee Corporation Malaysia Berhad** is responsible for offering a 60 to 80% financing guarantee to project companies and charges a 0.5% per annum guarantee fee to the government.
- **Local banks**: commercial and Islamic banks and Development Finance Institutions (DFIs) that provide the financing to the project company and receive a 2% interest subsidy from the government.

**Figure A B.1. Key players of Malaysia's GTFS**

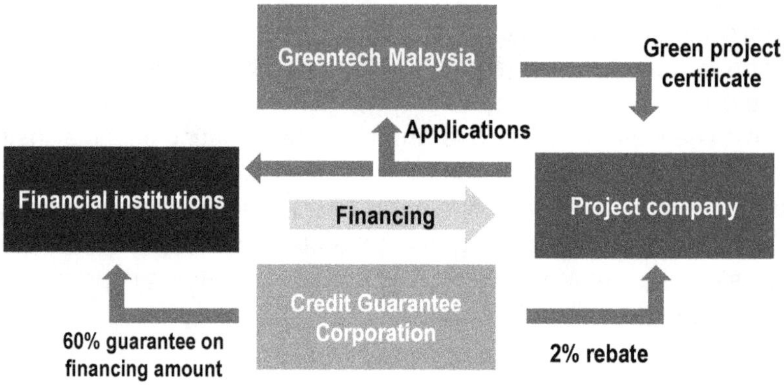


Source: Ministry of Natural Resources and Environment of Malaysia (2014[3]), Green Technology Financing Scheme (GTFS), untitled (unfccc.int).

## Outcomes

As of 2018, the GTFS resulted in the participation of 28 financial institutions in loans for 319 projects worth approximately United States Dollars (USD) 875 million (World Bank, 2020[4]). Most of the funding was allocated to solar power projects (Tu, Fan, 2016[5]). A recent study analysing the impact of the GTFS on the business performance of renewable energy producers shows that the scheme improves the financial and non-financial performance of participating companies, such as such as profitability, cash flow, product quality, customer satisfaction and environmental sustainability (Adebiyi et al., 2020[6]).

## Lessons learnt

The GTFS is an effective way to support green technology development in Malaysia by providing risk guarantees, interest subsidies and tax incentives to eligible companies. It helps to reduce the financial barriers and risks for green technology producers and users and encourages innovation and competitiveness in the green economy.

The case study reveals that the Green Technology Financing Scheme (GTFS) in Malaysia is driven by the collaborative efforts of diverse stakeholders, each contributing significantly to the success of the initiative. Funding agencies provide the necessary capital, technical support agencies validate the feasibility and sustainability of projects, financial institutions offer the needed liquidity with reduced risk thanks to the credit guarantee corporations, and project developers bring innovative green technologies to fruition. The interplay between these key players ensures that the GTFS can operate effectively.

The GTFS also faces some challenges and limitations, such as the complexity and bureaucracy of the application and approval process, the lack of awareness and promotion of the scheme, the limited scope and duration of the scheme and the need for more co-ordination and collaboration among the stakeholders.

The GTFS can be enhanced and improved by increasing the financing guarantee and expanding the scope of financing, especially to the electric vehicles and waste management sectors, providing more technical assistance and capacity building for the recipient companies, and strengthening the monitoring and evaluation of the scheme's impact and outcomes.

## Opportunities and challenges for the implementation of a risk guarantee in Thailand

Thailand's ESCO Revolving Fund once considered implementing a credit guarantee facility. The facility would have been part of the six financing tools under the fund, namely equity investment, equipment leasing, venture capital, GHG project facility and technical assistance. However, the ESCO fund decided to focus only on equity investment and equipment leasing due to their attractiveness and ease of implementation. Moreover, interviews with Thai stakeholders indicated that the government had previously launched a credit guarantee facility concurrently with other subsidy programs for green projects. However, most private sector entities opted to join the subsidy program rather than the credit guarantee one. Interview insights indicate that implementing a credit guarantee facility in itself would be the most effective way forward.

## Case study 2: Pay-as-you-go (PAYG) models in Thailand

Pay-as-you-go (PAYG) models can ease access to clean energy to off-grid communities, using mobile payment technologies to facilitate payment by instalments. PAYG models usually involve home solar systems that customers pay for using mobile payment technologies and mobile phone credit (IRENA, 2020[7]). PAYG models can be implemented at both household and community level. PAYG systems can also be implemented as a micro-grid solution, where a solar PV system with battery storage is used to provide electricity services to a community (IRENA, 2020[7]). PAYG schemes are often implemented in the context of community-ownership models, which refer to the collective ownership and management of energy-related assets. Through cost-sharing, community-ownership models enable individual participants to own assets with lower levels of investment requirements (IRENA, 2020[8]).

In Thailand, a pilot community-owned PAYG model was launched in 2017 through a collaborative effort between the Ministry of Energy, GIZ Thailand, and the social enterprise ReCharge Energy, aiming to develop sustainable electrification using solar home systems. The targeted areas include two off-grid islands in the Gulf of Thailand and the Andaman Sea, which currently rely on electricity generated by diesel engines: Bulon Don Island and Jik Island.

On Bulon Don Island, the PAYG model involves five key players: a funding agency, a technical support team, solar PV suppliers, a community enterprise and end-users. Meanwhile, on Jik Island, an additional player is involved, namely investors. Each player has a unique role to play, as illustrated in Figure A B.2 below.

### Figure A B.2. PAYG key actors

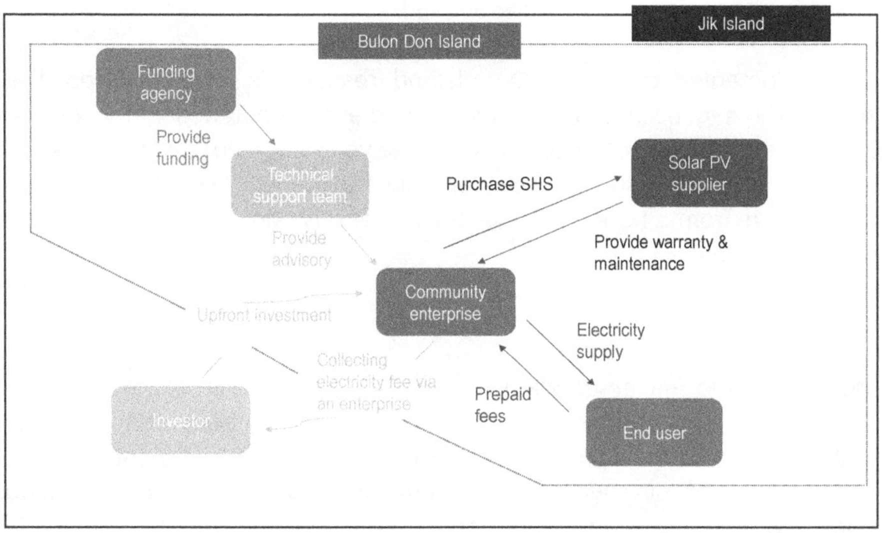


Source: Authors

## Bulon Don Island

### *Financing model*

The implementation of Pay-as-you-go (PAYG) Solar Home Systems (SHS) on Bulon Don Island marked a departure from the traditional *"Grant and Forget"* model, which faced challenges due to inadequate user feedback, technical knowledge and self-management. With financial support and technical assistance from development co-operation agencies, the new approach focused on a *"Financed and Sustained"* strategy. The new programme provided three different packages of solar home systems, operationalised and maintained by a local community enterprise through a revolving fund. A PAYG model was set up as a digital pre-payment scheme consisting of monthly instalments. The community enterprise was established to foster self-management, provide local technical support and establish an effective feedback mechanism. By adopting plug-and-play SHS, local technicians could easily troubleshoot and replace malfunctioning equipment. Ownership of the SHS assets was vested in the community, which leased them to end-users over a four-year period, collecting payments through a monthly PAYG scheme, thus ensuring sustainability and long-term viability of the project.

### *Key stakeholders*

Key stakeholders of the PAYG on Bulon Don Island include:

- the Ministry of Energy, GIZ Thailand and the social enterprise ReCharge Energy, who provided technical assistance to the community
- several development co-operation agencies which provided grants and technical assistance
- Fosera, a German based manufacturer of High-Quality Solar Home Systems, who is a supplier of solar PV panels and batteries
- the Koh Bulon Don renewable energy Community Enterprise, who is responsible for providing rental services of solar PV systems to villagers on the island, collecting prepaid fees, and managing a revolving fund for operating and maintaining the systems
- 79 households in Bulon Don Island that are the end-users who pay fees prior to employing the solar PV systems.

### *Outcomes*

The PAYG model implemented on Bulon Don Island resulted in significant positive environmental outcomes. These include a considerable reduction in diesel consumption by 2 994 litres annually, avoidance of approximately 8 tonnes of $CO_2$ emissions per year and a notable decrease in monthly energy expenses by Thai Baht (THB) 300 (USD 8.6) per household. Moreover, the model has substantially increased electricity access from 5 hours to 18-24 hours per day, significantly improving the community's quality of life and economic resilience.

### *Lessons learnt*

Key lessons learned from the implementation of the PAYG model on Bulon Don Island include the necessity of designing user-friendly systems that meet community energy demands, selecting communities with financial capability to sustain the project and ensuring that appropriate capacity building support is provided. Technical capacity-building within the community is crucial for the successful operation and maintenance of the system, reducing dependency on external support. Equally important is the development of financial management skills within the community to ensure transparent and sustainable fund management.

## Jik Island

### *Financing model*

Before 2004, Jik Island relied on individually-owned diesel generators for electricity. From 2004 to 2014, the government funded the island's electrification, allocating approximately USD 286 000 from the Energy Conservation Promotion Fund to establish a microgrid system managed by the community-owned company Koh Jik. However, due to limitations of the solar PV and wind turbine components, the ESCO incurred high expenses from diesel generator usage, resulting in minimal profitability. In 2014, a government-sponsored a USD 198 000 investment in a 40 kilowatt peak (kWp) solar PV system and lead-acid batteries significantly reduced ESCO's expenses in supplying electricity to the microgrid. As a result, the ESCO managed to start generating monthly profits.

In 2018, as critical components of the electricity generation system, such as batteries, reached the end of their lifespan, the community started to encounter challenges in securing funds for replacements. In response, GIZ Thailand, the Ministry of Energy, and ReCharge Energy collaborated to enhance the community's management and technical skills, preparing them to independently own, operate and maintain the system, thereby attracting private investors.

A joint venture between companies Blue Solar and Symbior Solar provided a 100% equity investment amounting to USD 172 000 for the installation of a 72-kWp solar PV system, LFP batteries with total capacity of 266 kWh, and a 60 kW backup diesel generator. A development co-operation agency provided a grant for the installation of 100 smart prepaid meters. Sales of Renewable Energy Certificates (RECs) facilitated by Allotrope Partners and its network of investors in renewable energy enabled the enterprise to lower electricity fees for end-users.

The Koh Jik renewable energy Community Enterprise manages operations and maintenance of the systems, supplies electricity to the community and handles the collection of prepaid fees at a rate of 13 THB/kWh, which are then remitted to the joint venture. Additionally, the enterprise serves as the fund manager for the Koh Jik Clean Energy for Environment Fund, which receives revenue from the sale of the RECs.

### *Key stakeholders*

Key stakeholders of the PAYG on Jik Island include:

- the Ministry of Energy, GIZ Thailand, and the ReCharge Energy, who all provided technical assistance to the community
- the joint venture between Blue Solar and Symbior Solar, who provided a 100% equity investment for the upgraded system
- A development co-operation agency, who provided a grant for the installation of 100 smart prepaid meters
- Allotrope Partners, which has a network of investors in renewable energy, and who entered into a 20-year agreement to purchase RECs from the Koh Jik renewable electricity project
- the Koh Jik renewable energy Community Enterprise, who is responsible for operating and maintaining the systems, providing electricity to the community, collecting prepaid fees, and managing the Koh Jik Clean Energy for Environment Fund, which receives revenues from the sale of RECs
- about 150 households on Jik Island, as the end-users who pay fees prior to consuming electricity from the microgrid system.

### *Outcomes*

The implementation of the upgraded energy system on Jik Island has yielded significant and multi-faceted benefits. The scheme resulted in annual savings of 31 500 litres of diesel, a substantial reduction representing 95% of the previous consumption. This not only signifies a significant decrease in reliance on fossil fuels but also translates to considerable cost savings and environmental benefits. The avoidance of approximately 1 725 tonnes of CO2 emissions over the project's lifetime underscores the project's positive environmental impact, contributing to mitigating climate change. Moreover, the upgraded system dramatically improved electricity access on the island, increasing from a mere 4 hours per day with personal generators to a consistent 24 hours per day, significantly enhancing the quality of life and economic opportunities for the community. Furthermore, the reduction in the cost of electricity from 30 THB/kWh to 13 THB/kWh demonstrates the improved affordability and financial sustainability of the energy supply, further enhancing the socio-economic well-being of the community.

### *Lessons learnt*

The electrification on Koh Jik Island provides several valuable lessons for sustainable energy projects:

- **Initial government investment in renewable energy infrastructure**: The government's initial investment in renewable energy infrastructure laid the foundation for electrification on the island. However, it is crucial to ensure that the installed systems have sufficient capacity to meet the community's energy needs effectively.
- **Financial sustainability through improved technology**: Upgrading the solar PV system in 2014 significantly reduced operational expenses and generated profits for the ESCO. This highlights the importance of regularly assessing and upgrading technology to enhance financial sustainability.
- **Community empowerment and capacity building**: Enhancing the community's management and technical skills was crucial to enable community members to independently own, operate, and maintain the energy system. This underscores the importance of community empowerment and capacity building for the long-term success of sustainable energy projects.
- **Public-private partnerships for investment**: Securing investment from private companies like Blue Solar Co., Ltd., and Symbior Solar Co., Ltd., demonstrates the added value of public-private partnerships in financing and implementing renewable energy projects.
- **Diversification and financial modelling**: Diversifying energy sources, such as blending solar and diesel, can provide more stability to the energy supply. Additionally, developing clear and transparent financial models, including strategies for revenue generation and cost reduction, is essential for attracting investors and ensuring the project's financial viability.

### *Opportunities and challenges for the implementation of pay-as-you-go (PAYG) models in Thailand*

The two case studies identified several potential challenges and potential solutions for the implementation of PAYG for renewable energy electrification on other off-grid islands in Thailand:

- **Technical durability**: The coastal environment can hasten the degradation of solar equipment. Frequent maintenance or replacement, particularly of sensitive components like batteries and inverters, is necessary.
- **Financial feasibility**: The substantial upfront investment and ongoing maintenance costs of the microgrid require financial support, often from government or donor sources, to be viable.
- **Consumption management**: Controlling the community's electricity usage is a complex task. As electricity becomes more available, consumption typically rises, potentially overwhelming the supply. A prepaid electricity model has been introduced to help manage this.

- **Supply reliability**: Solar energy's intermittent nature poses a challenge for consistent power delivery, especially during periods of reduced sunlight, necessitating backup solutions.
- **Affordability**: The cost of solar systems, both initial and recurring, may be prohibitive for some households, particularly where income is inconsistent due to reliance on seasonal revenues.
- **Service and repairs**: Remote island settings often lack access to skilled maintenance personnel, complicating the prompt repair and servicing of solar systems.
- **Community engagement**: Effective implementation depends on the community's understanding and engagement with the solar systems. This requires comprehensive and continuous education and training programs.

The primary targets for replicating both models include off-grid communities within national reserve parks, where constructing distribution systems is prohibited, and over 100 islands in the Gulf of Thailand and the Andaman Sea, where extending the grid is not economically viable.

Though initially developed for electrification in off-grid areas, the models are also applicable to on-grid communities seeking low-carbon solutions. By incorporating the PAYG model, on-grid communities can move towards greater energy independence, making them more resilient to grid outages and fluctuations in energy prices and allowing communities to transition towards greener, low-carbon energy sources, thus reducing their environmental impact.

To address the challenges associated with PAYG models and pave the way for successful renewable energy electrification projects in off-grid island communities in Thailand, the selection of high-quality systems, financial support from the government, the careful selection of the targeted community, and technical support on community empowerment and capacity building are the most crucial factors. To foster this initiative, providing a blend of technical expertise and financial backing is essential. Table A B.2 below outlines potential actors involved in the PAYG implementation in Thailand and the challenges they may encounter while Table A B.3 illustrates the roadmap for the implementation of Pay-As-You-Go (PAYG) model in Thailand.

## Table A B.2. Key players and potential challenges of implementation of PAYG in Thailand

| Key players | Potential Thai actors | Challenges |
|---|---|---|
| **Funding agencies** | **Domestic public fund:** Energy Conservation Promotion Fund (ENCON Fund) & Power Development Fund | • Eligibility criteria of the fund<br>• Political priorities |
| | **International agencies or funds**, e.g. GIZ, UNDP, ADB, GEF and bilateral development co-operation agencies | • Stringent eligibility criteria<br>• Complex application process<br>• Funding cycles and availability |
| **Technical support agencies** | **Ministry of Energy (MOEN) and ReCharge Energy** | • Limited financial and human resources<br>• Regulatory and policy constraints |
| **Investors** | • **Technology suppliers**<br>• **Existing power producers** | • Infrastructure constraints<br>• Market and demand uncertainty<br>• Very small size of project |
| **Community enterprise & end users** | **Off-grid communities** selected by project team with the key criteria including agreement on off-grid rules, affordability and willingness to pay | • Lack of management and technical skills<br>• Limited financial resources for upfront investment and limited access to financing |
| | **On-grid communities seeking low-carbon solutions** | • Lack of incentives<br>• Lack of technical capacity |

**Table A B.3. Roadmap for PAYG implementation in Thailand**

| Key areas | Activities | Responsible agency | Year 1: Preparation | Year 2-3: Pilot expansion | Year 4 onwards: Scale-up |
|---|---|---|---|---|---|
| **Stakeholder engagement and policy support** | 1.1 Establish a task force with representatives from the Ministry of Energy, private investors, international aid organisations, and community leaders. | MOEN & ReCharge Energy | X | | |
| | 1.2 Advocate for policy reforms that support microgrid developments in off-grid and on-grid areas. | MOEN & ReCharge Energy | X | | |
| | 1.3 Engage local communities throughout the project development process | Task Force | | X | X |
| | 1.4 Foster public-private partnerships to enhance investment and technology innovation. | Task Force | | X | X |
| **Technical and need assessment** | 2.1 Identify potential off-grid and on-grid communities that can benefit from PAYG. | MOEN & ReCharge Energy | X | | |
| | 2.2 Evaluate current technologies and identify the need for technical upgrades or adaptations to suit local conditions. | MOEN & ReCharge Energy | X | | |
| **Financing** | 3.1 Create a financial strategy suitable for scaling, including identifying sources for funding and investment. | MOEN & ReCharge Energy | X | | |
| | 3.2 Secure financing sources for project investment | Investors, Banks | | X | X |
| **Expansion** | 4.1 Deploy PAYG systems in selected off-grid / on-grid communities. | MOEN & ReCharge Energy | | X | X |
| **Capacity building and training** | 5.1 Develop local capacity in technical, managerial, and financial aspects of PAYG systems. | MOEN & ReCharge Energy | | X | X |
| | 5.2 Implement comprehensive education programs for end-users to ensure proper use and maintenance. | | | X | X |
| **Monitoring and evaluation** | 6.1 Set up systems to monitor usage, payments, and operational metrics. | | X | | |
| | 6.2 Regularly monitor and evaluate projects | | | X | X |

Source: Authors

## Case study 3: Energy savings insurance (ESI)

The ESI model was first developed by the Inter-American Development Bank (IDB) in Colombia in 2014, with the support of the Basel Agency for Sustainable Energy (BASE), as a mechanism to build investor confidence and improve access to low-cost finance for energy efficiency projects. Since its conceptualisation, the ESI model has been replicated in many other countries worldwide, usually in co-operation with multilateral or national development banks. See OECD report *Energy Savings Insurance: International Focus Group Discussion* for an overview of previous and ongoing ESI programmes (OECD, 2023[9]).

ESI is a de-risking package which combines four financial and non-financial elements to support the identification and structuring of technically robust and bankable projects: a **standard performance contract**, a **technical validation**, an **energy savings insurance product** and **concessional financing.** Table A B.4 below summarises the main functions and benefits of each of these four products.

## Table A B.4. Financial and non-financial elements of ESI: functions and benefits

| Element | Functions | Benefits |
|---|---|---|
| **Standard performance contract** | • Establishing the responsibilities of the supplier in terms of supply and installation of equipment, corresponding guarantees and the promised energy savings relative to a benchmark;<br>• Committing the customer to timely payments, access to facilities, and adequate maintenance of the equipment. | • Boost the confidence of the firms, insurance providers, and financial institutions in the technology provider's products<br>• Lower transaction costs |
| **Technical validation** | • Evaluating the project's technical potential to achieve the promised savings;<br>• Verifying that the project has been built according to agreed specifications;<br>• Determining which party is entitled to compensation in case of disagreements. | • Boost the confidence of the firms, insurance providers, and financial institutions in the technology provider's products<br>• Lower transaction costs |
| **Energy savings insurance** | • Partially covering the energy savings commitment made by the technology supplier under the performance contract for a specific period of time. | • Allow technology providers to back the performance of their products and distinguish themselves from lower-quality providers;<br>• Improve firms' trust and boosts their sales. |
| **Concessional financing** | • Financing insured projects with funding from international donor agencies and/or multilateral development banks (MDBs), with concessional elements such as such as longer loan terms or grace periods. | • Reduce the cost of capital<br>• Improve access to finance |

Source: OECD (2023[9]), Energy Savings Insurance: International Focus Group Discussion, https://www.oecd.org/environment/cc/cefim/cross-cutting-analysis/Discussion-paper-first-energy-savings-insurance-international-focus-group-discussion.pdf.

ESI schemes typically involve nine key players: Donors and/or multilateral development banks, a national development bank, local financial institutions, a local insurance company, a re-insurance agency, a technology provider, a technical validation agency and clients. A conceptual visualisation of the ESI model is shown in Figure A B.3 below.

## Figure A B.3. Key players of ESI

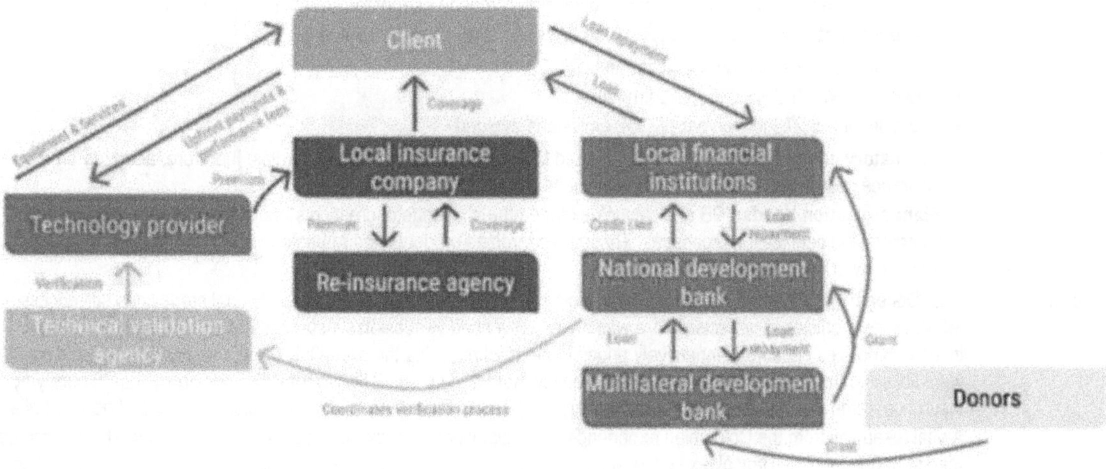


Source: Authors based on OECD (2023[9]), Energy Savings Insurance: International Focus Group Discussion, https://www.oecd.org/environment/cc/cefim/cross-cutting-analysis/Discussion-paper-first-energy-savings-insurance-international-focus-group-discussion.pdf.

### *Financing model, key stakeholders, outcomes and lessons learnt on ESI in Colombia, El Salvador and Mongolia*

Three cases in Colombia, El Salvador and Mongolia were reviewed, as illustrated in Table A B.5, A B.6 and A B.7.

## Table A B.5. ESI in Colombia

| Implementation dates | 2016 – 2022 |
|---|---|
| Implementation status | Pilot complete |
| Lead implementer | Bancóldex with the support from Inter-American Development Bank (IDB) |
| Funder | DEA, CTF, and IDB |
| Total project value | DEA provided initial technical support for ESI development with a budget of USD 300,000.<br>CTF and IDB providing an additional USD 48 million in the form of loans to Bancoldex to fund energy efficiency projects (both with and without the inclusion of ESI Financing model) |
| Financed activities | Twelve energy-efficient and renewable energy technologies with high potential in those sectors were eligible to be covered in the programme, namely light-emitting diode (LED) bulbs, heating, ventilation, and air conditioning (HVAC) systems, boilers, cogeneration units, solar thermal, motors, ovens, air compressors, cooling systems, motorcycle and cab fleets, biogas, and solar PV. |
| Targeted sectors | The ESI pilot programme initially covered MSMEs in the hospitality and healthcare sectors where significant market potential was identified. Eventually it was expanded to cover firms in the manufacturing, commercial, and other services sectors |
| EE landscape before implementation | In Colombia, there were no specific schemes to promote the adoption of energy-efficient technologies, leading to low trust and experience among firms regarding their benefits. The ESI pilot programme, launched in 2014 by IDB and the Colombian national development bank, Bancóldex, aimed to overcome these barriers and enhance the energy efficiency market. Bancóldex's goal is to foster sustainable growth in Colombian businesses, especially MSMEs, making the promotion of energy efficiency aligned with its mandate. |
| Financing model | Under the ESI pilot programme, Bancóldex offered three credit lines totaling USD 48 million for energy efficiency projects to MSMEs via 8 intermediary banks.<br>This funding blended equal resources from CTF and IDB, complemented by a USD 1 million grant from CTF for market development. This grant allowed for benefits like free project validation, technical advice, subsidized insurance, expedited credit processes, and specialized training. Blended international finance enabled Bancóldex to offer concessional credit terms and additional incentives to boost participation in the ESI programme. |
| Key Stakeholders | • **Validation and verification services:** Colombian Institute of Technical Standards and Certification<br>• **Local insurance company:** Salvadoran insurance company Aseguradora Suiza Salvadoreña<br>• **Disbursement of energy efficiency credit lines:** 11 local financial institutions |
| Outcomes | • 262 energy savings insurance policies issued<br>• Investments worth USD 29.8 million mobilised<br>• Approximately 6,273 tonne/year of CO2 emissions avoided |
| Challenges | • **Regulatory complications:** There was a need to avoid potential regulatory hurdles; therefore, adapting an existing insurance policy was time and resource efficient.<br>• **Standardisation Needs:** IDB and Bancóldex faced the challenge of creating standardized energy performance contracts and certification processes. These standardized products had to be flexible enough to cater to specific technology or sector need |
| Lessons learnt | After December 2022, the ESI programme in Colombia progressed with IDB's concessional credit lines still accessible for MSME energy efficiency projects. There was no longer a need to subsidize insurance costs since energy savings insurance policies became competitively priced in the market during the pilot. Only 5% of the 262 policies sold by SURA were linked to the IDB-Bancóldex credit line. The low default ratio led SURA to transition the policy from a surety bond to insurance, removing the obligation for technology suppliers to contribute to insurance claims in case of non-compliance.<br>A vital takeaway from the Colombian experience is the significance of forming robust, strategic partnerships informed by market understanding. Bancóldex successfully harnessed these partnerships to create demand and address market gaps. |

Source: OECD (2023[9]), Energy Savings Insurance: International Focus Group Discussion, https://www.oecd.org/environment/cc/cefim/cross-cutting-analysis/Discussion-paper-first-energy-savings-insurance-international-focus-group-discussion.pdf.

## Table A B.6. ESI in El Salvador

| | |
|---|---|
| **Implementation dates** | 2019 – 2022 |
| **Implementation status** | Pilot complete |
| **Lead implementer** | National development bank Banco de Desarrollo de El Salvador (BANDESAL) in partnership with IDB |
| **Funder** | IDB & GCF |
| **Total project value** | USD 41.7 million |
| **Financed activities** | Replacement of energy-intensive motors, air conditioners (ACs), refrigerators, and boilers used by MSMEs |
| **EE landscape before implementation** | Energy efficiency investments in El Salvador were minimal because of low demand and unsatisfactory financing conditions. Especially among MSMEs, there was a significant lack of confidence in the returns on energy efficiency investments and skepticism regarding the reliability of technology or service providers.<br>The absence of mandates for energy efficiency and the lack of Energy Service Companies (ESCOs) in the nation further stifled market demand. The availability of financing for energy efficiency, and for MSMEs in particular, was also sparse. The country's financial system suffered from limited liquidity and a focus on short-term assets, making long-term loans for productive endeavors, like equipment upgrades, a rarity. |
| **Financing model** | The program, valued at USD 41.7 million, consisted of both reimbursable and non-reimbursable components. The GCF extended a USD 20 million concessional loan to IDB, which was passed on to BANDESAL, backed by a sovereign guarantee from El Salvador. BANDESAL matched this with its own USD 20 million, establishing a concessional credit line for local institutions to offer favorable loans to MSME energy efficiency projects.<br>Repayments from these loans fueled a dedicated revolving fund for more projects. The GCF loan aimed to offer MSMEs benefits like lower interest rates (3.17%) and extended maturity periods in line with eligible technologies. Some of the loan's benefits were also given as a "success fee", enabling MSMEs to access more affordable credit.<br>Alongside the loan, GCF provided a USD 1.7 million non-reimbursable grant to create and implement non-financial tools and risk-sharing methods under the ESI model. This included strategies for financing, development of energy performance contracts, engagement with local financial institutions, and collaboration with tech providers for robust project development. |
| **Stakeholders involved** | • Validation and verification services: ICONTEC, which had previously been involved in the ESI programme of Colombia and the Spanish Association for Standardisation (AENOR)<br>• Local insurance company: Seguros de Vida Suramericana (SURA), Colombia's largest insurance company<br>• Disbursement of energy efficiency credit lines: Several private banks with some existing interest and technical capacity in energy efficiency lending and project evaluation, such as Bancolombia, Davivienda, BBVA, and Banco de Bogotá. |
| **Outcomes** | Insuring 100 firms, achieving 36.5 GWh of energy savings, and avoiding 562,037 tonnes of $CO_2$ equivalent of emissions over a 15-year period |
| **Challenges** | Regulatory challenge: Regulations in the local insurance sector dictate the maximum coverage period and extent of energy savings insurance policies available to technology providers, based on their size and characteristics. This constrains their effectiveness as confidence-building tools.<br>Market challenge: Due to an emphasis on capacity building over marketing, the ESI programme faced low demand, leading insurance companies to eventually exit the programme and independently offer the ESI insurance policy. |
| **Lessons learnt** | The ESI programme in El Salvador highlights the need to customize program components to fit the national context while integrating global best practices. Using existing templates from other countries can enhance efficiency, but it's essential to gather feedback from local stakeholders for a context-specific design.<br>Regulatory differences, like those in the insurance sector, can influence the structuring of energy-saving insurance products, making early engagement with experts and regulators vital. Additionally, while designing tools and building capacity are crucial, continuous marketing and communication are needed to maintain demand. Effective demand generation requires thorough market research, awareness campaigns, and sharing success stories. The Salvadoran experience underscores the significance of a comprehensive demand creation strategy. |

Source: OECD (2023[9]), Energy Savings Insurance: International Focus Group Discussion, https://www.oecd.org/environment/cc/cefim/cross-cutting-analysis/Discussion-paper-first-energy-savings-insurance-international-focus-group-discussion.pdf.

## Table A B.7. ESI in Mongolia

| | |
|---|---|
| **Implementation dates** | 2020 - ongoing |
| **Implementation status** | Design started in 2020;<br>Pilot launched in 2023 |
| **Lead implementer** | XacBank, a Mongolian commercial bank, with support from BASE |
| **Funder** | GCF |
| **Total project value** | XacBank received a USD 296,300 grant from the GCF in 2020 to implement the program by tailoring and developing the ESI model elements for the Mongolian context. This will complement an existing USD 60 million credit line, operated by XacBank and co-funded by GCF, known as the "Micro, Small, and Medium Enterprises (MSME) Business Loan Programme for Greenhouse Gas (GHG) Emissions Reduction" |
| **Financed activities** | Use of energy efficient and renewable energy solutions in the Mongolian MSME market. |
| **EE landscape before implementation** | National energy consumption in Mongolia has been experiencing a rising trend over 2010-2018, and several energy efficiency and conservation policies have been enacted to mitigate this trend.<br>A 2016 energy audit of 15 large energy users in Mongolia demonstrated that the country has high potential for energy efficiency – power saving measures alone can conserve 260 million kWh worth USD 10.3 million (MNT 35 billion)<br>Despite the high potential for energy efficiency projects to decrease energy costs of businesses and increase production efficiency, there remain significant investment barriers such as limited awareness and priority, lack of trust in technology/providers, difficulty with access to finance. |
| **Financing model** | In June 2017, XacBank acquired a USD 20 million concessional loan from GCF to launch the MSME Business Loan Program for GHG Emissions Reduction in Mongolia, promoting energy efficiency and renewable energy solutions. Leveraging this, XacBank established a USD 60 million concessional credit line for MSMEs, which serves as the primary finance avenue for Mongolia's forthcoming ESI programme, setting a practical minimum project cost at USD 20,000.<br>By 2020, XacBank received a USD 296,300 grant from GCF to develop the ESI model's non-financial components for the Mongolian market, encompassing the creation of standard contracts, insurance policies, systems, and training initiatives, along with enhancing outreach, especially in remote areas. |
| **Key Stakeholders** | • Validation and verification services: Société Générale de Surveillance SA (SGS) and Bureau Veritas (BV),<br>• Local insurance company: Tenger Insurance one of the top 5 insurance companies in Mongolia<br>• Disbursement of energy efficiency credit lines: XacBank |
| **Outcomes** | Mobilising a total of USD 36 million in energy efficiency investments<br>Contributing to energy savings of 39 GWh and GHG emissions reductions of 234,206 tonnes of $CO_2$ equivalent within 5 years of its inception |
| **Challenges** | • The need to adapt international templates and best practices to local contexts, considering Mongolian laws, regulations, and language.<br>• The involvement of multiple stakeholders, like BASE, to ensure quality outcomes and integration of tools with the risk coverage product.<br>• The recommendation to centralize paperwork, formalities, and information sharing through an online management information system (MIS).<br>• The need to design a risk coverage product, weighing options between a surety product and a bank guarantee, given local market experience and preferences.<br>• The inexperience of the local insurance industry in Mongolia with third-party surety policies, necessitating training. |
| **Lessons learned** | The ESI programme in Mongolia is in its early stages and is unique as it is implemented by a private bank instead of a national development bank. The program employs strategies like incorporating insurance products as prerequisites for accessing favorable credit rates and focuses on first-mover MSMEs. |

Source: OECD (2023[9]), Energy Savings Insurance: International Focus Group Discussion, https://www.oecd.org/environment/cc/cefim/cross-cutting-analysis/Discussion-paper-first-energy-savings-insurance-international-focus-group-discussion.pdf.

### *Opportunities and challenges for the implementation of ESI in Thailand*

One of the barriers to implementing energy efficiency projects in Thailand is the uncertainty about their performance. ESI directly addresses this challenge by enabling ESCOs to confidently back their contractual guarantees while providing clients with assurance of compensation if expected energy savings are not met. In addition to addressing scepticism regarding technology providers' claims, ESI alleviates the challenge of accessing financing for energy projects. Implementation of the ESI model could significantly ease barriers to investment in energy efficiency for Thai firms. Table A B.8 below outlines potential actors involved in the ESI implementation in Thailand and the challenges they may encounter while Table A B.9 illustrates the roadmap for the implementation of ESI model in Thailand.

## Table A B.8. Key players and potential challenges of implementation of an ESI in Thailand

| Key players | Potential Thai actors | Challenges |
|---|---|---|
| **Donor** | **Domestic public funding:** Energy Conservation Promotion Fund (ENCON Fund) | • Eligibility criteria of the fund<br>• Political priorities |
| | **Multilateral development Banks:** World Bank, ADB, etc. | • Stringent eligibility criteria<br>• Complex application process<br>• Currency and repayment risks<br>• Competitive funding environment |
| **Financial institutions** | Local commercial banks | • Limited technical capacity to offer energy efficiency financing<br>• Lack of confidence in the new business model<br>• Stringent eligibility criteria |
| **Insurance regulator** | Office of Insurance Commission | • Lack of understanding on EE |
| **Insurance company** | Local insurance companies | |
| **Re-insurance agency** | e.g. Thai Reinsurance Public Co., Ltd. | |
| **Technology Provider** | ESCOs<br>RE & energy efficiency equipment supplier | • Difficult access to market |
| **Technical validation Agency** | DEDE | • Limited resources |
| | **Academic and research institutions,** e.g. Joint Graduate School of Energy and Environment, Chulalongkorn University | |
| | **International agencies,** e.g. GIZ, UNDP | |

Source: Authors

## Table A B.9. Roadmap for ESI implementation in Thailand

| Key areas | Activities | Responsible agency | Year 1-2: Preparation | Year 3-5: Pilot | Year 6 onwards: Scale-up |
|---|---|---|---|---|---|
| **Market assessment, and feasibility study** | | DEDE | X | | |
| **Financing structure** | 1. Design financing model | DEDE , donors, FIs, insurance companies | X | | |
| | 2. Secure funding | | | X | X |
| **Regulatory framework** | 3. Explore existing laws to provide a legal basis for ESI operations | DEDE, insurance regulator | X | | |
| **Standard performance contract & Energy savings insurance** | 4. Create standardised energy performance contracts to be used by businesses, specifying<br>(i) the basic responsibilities of all parties,<br>(ii) monitoring and reporting procedures,<br>(iii) dispute resolution mechanism, and<br>(iv) internal risk mitigation structures | DEDE, technical validation agency, technology providers and insurance regulator | X | | |
| | 5. Determine the appropriate structure for an ESI product | | X | | |

| | | | | | |
|---|---|---|---|---|---|
| | 6. Identify insurance and reinsurance companies willing to participate in the programme | | X | | |
| | 7. Develop a risk coverage structure and pricing methodology | DEDE, insurance regulator, insurance and reinsurance companies | X | | |
| **Validation & verification procedure** | 8. Define appropriate validation and verification procedures | All key stakeholders | X | | |
| **Marketing and communication plan** | 9. Conduct market research and develop a targeted strategy to inform potential clients about the ESI pilot programme and build their confidence in its ability to deliver results | DEDE | X | X | X |
| **Capacity building** | 10. Equip key stakeholders (technology providers, insurance providers, financial institutions) with the necessary tools and train to participate in the ESI programme | DEDE | X | X | X |

Source: Authors

## Case study 4: On-bill financing

**On-bill financing (OBF)** is a financing mechanism whereby utilities or private lenders provide customers with capital for energy-efficient, renewable, or other power-related projects, with repayment being made through the customer's regular utility bill payments. The typical on-bill financing or repayment structure comprises investors, utilities, contractors or ESCOs, and customers as shown in Figure A B.4 below.

### Figure A B.4. On-bill financing structure

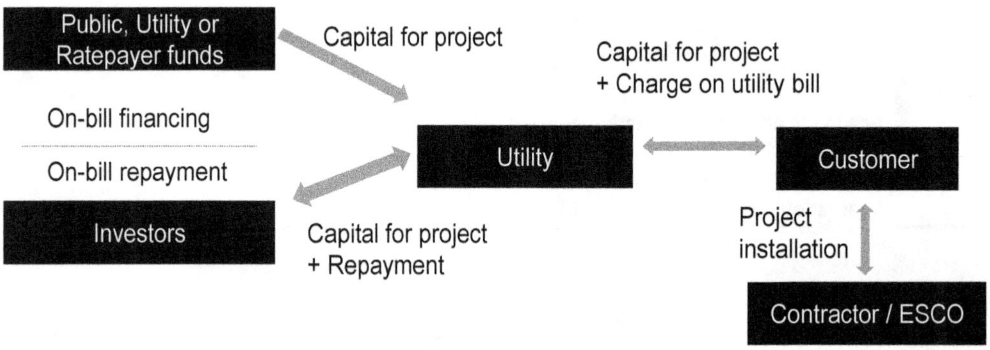


Source: US Department of Energy (2023[10]), On-Bill Financing / Repayment, https://betterbuildingssolutioncenter.energy.gov/financing-navigator/option/bill-financingrepayment#case-studies.

The OBF model has multiple advantages:

- **Improved energy efficiency:** OBF programs help customers invest in energy efficiency improvements, such as upgrading to a high-efficiency air conditioner or adding insulation, yielding mutual advantages like lowered energy bills and enhanced property values, amongst others.
- **Convenient repayment:** Regular monthly loan payments are collected by the utility on the utility bill until the loan is repaid. This makes it easier for customers to repay the loan and helps ensure that the loan is repaid on time.
- **Reduced risk of loan default risk:** OBF schemes authorise utilities to discontinue services for non-payment, thereby reducing the risk of loan defaults and assuring repayment.

- **Bill neutrality**: Energy efficiency improvements financed through OBF can be structured to match or exceed loan payments, confirmed by energy audits, ensuring that the customer's utility bill remains neutral or decreases post-upgrade.
- **Wider adoption of energy efficiency measures:** The unique characteristics of on-bill loans, particularly their tie to utility services and the assurance of bill neutrality, provide tangible benefits that can encourage more customers to invest in energy efficiency upgrades.

### *Financing model*

The past decade saw the introduction of several on-bill programs, notably in the United States' residential sector and later in Europe. A notable OBF example is that of Southern California Edison (SCE), which offered qualified non-residential customers 0% financing from USD 5 000 to USD 1 000 000 for a wide variety of efficiency improvement projects. The monthly loan payments are added directly to the customer's bill over a period of up to five years. Monthly energy savings help to offset the monthly loan charges. The program was delivered by a dedicated third-party contractor, who provided energy audits, technical assistance and project implementation to customers.

After pilot tests in 2007 – 2008, the SCE on-bill financing program was launched in 2010, offering 0% interest loans to customers in government and institutional, multifamily and business sectors. Customers may participate by retrofitting buildings or installing energy-efficient equipment. The high demand and success of the programme prompted SCE to broaden it for non-residential customers and introduce a new Tariffed On-Bill (TOB) program for residential customers. The TOB would consist of a tariff charge, expected to be lower than the reduction in the customer's energy bills, attached to the site meter, rather than a loan to individual customers (Southern California Edison, 2024[11]). Two advantages of this model are that it can be utilised by renters and is more easily accessible for customers with limited credit or low credit scores (Southeast Energy Efficiency Alliance, 2024[12]).

### *Key stakeholders*

The key stakeholders of SCE's OBF model include:

- **Southern California Edison Company (SCE):** SCE is the primary stakeholder and the proposer of the OBF program to the California Public Utilities Commission (CPUC).
- **California Public Utilities Commission (CPUC):** CPUC is the regulatory agency that oversees the OBF program and approves the program design, funding, and implementation.
- **Non-residential customers:** Non-residential customers are eligible to participate in SCE's OBF program and can use it to finance energy efficiency and renewable energy projects.
- **Residential customers:** Residential customers are expected to be eligible for SCE's OBF program once the program is developed and approved by the CPUC.
- **Third-party lenders:** Third-party lenders can partner with SCE to provide financing for the OBF program and receive a return on investment.
- **Energy service companies (ESCOs):** ESCOs can partner with SCE to provide energy efficiency and renewable energy services to customers and receive payments through the OBF program.
- **Other investor-owned utilities in California:** Under the CPUC's leadership, SCE has partnered with other utilities to develop a statewide model for OBF in California.

### *Outcomes*

Within SCE on-bill financing programme, over 2 400 loans were issued, worth USD 99 million, with a 99.3% collection rate (Southern California Edison, 2024[11]).

### *Lessons learnt*

The On-Bill Financing (OBF) program by SCE, through its pilot and subsequent expansions, offers critical insights into fostering clean energy adoption with a blend of strategic financial mechanisms, program design and stakeholder engagement. Key to its initial and ongoing success is the bundling of loan payment obligations with utility bills. This method, coupled with targeted support to specific customer segments like grocery and convenience stores, and the provision of a holistic package comprising new equipment, financial incentives and a repayment structure tied to electricity bill savings, has proven pivotal.

The expansion of the OBF program to include non-residential customers and the development of a Tariffed On-Bill (TOB) program for residential customers reflect the program's adaptability and responsiveness to demand. Incorporating a wide range of eligible technologies and making the program cash positive, transparent and affordable, are essential elements for scaling up and achieving broader clean energy goals. Key improvements, such as reducing dependency on a limited number of third-party implementers and introducing standardised credit criteria, have further strengthened the program.

### *Opportunities and challenges for the implementation of an on-bill financing in Thailand*

Interviews with key stakeholders, such as commercial banks, the ESCO association, ESCO companies, the Federation of Thai Industries, and the Ministry of Energy, reveal that while Thailand has made significant strides in the development of renewable energy and energy efficiency, progress remains concentrated at the large-scale level. Small-scale projects, in contrast, still encounter barriers, such as:

- **Limited capital and access to finance:** Large developers can get finance easily, but it is more challenging for small and medium firms. Issues such as collateral constraints and a lack of credit history limit their access to bank loans, often forcing them to rely on limited internal equity.
- **Lack of expertise:** Small and medium-sized enterprises often struggle with a shortage of technical expertise and skilled personnel needed to execute clean energy projects. Moreover, commercial banks exhibit hesitancy in engaging with renewable energy and energy efficiency initiatives, stemming from their own limited technical evaluation capabilities.

Likewise, the residential sector confronts financial and technical challenges, which are further exacerbated by a general lack of awareness regarding energy efficiency. Public buildings managed by local governments face similar issues, with funding constraints due to limited government budgets and regulatory barriers that inhibit their ability to obtain commercial bank loans or private ESCO investments. **OBF serves as a solution that simultaneously addresses these financial and technical barriers across MSMEs, the residential sector and local government entities.** For the implementation of OBF in Thailand, Table A B.10. below outlines potential actors and the challenges they may encounter and Table A B.11 illustrates the roadmap for the implementation of the OBF model in Thailand.

## Table A B.10. Key players and potential challenges of implementation of an OBF in Thailand

| Key players | Potential Thai actors | Challenges |
|---|---|---|
| Funding agencies, Investors | **Domestic public fund:** Energy Conservation Promotion Fund (ENCON Fund) & Power Development Fund | • Eligibility criteria of the fund<br>• Competing political priorities |
| | **Utilities:** Metropolitan Electricity Authority (MEA) & Provincial Electricity Authority (PEA) | • Budget constraint<br>• Lack of incentives |
| | **International Development Banks:** World Bank, ADB, etc. | • Stringent eligibility criteria<br>• Complex application process<br>• Currency and repayment risks<br>• Competitive funding environment |
| Utilities | • **MEA**<br>• **PEA** | • Regulatory constraints<br>• Technical and logistical challenges to integrate with billing systems<br>• Lack of expertise to assess credit risk<br>• Limited resources for program administration |
| Contractor / ESCO | **Local ESCO companies** | • Lack of the necessary expertise and experience to deliver high-quality energy efficiency services |
| Customers | • **MSMEs,**<br>• **Residential sector, and**<br>• **Local government entities** | • Lack of awareness on clean energy investment |

Source: Authors

## Table A B.11. Roadmap for OBF implementation in Thailand

| Key areas | Activities | Responsible agency | Year 1-2: Preparation | Year 3-5: Pilot | Year 6 onwards: Scale-up |
|---|---|---|---|---|---|
| **1. Program feasibility** | 1.1 Market analysis and feasibility study | DEDE | X | | |
| | 1.2 Regulatory review and policy development | DEDE | X | | |
| | 1.3 Financial modelling and risk assessment | DEDE | X | | |
| **2. Program design** | 2.1 Secure funding for the program | Utilities | X | | |
| | 2.2 Engage all key stakeholders | Utilities | X | | |
| | 2.3 Design of program structure and key elements | DEDE and utilities | X | | |
| | 2.4 Development of standardised contracts and agreement for customers, contractors, and utilities | DEDE and utilities | X | | |
| | 2.5 Readiness assessments of key stakeholders | DEDE and utilities | X | | |
| **3. Pilot project** | 3.1 Marketing and outreach | Utilities | | X | |
| | 3.2 Training and capacity building | DEDE, Utilities, Think tanks | | X | |
| | 3.3 Financing setup | Utilities & Investors | | X | |
| | 3.4 Installation of clean energy technologies | ESCO | | X | |
| | 3.5 Monitoring and data collection | ESCO & Customers | | X | |
| | 3.6 Evaluation and adjustment | DEDE and utilities | | X | |
| **4. Scale up** | 4.1 Program revision and finalisation | DEDE and utilities | | | X |
| | 4.2 Capacity building and marketing | DEDE and utilities | | | X |
| | 4.3 Continuous monitoring and evaluation | DEDE and utilities | | | X |

Source: Authors

## Case study 5: Bulk procurement and demand aggregation

Typically, energy efficiency projects struggle to obtain access to financing due to their small size, high upfront cost, the lack of awareness and trust among consumers, and the absence of a supportive policy environment. Bulk procurement is a strategic approach to improving energy efficiency and stimulating the market for energy-efficient technologies. The primary aim of bulk procurement is to harness economies of scale, lower costs, enhance the availability of energy-efficient technologies and catalyse a transformation in the market. It benefits large organisations through cost savings and operational efficiency while encouraging manufacturers to innovate and produce more competitive and efficient products. In a bulk procurement mechanism, the key players include the following (see Figure A B.5):

- The aggregator: an entity responsible for aggregating demand and coordinating the procurement process (e.g. a government agency or an ESCO).
- Suppliers: manufacturers or distributors of energy-efficient technologies and equipment.
- End-users: businesses, government entities, households, or other entities looking to improve energy efficiency.
- Financial institutions: banks or lending institutions that provide financing options (loans, grants, etc) or incentives to help end users acquire energy-efficient products.

### Figure A B.5. Bulk procurement structure

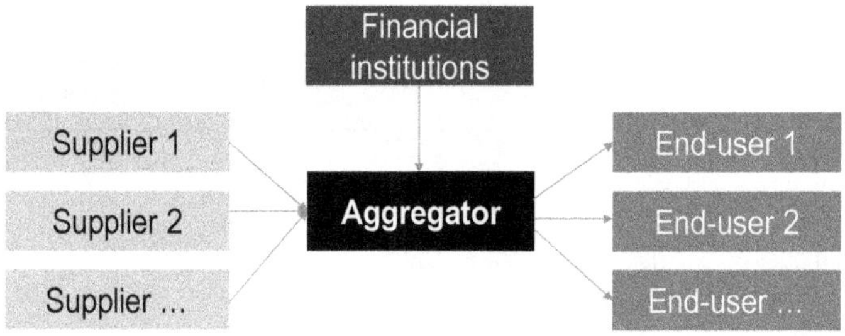


Source: Authors

A notable example of a bulk procurement model that delivered significant efficiency improvements in an emerging economy is India's UJALA programme. The Government of India launched the UJALA light-emitting diode (LED) scheme in 2015 to help households to save money on their electricity bills through efficient lighting (OECD, 2022[13]).

### *Financing model*

The UJALA programme aimed to decrease national energy consumption by enhancing the market acceptance of energy-efficient Light Emitting Diode (LED) bulbs. It was established as a joint project between the Government of India's Public Sector Undertakings, the Union Ministry of Power's Energy Efficiency Services Limited (EESL) - a super Energy Service Company (ESCO) - and India's power distribution companies.

EESL uses concessional financing to cover all initial costs for the bulk procurement of LED bulbs. This strategy enables EESL to avail volume discounts, manage sales and consumer repayment risks and subsequently lower the retail price of LED bulbs for consumers, thereby passing on the cost savings. Figure A.B.6 illustrates the operating model of UJALA.

EESL received a USD 220 million programme-for-results loan from the International Bank for Reconstruction and Development (IBRD), with a 5-year grace period and a maturity of 19 years, as well as an USD 80 million IBRD guarantee, to partially cover re-payment risks to commercial lenders or investors and to enable EESL to raise additional funds (World Bank, 2018[14]).

The UJALA scheme provides consumers with two payment options for purchasing LED bulbs. The first option allows full payment upfront at 40% of market price, while the second is a pay-as-you-go scheme. This scheme requires an initial payment of USD 0.15 (INR 10) per bulb, with the remaining amount recuperated in monthly instalments of USD 0.15 (Rs. 10) added to the electricity bill. Customers can purchase a maximum of eight LED bulbs per electricity bill under this programme.

Under the UJALA scheme, 20W LED tube lights offer a 50% energy efficiency improvement over traditional 40W tube lights and are priced at Rs. 220 each, compared to their market price range of Rs. 400-600 (USD 6-9). Additionally, the scheme provides energy-efficient ceiling fans with a BEE 5 Star rating, denoting a 30% increase in energy efficiency relative to standard fans, and these are available at Rs. 1200 (USD 18) per fan.

### *Key stakeholders*

As illustrated in Figure A B.6, the key actors of UJALA bulk procurement programme are:

- **Ministry of Power** is the nodal government body that plans and coordinates India's energy efficiency efforts through the National Mission for Enhanced Energy Efficiency (NMEEE).
- **Bureau of Energy Efficiency (BEE)** is the nodal agency for implementing the NMEEE.
- **EESL** is the implementer of the UJALA program with a target to distribute 770 million LEDs.
- **The World Bank** provided a concessional loan to EESL under the India Energy Efficiency Scale-up Program.
- **State Electricity Distribution Companies (DISCOMS)** are the partners of EESL for implementing UJALA in each state.

## Figure A B.6. Operating Model of UJALA

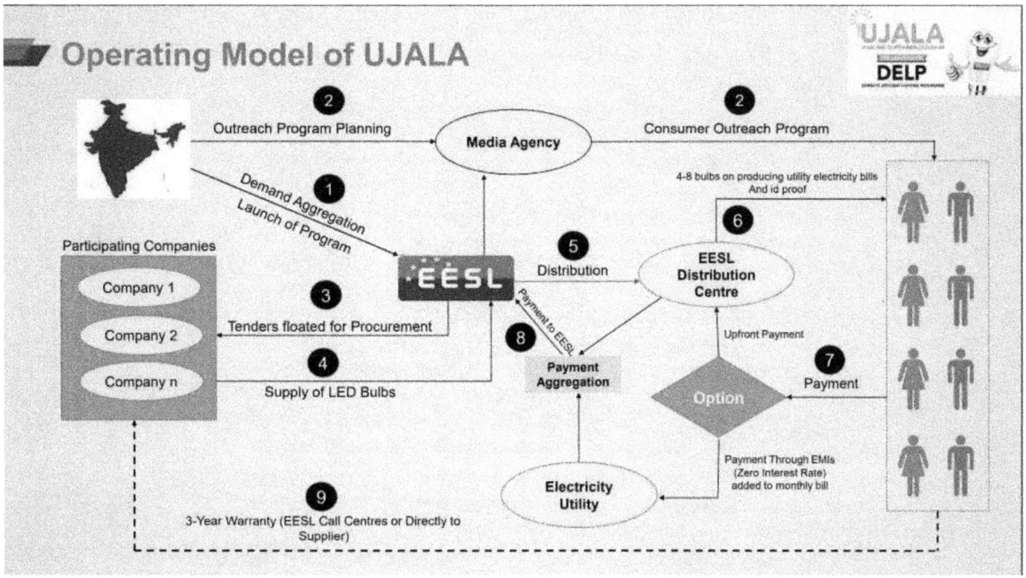


Source: EESL (2023[15]), Market Transformation through Domestic Efficient Lighting Program (UJALA) in India, https://sacreee.org/sites/default/files/2023-11/S%20P%20Garnaik_EESL%20India.pdf.

### Outcomes

As of 31 March 2022, EESL cumulatively distributed 368 million LED light bulbs, 7.2 million LED tube lights, and 2.4 million energy-efficient fans across India, leading to a total energy savings of 48.3 billion kWh per year with avoided peak demand of 9 770 MW. The annual energy savings are estimated at USD 2 700 million and the annual $CO_2$ emissions reductions at 35.5 million tonnes.

### Lessons learnt

The success of Energy Efficiency Services Limited's (EESL) UJALA program underscores several key lessons in promoting energy efficiency at scale. Firstly, its robust business model, which involved EESL taking on the upfront investment risk for bulk procurement of energy-efficient appliances, was instrumental in creating a conducive environment for market growth. By demonstrating tangible benefits and significantly lowering retail prices through volume discounts, EESL effectively stimulated demand and fostered widespread adoption of energy-efficient technologies among consumers. Moreover, the program's comprehensive support from the Indian government and prominent public energy sector entities lent credibility and legitimacy, crucial for securing buy-in from various stakeholders and ensuring sustained momentum.

Secondly, the UJALA program's emphasis on building awareness and trust in energy-efficient products played a pivotal role in its success. Through transparent reporting mechanisms such as the UJALA Dashboard and regular stakeholder engagements, EESL effectively communicated the program's impact and built confidence in its efficacy. Additionally, stringent quality specifications and robust after-sales services bolstered consumer trust in the reliability and durability of energy-efficient appliances, further enhancing adoption rates. Overall, the UJALA program serves as a compelling example of how strategic partnerships, innovative financing mechanisms, and concerted efforts to raise awareness can drive transformative change in promoting energy efficiency on a national scale.

### Opportunities and challenges for the implementation of a bulk procurement in Thailand

The implementation of bulk procurement in Thailand presents a significant opportunity to streamline energy efficiency across various sectors, leveraging the collective power of bulk procurement and economies of scale. For the implementation of a bulk procurement in Thailand, Table A B.12 below outlines potential actors and the challenges they may encounter and Table A B.13 illustrates the roadmap for the implementation of OBF model in Thailand.

## Table A B.12. Key players and potential challenges of implementation of a bulk procurement in Thailand

| Key players | Potential Thai actors | Challenges |
|---|---|---|
| **Aggregator** | • ESCOs | • Limited capacity of existing ESCOs to become super ESCOs |
| | • Large corporate: Retail | • Lack of government incentives |
| | • Bangkok Metropolitan Administration (BMA) or other provincial administration | • Lack of technical expertise<br>• Limited own budget<br>• Regulatory barriers in access to financing<br>• Bureaucratic barriers |
| **Financial Institutions** | • Commercial banks in Thailand | • Limited technical capacity to offer energy efficiency financing<br>• Lack of confidence in the new business model<br>• Stringent eligibility criteria |
| | • Multilateral development banks: World Bank, ADB, etc. | • Stringent eligibility criteria<br>• Complex application process<br>• Currency and repayment risks<br>• Competitive funding environment |
| **EE technology manufacturers** | • Local manufacturers | • Difficult access to market |
| **End users who adopt the technology** | • Residential sector,<br>• Hospitality and retail<br>• Municipalities and local governments. | • Difficult access to finance<br>• Limited awareness |

Source: Authors

## Table A B.13. Roadmap for bulk procurement implementation in Thailand

| Key areas | Activities | Responsible agency | Year 1-2: Preparation | Year 3-5: Pilot | Year 6 onwards: Scale-up |
|---|---|---|---|---|---|
| **1. Idea generation** | 1.1 Prioritisation of energy efficiency actions as per national or provincial plan | DEDE and provincial authorities as an aggregator | X | | |
| | 1.2 Provide guidance on best practices | DEDE, academic institutions, research institutes, or international agencies like USAID and GIZ | | | |
| | 1.3 Connect to partners, networks, sources | Provincial authorities as an aggregator | X | | |
| | 1.4 Assess in ideas scoping | | X | | |
| **2. Technical and financial evaluation** | 2.1 Prepare standard template for project ideas | DEDE, provincial authorities as an aggregator with technical support | X | | |
| | 2.2 Conduct the feasibility assessment | | X | | |
| **3. Business modelling and financing** | 3.1 Select the most suitable business model and financing scheme for the energy efficiency project bundle, based on the technical and economic assessment and the local context | Provincial authorities as an aggregator with technical support | X | | |
| | 3.2 Design the right financing solution for each municipal energy efficiency project bundle, based on a decision tree and a checklist tool | | X | | |
| | 3.3 Develop project proposal in a standardized format | | X | | |
| **4. Strategic procurement** | 4.1 Develop a procurement strategy | Provincial authorities as an aggregator with technical support | | X | |
| | 4.2 Prepare the tender process including process of identifying and selecting contractors | | | X | |
| | 4.3 Organize the tender process | | | X | |

| | | | | | |
|---|---|---|---|---|---|
| **5. Investing in infrastructure** | 5.1 Oversee the installation process, ensuring adherence to performance standards | Provincial authorities as an aggregator with technical support | | X | |
| | 5.2 Facilitate the disbursement of funds to the individual projects within the aggregation | | | X | |
| | 5.3 Maintain customer satisfaction through the project lifecycle | | | X | |
| **6. Performance and impact assessment** | 6.1 Establish a system for measuring, reporting, and verifying (MRV) the effectiveness and benefits of the energy efficiency project aggregation | Provincial authorities as an aggregator with technical support | | X | |
| | 6.2 Track performance metrics and evaluate the overall impact of the aggregation initiative | | | X | |
| **7. Scale-up** | 7.1 Programme revision and finalisation | DEDE and provincial authorities as an aggregator | | | X |
| | 7.2 Capacity building and marketing | | | | X |
| | 7.3 Continuous monitoring and evaluation | | | | X |

Source: Authors

## References


Adebiyi, O. et al. (2020), "Impact of Malaysian Green Technology Financial Scheme on Business Performance of Renewable Energy Producers", *Journal of Southwest Jiaotong University*, Vol. 55/6, https://doi.org/10.35741/issn.0258-2724.55.6.19. [6]

Alliance for Financial Inclusion (2022), "Green Credit Guarantee Schemes for MSMEs", https://www.afi-global.org/wp-content/uploads/2022/06/Green-credit-schemes-for-MSMEs_260722.pdf (accessed on 20 December 2023). [1]

EESL (2023), *Market Transformation through Domestic Efficient Lighting*, https://sacreee.org/sites/default/files/2023-11/S%20P%20Garnaik_EESL%20India.pdf. [15]

IRENA (2020), *Community-ownership models: Innovation Landscape Brief*, https://www.irena.org/-/media/Files/IRENA/Agency/Publication/2020/Jul/IRENA_Community_ownership_2020.pdf. [8]

IRENA (2020), *Pay-as-you-go Models: Innovation Landscape Brief*, https://www.irena.org/-/media/Files/IRENA/Agency/Publication/2020/Jul/IRENA_Pay-as-you-go_models_2020.pdf. [7]

Malaysian Sustainable Finance Initiative (2023), *Green Technology Financing Scheme (GTFS)*, https://www.msfi.com.my/incentives-green-technology-financing-scheme-gtfs/. [2]

Ministry of Natural Resources and Environment of Malaysia (2014), *Green Technology Financing Scheme (GTFS)*, https://unfccc.int/files/focus/mitigation/application/pdf/malaysia_presentation.pdf. [3]

OECD (2023), *Energy Savings Insurance: International Focus Group Discussion*, https://www.oecd.org/environment/cc/cefim/cross-cutting-analysis/Discussion-paper-first-energy-savings-insurance-international-focus-group-discussion.pdf. [9]

OECD (2022), *Clean Energy Finance and Investment Roadmap of India: Opportunities to Unlock Finance and Scale up Capital*, Green Finance and Investment, OECD Publishing, Paris, https://doi.org/10.1787/21b6e411-en. [13]

Southeast Energy Efficiency Alliance (2024), *On-Bill Finance*, https://www.seealliance.org/initiatives/low-income-financing/. [12]

Southern California Edison (2024), *Energy Efficiency Financing*, https://www.sce.com/business/Energy-Efficiency-Financing. [11]

Tu, Fan (2016), *Promoting urban sustainability through green technology in Malaysia*, https://scienceimpact.mit.edu/sites/default/files/documents/Tu.pdf. [5]

US Department of Energy (2023), *On-Bill Financing / Repayment*, https://betterbuildingssolutioncenter.energy.gov/financing-navigator/option/bill-financingrepayment#case-studies. [10]

World Bank (2020), *Green loans: Financing the transition to a low-carbon economy*, https://blogs.worldbank.org/climatechange/green-loans-financing-transition-low-carbon-economy. [4]

World Bank (2018), *Project Signing: Government of India, EESL and World Bank Sign $300 Million Agreement to Scale Up India's Energy Efficiency Program*, https://www.worldbank.org/en/news/press-release/2018/08/28/agreement-scale-up-indias-energy-efficiency-program. [14]

# Annex C. Methodology for modelling Thailand's clean energy finance and investment needs

In the process of developing the Clean Energy Finance and Investment Roadmap, The Creagy ran models to estimate the financing and investment required to meet Thailand's renewable energy and energy efficiency goals. In particular, the models estimated the following elements:

1. the investment and financing needs required for implementing the Alternative Energy Development Plan (AEDP) 2018 and the draft Energy Efficiency Plan (EEP) 2022, the level of financial assistance needed by public and private financing sources, as well as the distribution of investment costs across the supply chain for the selected renewable energy and energy efficiency technologies
2. the economic impact, including employment and value added, that would be generated from the implementation of the AEDP 2018 and the draft EEP 2022.

The following sections outline the estimation methodology and assumptions.

## Model on the investment and financing needs for the implementation of the Alternative Energy Development Plan (AEDP) 2018 and the draft Energy Efficiency Plan (EEP) 2022

This model has two main objectives: (i) estimating the investment needed for the implementation of the AEDP 2018 and the draft EEP 2022; and (ii) estimating the level of financial assistance provided by the government (in the form of subsidies, incentives and grants) and by the private sector, to promote clean energy initiatives.

As shown in Figure A C.1, the assessment involved the following steps:

- Step 1: Identifying the annual plan for new renewable energy installations by fuel type, as per AEDP 2018, and the annual plan for promoting energy efficiency improvements by economic sector, according to the draft EEP 2022
- Step 2: Collecting data on capital expenditures (CAPEX) and operating expenditures (OPEX) for each renewable energy technology used for generating electricity, along with their trends over time, as well as the cost of energy efficiency investments by economic sector
- Step 3: Using data from steps 1 and 2, assess the annual magnitude of the investment needed to reach the targets of the AEDP 2018 and the draft EEP 2022
- Step 4: Determining the extent of government support, private equity and private debt required to achieve the AEDP 2018 and the draft EEP 2022 by using the debt-to-equity ratio and the co-financing ratio at the different technology readiness levels summarised in Figure A C.1.

## Figure A C.1. Process in assessing investment and financing needs for implementation of the AEDP 2018 and the draft EEP 2022

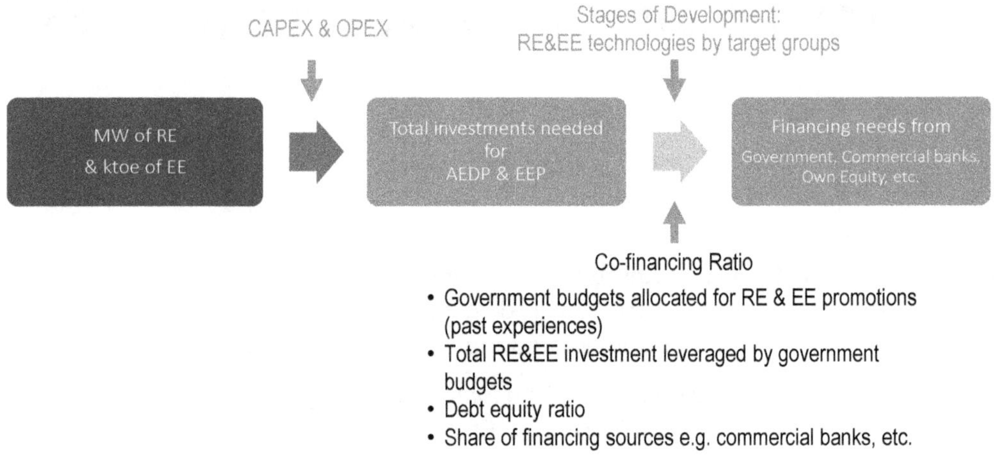


Source: Authors

Access to various financial sources is significantly influenced by the level of technological readiness. Lower levels of readiness are associated with higher risks and uncertainties. As technology progresses through readiness levels, private entities exhibit greater confidence, leading to increased reliance on private debt and reduced dependence on government support. Figure A C.2 illustrates the debt-to-equity ratio for projects with different technology readiness levels, based on previous private investments in renewable energy and EE, as well as the co-financing ratio for each financial instrument provided by the government. This co-financing ratio represents the proportion of the total project investment and the total amount of support funded by the government, relative to the shared financed by the private sector. In this modelling, five financial instruments implemented by the government were analysed, namely grants, investment subsidies, performance subsidies, debt and equity financing, and carbon markets.

## Figure A C.2. Past financial support provided by the government at the different technology readiness levels

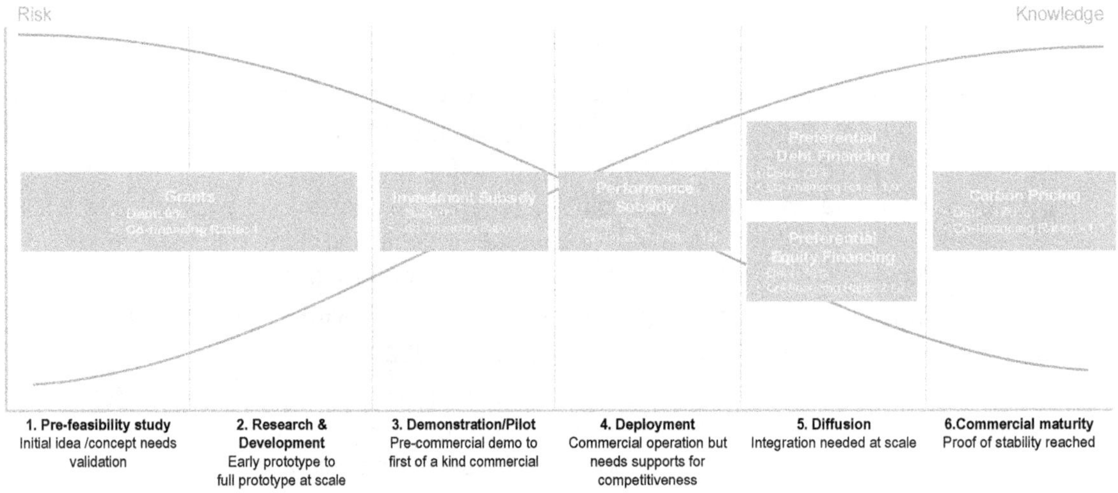


Source: Authors (Creagy)

Data on the co-financing ratios for the five government financial instruments were obtained from various sources, as described in Table A C.1.

**Table A C.1. Co-financing ratio for five government financial instruments**

| Financial Instrument | Government's scheme | Project Activities | Investment Cost (million THB) | Amount of support (million THB) | Co-financing Ratio | Debt-equity ratio |
|---|---|---|---|---|---|---|
| Grant | Grants for R&D | Waste to Energy (MBT, RDF, Pyrolysis, Power Plant, Refinery) | 570 | 570 | 1.0 | N/A |
| Investment Subsidy | Direct Subsidy (70:30 / 80:20) for energy efficiency investment | 20% and 30% subsidy for energy efficiency investments | 881 | 378 | 3.3 | N/A |
| Performance Subsidy | DSM Bidding | Subsidy per energy savings for 152 projects | 2,687 | 309 | 8.7 | 70% |
| Preferential Debt Financing | EERF | Revolving fund for renewable energy & EE | 14,643 | 6,057 | 2.4 | 70% |
| Preferential Equity Financing | ESCO Revolving Fund | 3 x 6.123 MW Solar PV Farm | 2,412 | 111 | 21.7 | 70% |
| Carbon Market | CDM | 38-MW Solar PV Farm | 4,220 | 46 | 91.1 | >70% |

Sources: (DEDE, 2023[1]; Energy For Environment Foundation, 2011[2]; Asian Power, 2011[3])

### *Key assumptions on the investment and financing needs for the implementation of the AEDP 2018*

Data on the cumulative installed capacity of renewable energy power plants during 2021-2037 was collected from different sources. The data for 2021 was sourced from the DEDE database while the data for 2037 is the target as per the AEDP 2018. The data between 2022 -2036 was obtained from the PDP 2018 (rev.1). Based on Table A C.2, the new installation of renewable energy power plants can be calculated, as illustrated in Table A C.3.

## Table A C.2. New installation of renewable energy power plants during 2022-2037 (MW)

| RE Type | 2022 | 2023 | 2024 | 2025 | 2026 | 2027 | 2028 | 2029 | 2030 | 2031 | 2032 | 2033 | 2034 | 2035 | 2036 | 2037 | Total |
|---|---|---|---|---|---|---|---|---|---|---|---|---|---|---|---|---|---|
| **Large hydro** | - | - | - | - | - | - | - | - | - | - | - | - | - | - | - | - | - |
| **Small hydro** | 23* | 18 | - | 6 | 4 | 4 | 6 | 2 | 4 | 2 | 3 | 3 | 28 | 5 | 1 | 55 | 141 |
| **Onshore wind** | 49 | 90 | 90 | - | - | - | - | - | - | - | 130 | - | - | 300 | 657 | 128 | 1 444 |
| **Solar PV** | 264 | 130 | 130 | | | | 850 | 1 650 | 900 | 2,250 | 450 | 1 600 | | 400 | 390 | 110 | 9 124 |
| **Floating Solar PV** | - | - | - | - | 298 | 50 | - | 280 | 300 | 250 | 300 | 438 | 140 | 325 | 100 | 175 | 2 680 |
| **Biomass** | 896* | 24 | 18 | 146* | 58* | 56* | 196* | 179* | 297 | 237 | 17 | 926 | 177 | 492 | 277 | 1 074 | 3 675 |
| **Biogas** | 330 | 160 | 100 | - | - | - | - | - | - | 50 | 100 | 150 | - | - | 50 | 50 | 930 |
| **Waste** | 395 | 100 | - | - | - | - | - | - | - | - | - | - | 6 | 15 | 14 | 156 | 586 |
| **Total new installations (MW)*** | 1 037 | 522 | 388 | 6 | 302 | 51 | 856 | 1 932 | 1 501 | 2 789 | 1 000 | 3 117 | 351 | 1 537 | 1 489 | 1 748 | 18 579 |

Note: The total capacity includes only the newly installed units, excluding the retired capacity (noted with a *) of 1 554 MW.

Data regarding CAPEX, OPEX and capacity factor for renewable energy technologies was sourced from multiple references, including IRENA's Renewable Power Generation Costs in 2022 (August, 2023), Ambition to Action's Domestic Expenditure and Employment Impacts of Power Sector Development in Thailand (A2A, November, 2019), and Clean, Affordable and Secure Energy for Southeast Asia (CASE)'s study on Towards a collective vision of Thai energy transition: National long-term scenarios and socioeconomic implications (November, 2022). Details are described in Table A C.3.

### Table A C.3. CAPEX and OPEX for renewable energy power plants

| RE Types | CAPEX (THB/kW) | | | | Fixed OPEX (THB/kW) | | | | Capacity Factor (%) | | | |
|---|---|---|---|---|---|---|---|---|---|---|---|---|
| | 2022 - 2024 | 2025 - 2029 | 2030 - 2036 | 2037 | 2022 - 2024 | 2025 - 2029 | 2030 - 2036 | 2037 | CASE | A2A | IRENA | AVG |
| Small hydro | 61 469 | 61 469 | 61 469 | 61 469 | 1 229 | 1 229 | 1 229 | 1 229 | | 37% | 56% | 47% |
| Onshore wind | 45 152 | 39 716 | 33 287 | 28 557 | 1 402 | 1 302 | 1 202 | 1 202 | 24% | 23% | 25% | 24% |
| Solar PV | 38 096 | 47 187 | 36 474 | 37 460 | 508 | 451 | 378 | 360 | 20% | 14% | 21% | 18% |
| Floating Solar PV | 38 875 | 33 232 | 27 589 | 27 589 | 445 | 366 | 287 | 287 | 20% | 14% | 21% | 18% |
| Biomass | 59 687 | 57 299 | 54 912 | 54 912 | 1 652 | 1 585 | 1 519 | 1 519 | 60% | 70% | 75% | 68% |
| Biogas | 59 687 | 57 299 | 54 912 | 54 912 | 1 652 | 1 585 | 1 519 | 1 519 | 60% | 70% | 75% | 68% |
| Waste | 59 687 | 57 299 | 54 912 | 54 912 | 1 652 | 1 585 | 1 519 | 1 519 | 60% | 70% | 75% | 72% |

Notes:
1. CAPEX and OPEX for Small Hydro were sourced from A2A (2019)
2. CAPEX and fixed OPEX for onshore wind, solar PV, and biomass were sourced from CASE (2022).
During 2022-2024, the CAPEX and OPEX of solar PV were estimated from the following sources: 50% solar rooftop, 50% utility solar, and 0% solar with battery. This ratio was adjusted to 37.5% solar rooftop, 37.5% utility solar, and 25% solar with battery from 2025 to 2029, and 25% solar rooftop, 25% utility solar, and 50% solar with battery from 2030 onwards.
4. The CAPEX of floating solar PV is estimated to be 25% higher than utility solar, while its OPEX is estimated to be 14% lower.
5. CAPEX and fixed OPEX for biomass are used for both biogas and waste.

Table A C.4 illustrates the estimated annual investment needed for the implementation of the AEDP 2018 by multiplying CAPEX data from Table A C.3 and new installations from Table A C.2.

### Table A C.4. Investments needed for the implementation of the AEDP 2018 (unit: million THB)

| RE Type | 2022 | 2023 | 2024 | 2025 | 2026 | 2027 | 2028 | 2029 | 2030 | 2031 | 2032 | 2033 | 2034 | 2035 | 2036 | 2037 | Total |
|---|---|---|---|---|---|---|---|---|---|---|---|---|---|---|---|---|---|
| Small Hydro | - | 1.11 | - | 0.37 | 0.25 | 0.25 | 0.37 | 0.12 | 0.25 | 0.12 | 0.18 | 0.18 | 1.72 | 0.31 | 0.06 | 3.38 | **8.67** |
| Onshore Wind | 2 198 | 4 064 | 4 064 | - | - | - | - | - | - | - | 4 327 | - | - | 9 986 | 21 870 | 3 655 | **50 163** |
| Solar PV | 10 046 | 4 952 | 4 952 | - | - | - | 40 109 | 77 859 | 32 826 | 82 066 | 16 413 | 58 358 | - | 14 590 | 14 225 | 4 121 | **360 517** |
| Floating Solar PV | - | 933 | - | - | 9 903 | 1 662 | - | 9 305 | 8 277 | 6 897 | 8 277 | 12 084 | 3 862 | 8 966 | 2,759 | 4 828 | **77 752** |

| | | | | | | | | | | | | | | | | | |
|---|---|---|---|---|---|---|---|---|---|---|---|---|---|---|---|---|---|
| Biomass | - | 9 550 | 1 074 | - | - | - | - | - | 16 309 | 13 014 | 933 | 50 848 | 9 719 | 27 017 | 15 211 | 58 975 | **202 650** |
| Biogas | 19 673 | 5 969 | 5 969 | - | - | - | - | - | - | 2 746 | 5 491 | 8 237 | - | - | 2 746 | 2 746 | **53 575** |
| Waste | 23 605 | - | - | - | - | - | - | - | - | - | - | - | 329 | 824 | 769 | 8 566 | **34 093** |
| **Total investment (million THB)** | **55 522** | **25 469** | **16 059** | **0.37** | **9 903** | **1 662** | **40 109** | **87 164** | **57 412** | **104 723** | **35 442** | **129 527** | **13 913** | **61 382** | **57 578** | **82 894** | **778 761** |

As mentioned previously, the government employs various financial instruments to promote the adoption of renewable energy, depending on the technological readiness level. The investment needed for each readiness level of AEDP 2018 was estimated using the assumptions described in Table A C.5, which outlines the readiness levels of renewable energy technologies for generating electricity. Table A C.6 displays the estimated investment required for each readiness level.

## Table A C.5. Extent of renewable energy investments at each readiness level of renewable energy technologies

| RE Type | 2022-2025 | | | | 2026-2030 | | | | 2031-2037 | | | |
|---|---|---|---|---|---|---|---|---|---|---|---|---|
| | Demonstration/ pilot | Deployment | Diffusion | Commercial maturity | Demonstration/ pilot | Deployment | Diffusion | Commercial maturity | Demonstration/ pilot | Deployment | Diffusion | Commercial maturity |
| Small Hydro | | 50% | 50% | | | | 50% | 50% | | | | 100% |
| Onshore Wind | | 50% | 50% | | | | | 0% | | | 50% | 50% |
| Solar PV | | 50% | 50% | | | 20% | 50% | 30% | | | 30% | 70% |
| Floating Solar PV | 50% | 50% | | | | 20% | 50% | 30% | | | 30% | 70% |
| Biomass | | | 30% | | | 20% | 50% | 30% | | | 30% | 70% |
| Biogas | | | 30% | 70% | | 0% | 0% | 0% | | | 30% | 70% |
| Waste | | | 30% | 70% | | 0% | 0% | 0% | | | 30% | 70% |

## Table A C.6. Amount of renewable energy investments at each readiness level of renewable energy technologies (Unit: million THB)

| RE Type | 2022-2025 | | | | 2026-2030 | | | | 2031-2037 | | | |
|---|---|---|---|---|---|---|---|---|---|---|---|---|
| | Demonstration/ pilot | Deployment | Diffusion | Commercial maturity | Demonstration/ pilot | Deployment | Diffusion | Commercial maturity | Demonstration/ pilot | Deployment | Diffusion | Commercial maturity |
| Small Hydro | - | 1 | 1 | - | - | | 1 | 1 | - | - | - | 6 |
| Onshore Wind | - | 5,163 | 5,163 | - | - | | | | - | - | 19,919 | 19,919 |
| Solar PV | - | 9,976 | 9,976 | - | - | 30,159 | 75,397 | 45,238 | - | - | 56,932 | 132,841 |
| Floating Solar PV | 466 | 466 | - | - | - | 5,829 | 14,573 | 8,744 | - | - | 14,302 | 33,371 |
| Biomass | - | - | 3,187 | 7,437 | - | 3,262 | 8,154 | 4,893 | - | - | 52,715 | 123,002 |
| Biogas | - | - | 9,483 | 22,127 | - | | | | - | - | 6,589 | 15,375 |
| Waste | - | - | 7,082 | 16,524 | - | | | | - | - | 3,146 | 7,342 |
| **Total investments** | **466** | **15,605** | **34,891** | **46,088** | **-** | **39,250** | **98,125** | | **-** | **-** | **153,604** | **331,856** |

The amount of government support for renewable energy investments was estimated by mapping the co-financing ratio of each financing instrument (Table A C.1) to the amount of investments allocated based on the technology's readiness level. The remaining investments were then split into private debt and private equity by multiplying it with the debt-equity ratio (Table A C.1) at the specific readiness level of technology. Table A.C.7 shows the proportion of financing from each source for renewable energy investment, based on the data and assumptions above.

## Table A C.7. Renewable energy investments during 2022 – 2037 by source of finance (Unit: million THB)

| Source of Finance | Investment (million THB) | | | | Share (%) | | | |
|---|---|---|---|---|---|---|---|---|
| | 2022-2025 | 2026-2030 | 2031-2037 | Total | 2022-2025 | 2026-2030 | 2031-2037 | Total |
| Government support | 5,331 | 13,290 | 16,369 | **34,990** | 5.5% | 6.8% | 3.4% | 4.5% |
| Private debt | 68,533 | 133,895 | 361,185 | **563,613** | 70.6% | 68.2% | 74.4% | 72.4% |
| Private equity | 23,186 | 49,065 | 107,906 | **180,157** | 23.9% | 25% | 22.2% | 23.1% |
| Total investment (million THB) | **97,051** | **196,250** | **485,460** | **778,761** | 100% | 100% | 100% | 100% |

### *Key assumptions on the investment and financing needs for the implementation of the draft EEP 2022*

Table A C.8 shows the estimated investment cost per ktoe of energy savings for each sector based on data from the different government programmes.

**Table A C.8. Estimated investment cost per ktoe of energy savings for each sector**

| Sector | Government Program | Total Investment (million THB) | Total energy savings (ktoe) | Investment Cost (Million THB/ktoe) |
|---|---|---|---|---|
| Industrial | DSM Bidding (2019) | 2,687.0 | 79.6 | 33.76 |
| Commercial | 30% Subsidy & 20% Subsidy | 1,960.0 | 26.9 | 72.86 |
| Residential | Matching Fund | 1,008.0 | 8.5 | 119.15 |
| Agricultural | Assume the same cost as residential sector | | | 119.15 |

Source: Source: (Creagy, 2018[4])

**Table A C.9. Energy efficiency investments during 2022 – 2037 by sector (Unit: million THB)**

| Sector | Saving Targets at 2037 (ktoe) | Investment Cost (Million THB/ktoe) | Total Investment Cost during 2022 -2037 (Million THB) |
|---|---|---|---|
| Industrial | 12,432 | 33.76 | 419,658 |
| Commercial | 3,542 | 72.86 | 258,079 |
| Residential | 1,774 | 119.15 | 211,370 |
| Agricultural | 710 | 119.15 | 84,596 |
| **Total energy efficiency investments** | **18,458** | | **973,703** |

As mentioned previously, the government employs various financial instruments to promote the adoption of EE, depending on the technological readiness level. The investment needed for each readiness level of the draft EEP 2022 was estimated using the assumptions described in Table A C.10, which outlines the readiness levels of energy efficiency technologies for different sectors. Table A C.11 displays the estimated investment required for each readiness level.

**Table A C.10. Extent of energy efficiency investments at each readiness level of energy efficiency technologies**

| Sector | Demonstration/pilot | Deployment | Diffusion | Commercial maturity | Total |
|---|---|---|---|---|---|
| Industrial | 15% | 15% | 20% | 50% | 100% |
| Commercial | 15% | 15% | 20% | 50% | 100% |
| Residential | 15% | 15% | 20% | 50% | 100% |
| Agricultural | 15% | 15% | 20% | 50% | 100% |

**Table A C.11. Amount of energy efficiency investments at each readiness level of energy efficiency technologies (Unit: million THB)**

| Sector | Demonstration/pilot | Deployment | Diffusion | Commercial maturity | Total |
|---|---|---|---|---|---|
| Industrial | 62,949 | 62,949 | 83,932 | 209,829 | 419,658 |
| Commercial | 38,712 | 38,712 | 51,616 | 129,039 | 258,079 |
| Residential | 31,706 | 31,706 | 42,274 | 105,685 | 211,370 |
| Agricultural | 12,689 | 12,689 | 16,919 | 42,298 | 84,596 |
| **Total** | **146,055** | **146,055** | **194,741** | **486,851** | **973,703** |

The amount of government support for energy efficiency investments was estimated by mapping the co-financing ratio of each financing instrument (Table A C.1) to the amount of investments allocated based on the technology's readiness level. The remaining investments were then split into private debt and private equity by multiplying it with the debt-equity ratio (Table A C.1) at the specific readiness level of technology. Table A.C.12 shows the proportion of financing from each source for energy efficiency investment, based on the data and assumptions above.

**Table A C.12. Amount of energy efficiency investments at each readiness level of energy efficiency technologies (Unit: million THB)**

| Source of Finance | Amount (million THB) | Share (%) |
|---|---|---|
| Government support | 82,091 | 8% |
| Private debt | 600,712 | 62% |
| Private equity | 290,900 | 30% |
| **Total investment (million THB)** | **973,703** | **100%** |

## Model on the economic impacts from the implementation of the AEDP 2018 and the draft EEP 2022

The purpose of this analysis is to evaluate the economic impact, including employment and value added, resulting from the implementation of the AEDP 2018 and the draft EEP 2022.

As shown in Figure A C.2, the assessment method can be illustrated as follows:

- The total jobs generated from the implementation of the AEDP 2018 can be estimated from the sum of manufacturing jobs, construction and installation jobs, and operation and maintenance jobs. The calculation method is shown in Figure A C.3 and the employment factors are listed in Figure A C.5. For the power plant using biomass, waste, the fuel jobs will be added into the total job.
- The total number of jobs created by implementing the draft EEP 2022 was estimated by multiplying the total investment with the employment factor, measured in jobs per one million United States Dollars (USD) of investment. The employment factor of each economic sector is shown in Figure A C.6.
- The value added generated from the implementation of the AEDP 2018 was estimated using the Economic Impact Model for Electricity Supply developed under the Ambition to Action project, funded by the International Climate Initiative.
- The value added generated from the implementation of the draft EEP 2022 was estimated by using input-output matrix and the Leontief inverse to calculate the value added of each sector.

**Figure A C.3. Process of assessing the economic impact from the implementation of the AEDP 2018 and the draft EEP 2022**

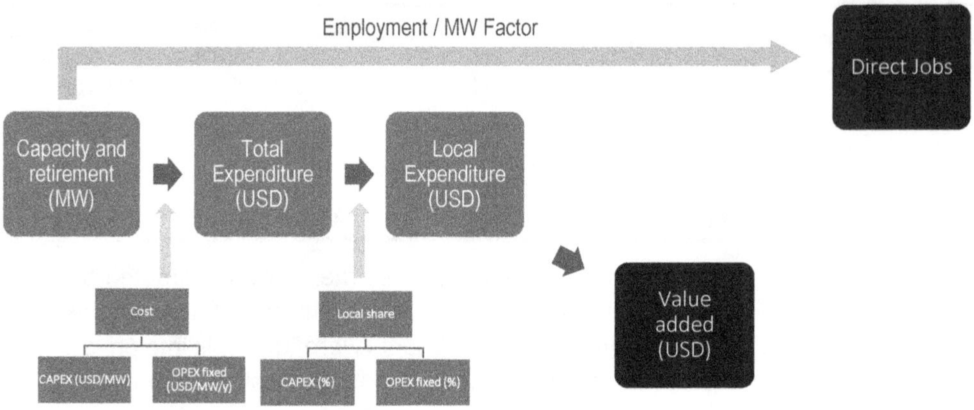


Source: Authors

### *Key assumptions on the economic impacts from the implementation of the AEDP 2018*

The method for estimation of job generated from the implementation of the AEDP 2018 is shown in Figure A C.4. Key assumptions on employment factors and decline factors are described in Table A C.134. The total jobs generated from the implementation of the AEDP 2018 can be estimated from the sum of manufacturing jobs, construction and installation jobs, and operation and maintenance jobs.

**Figure A C.4. Method for estimation of job generated from the implementation of the AEDP 2018**

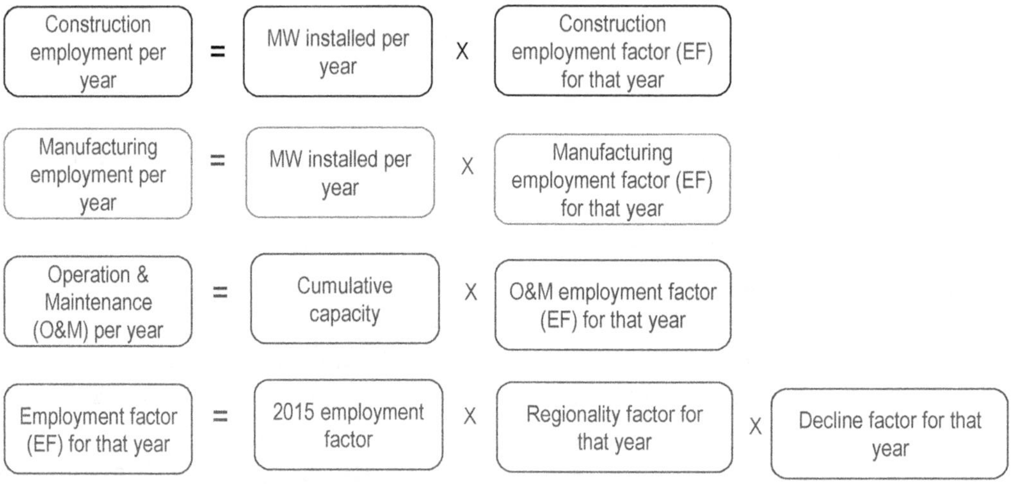


Source: (ASEAN Centre for Energy, 2024[5])

## Table A C.13. Employment factors

| | Employment factors | | | | Decline factors | | | | | |
|---|---|---|---|---|---|---|---|---|---|---|
| | Construction times | Construction | Manufacturing | O&M | 2020 | 2021 | 2022 | 2023 | 2024 | 2025 |
| Technology | Years | Job Years / MW | | Jobs / MW | | | | | | |
| Hydro | 2 | 7.4 | 3.5 | 0.2 | 98% | 98% | 97% | 97% | 96% | 96% |
| Geothermal | 2 | 6.8 | 3.9 | 0.4 | 84% | 81% | 78% | 74% | 71% | 68% |
| Solar | 1 | 13 | 6.7 | 0.7 | 86% | 84% | 81% | 78% | 75% | 73% |
| Wind | 1 | 3.2 | 4.7 | 0.3 | 99% | 99% | 99% | 98% | 98% | 98% |
| Regionality factors | | | | | 2.30 | 2.26 | 2.22 | 2.18 | 2.14 | 2.10 |

Source: (ASEAN Centre for Energy, 2024[5])

The value added generated from the implementation of the AEDP 2018 was estimated using the Economic Impact Model for Electricity Supply developed under the Ambition to Action project, funded by the International Climate Initiative.

### *Key assumptions on the economic impacts from the implementation of the draft EEP 2022*

The job generated from the implementation of the draft EEP 2022 is estimated by using the employment factor, measured in jobs per one million USD of investment as shown in Figure A C.5.

## Figure A C.5. Employment factors, measured in jobs per USD one million USD (USD 2015)

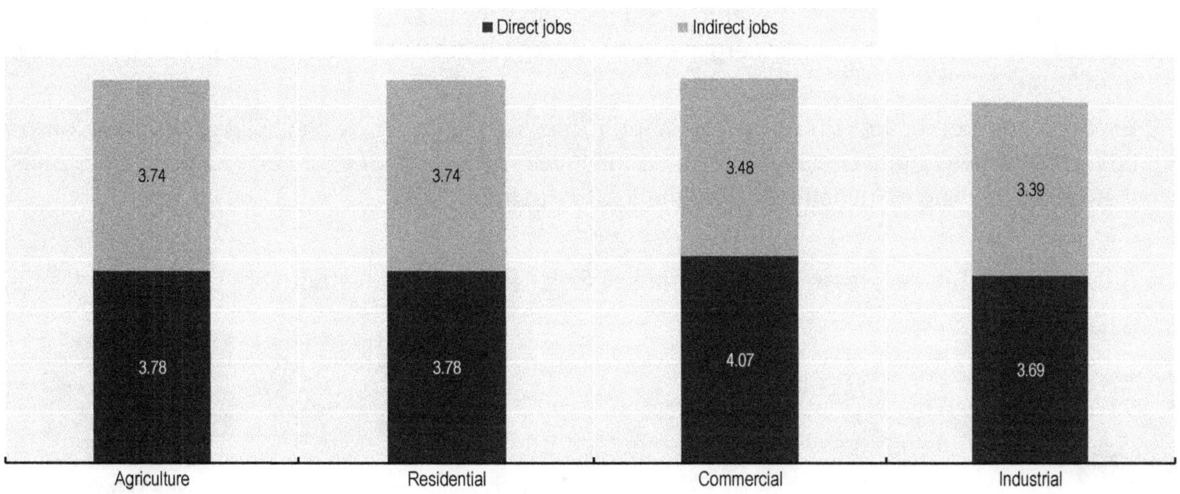


Source: Authors based on data from https://ars.els-cdn.com/content/image/1-s2.0-S2215016120301758-fx1_lrg.jpg.

The value added generated from the implementation of the draft EEP 2022 was estimated by using input-output matrix and the Leontief inverse to calculate the value added of each sector. The energy efficiency investments were allocated to each sector using the assumptions as shown in Table A C.13.

**Table A C.14. Allocation of energy efficiency investments across economic sectors based on input/output table**

| Economic Sector in I/O table | Industrial | Commercial | Residential | Agriculture |
|---|---|---|---|---|
| D16: Wood and products of wood and cork | 1.5% | 0% | 2% | 2% |
| D20T21: Chemicals and pharmaceutical products | 2.5% | 2.8% | 6% | 6% |
| D22: Rubber and plastic products | 0.0% | 0.5% | 0% | 0% |
| D23: Other non-metallic mineral products | 1% | 2.5% | 4% | 4% |
| D25: Fabricated metal products | 1% | 1.3% | 0.0% | 0.0% |
| D26: Computer, electronic and optical products | 20% | 18% | 15% | 15% |
| D27: Electrical equipment | 12% | 5% | 5% | 5% |
| D28: Machinery and equipment, etc | 41% | 38% | 36% | 36% |
| D31T33: Other manufacturing | 0% | 0% | 6% | 6% |
| D41T43: Construction | 9% | 20% | 14% | 14% |
| D64T66: Financial and insurance activities | 2% | 2% | 2% | 2% |
| D69T82: Other business sector services | 10% | 10% | 10% | 10% |
| Total | 100% | 100% | 100% | 100% |

Source: (Brown, Soni and Li, 2020[6])

## Model on the value chain of solar PV and highly efficient cooling systems

The purpose of this analysis is to assess the investment gaps for selected clean technologies including solar PV rooftops and high-efficiency cooling systems.

As shown in Figure A C.6, the assessment process involves the following steps.

- Gather information on investment allocation and the distribution of local content across the supply chain. The distribution of investment cost for solar PV systems and high-efficiency cooling systems across the supply chain as well as its local content are shown in Table A C.14 and Table A C.15 respectively.
- Draw capacity of new installation and investment costs of solar PV systems from Table A C.2 and Table A C.4 respectively and energy efficiency targets and investments for commercial sectors from Table A C.8.
- Estimate the domestic value of investment in the supply chain by multiplying the ratio of local content and investment costs and estimate the investment gaps of each technology by subtracting the domestic value of investment from the total investment.

**Figure A C.6. Process in Assessing Value Chain of Solar PV and High-efficiency Cooling Systems**

Source: Authors

## Table A C.15. Allocation of energy efficiency investments across economic sectors based on input/output table

| | Share | Local content |
|---|---|---|
| PV module | 34% | 10% |
| Inverter | 6% | 10% |
| Racking | 9% | 47% |
| BOS and grid connection | 17% | 32% |
| Installation | 12% | 63% |
| Developer | 12% | 76% |
| Fees and contingencies | 9% | 89% |
| **Total** | **100%** | - |

Source: (Ambition to Action, 2019[7])

## Table A C.16. Allocation of energy efficiency investments across economic sectors based on input/output table

| | Raw materials | Manufacturing | Assembling | Engineering | Total |
|---|---|---|---|---|---|
| Share | 42.25% | 22.75% | 15% | 20% | 100% |
| Local content | 0% | 43% | 100% | 100% | - |

Source: (KMUTT, n.d.[8])

## References


Ambition to Action (2019), *Domestic expenditure and employment impacts of power sector development in Thailand*, https://ambitiontoaction.net/wp-content/uploads/2019/12/Domestic-expenditure-and-employment-in-the-Thai-power-sector-November-2019.pdf. [7]

ASEAN Centre for Energy (2024), *Job Creation Towards Achieving the Regional Renewable Energy Target*, https://aseanenergy.org/job-creation-towards-achieving-the-regional-renewable-energy-target/. [5]

Asian Power (2011), *ADB lends $140M for Thai solar projects*, https://asian-power.com/project/in-focus/adb-lends-140m-thai-solar-projects. [3]

Brown, M., A. Soni and Y. Li (2020), "Estimating employment from energy-efficiency investments", *MethodsX*, Vol. 7, p. 100955, https://doi.org/10.1016/j.mex.2020.100955. [6]

Creagy (2018), *Partnership for Market Readiness*, https://ghgreduction.tgo.or.th/th/pmr-news-and-activities/download/1556/1036/17.html. [4]

DEDE (2023), *Thailand's renewable energy policy and plan*, https://www.thailand-energy-academy.org/assets/upload/coursedocument/file/Renewable%20Energy%20Policy.pdf. [1]

Energy For Environment Foundation (2011), *ESCO Revolving Fund*, http://www.efe.or.th/escofund.php?task=&sessid=&lang=en. [2]

KMUTT (n.d.), *Percentages*, https://www.thailog.org/wp-content/uploads/2019/01/54-68.pdf. [8]

# Annex D. Building Energy Code standards

The Building Energy Code (BEC) provides standards and specifications for: building envelope, lighting system, air conditioning (AC) system, hot water generating system and renewable energy performance. The BEC allows for either conformity on system standards on building envelope, lighting system and air conditioning systems, or alternatively on whole-of-building energy performance. For whole building, compliance designed buildings must be lower or equal to a reference building for the category. In case the building uses renewable energy, this is taken into consideration for the calculation of the energy performance of the building.

## Building Envelope

The BEC evaluates the building envelope by assessing the overall thermal transfer value (OTTV) and roof thermal transfer value (RTTV) of the enveloped area in a building with air conditioning. This value depends on the thermal properties of the material and the envelope composition, both opaque and transparent. The standard sets the calculation methodology based on factors such as the heat transfer coefficient value, window-to-wall ratio and equivalent temperature. For transparent materials, the solar heat gain, shading coefficient and solar radiation are also considered (Ananwattanaporn et al., 2021[1]).

### Table A D.1. Building envelope

| Buildings grouping | Hours per day | System standards |
|---|---|---|
| Education and Office | 8 hours/ day | OTTV = 50 W/m2<br>RTTV = 15 W/m2 |
| Theatre, Convention Hall, Entertainment, Department store | 12 hours/ day | OTTV = 40 W/m2<br>RTTV = 12 W/m2 |
| Hotel, Hospital, Condominium | 24 hours / day | OTTV = 30 W/m2<br>RTTV = 10 W/m2 |

Note: Overall Thermal Transfer Value (OTTV), Roof Thermal Transfer Value (RTTV)
Source: Ministry of Energy (2022[2]), Building Energy Code, https://bec.dede.go.th/wp-content/uploads/2022/05/ebook.pdf

Air conditioning systems in the BEC are evaluated through the energy performance for each individual unit for both split types and packaged air conditioning units using the seasonal energy efficiency ratio as an index. In the case of central systems, the evaluation is separated into chiller and other components. The chiller needs to have a coefficient of performance according to the standard, while other equipment in the system needs to have a total power consumption below 0.5 kW per refrigerator tonnes. Other considerations on space cooling system performance (for example shorter ducts on an AC unit can improve its efficiency) are not considered.

Under the BEC, for air conditioners with a capacity of less than 12 000 watts, the Seasonal Energy Efficiency Ratio must be under the current EGAT Label No. 5 Certification Criteria. The water cooler of a vapor-compression air conditioning system must have an electric power per Ton of Refrigeration no greater than the value specified in the notification.

## Whole-of-building energy consumption

In cases where one or more systems do not meet minimum efficiency requirements, then the building may be evaluated according to overall building energy consumption criteria. This is done by calculating the building's overall annual energy consumption and comparing to the overall energy consumption of the reference building.

If the building's overall energy consumption value is lower than that of the reference building, then the building is compliant with the BEC. To evaluate this criterion, the reference building must have the same usage area, direction for the building perimeter system on each side as the evaluated new building or renovate building (Table A D.2). In addition, the reference building must have the minimum requirements for the building envelope system, lighting system and air conditioning systems according to the requirements for each system.

The whole of building approach aimed to allow more flexibility regarding the building design but can mean that individual standards particularly for building envelope are not met.

### Table A D.2. Efficiency coefficient of cooling load in building energy code

| Buildings grouping | Coefficient of cooling load from lighting system | Coefficient of cooling load from electrical equipment | Coefficient of cooling load from occupants | Coefficient of cooling load from air ventilation | Number of hours of building usage |
|---|---|---|---|---|---|
| **Education and Office** | 0.84 | 0.85 | 0.90 | 0.90 | 2340 |
| **Theatre, Convention Hall, Entertainment, Department store** | 0.84 | 0.85 | 0.90 | 0.90 | 4380 |
| **Hotel, Hospital, Condominium** | 1.0 | 1.0 | 1.0 | 1.0 | 8760 |

Source: Ananwattanaporn et al (2021[1]), Retrofitted Existing Residential Building Design in Energy and Economic Aspect According to Thailand Building Energy Code, 10.3390/app11041398

## Renewable energy

Under the BEC, in case the building consumes energy from a renewable source the power generation from the renewable system can be deducted from the whole building energy performance value.

In case there is a renewable power generation in the building (e.g. a solar PV system), it is possible to deduct the amount of renewable electricity power generated from the overall building energy consumption of the building, prior to comparing to the reference building energy consumption value. The renewable energy of solar power generation is to be calculated from the average annual electricity produced by the solar PV system. The use of renewable energy heat for buildings can be calculated equivalent to the heat to electrical energy, in kWh/y. Buildings can take the amount of equivalent electrical energy to deduct from the overall energy consumption of the buildings.

## Procedure for construction permit under BEC compliance

Following the BEC compliance regulation, building owners must apply for building permits by preparing an application document with a building design that is compliant with the BEC standards detailed in Ministerial Regulation B.E. 2563. This permit must be approved by an authorised person holding BEC-certified professional license (for professional engineer/architect) before being submitted to the local building administration. To support this process in 2018, DEDE launched a training programme to certify over 2 500 BEC auditors (DEDE, 2018[3]) (Figure A D.1).

### Figure A D.1. Owner approval under BEC standards

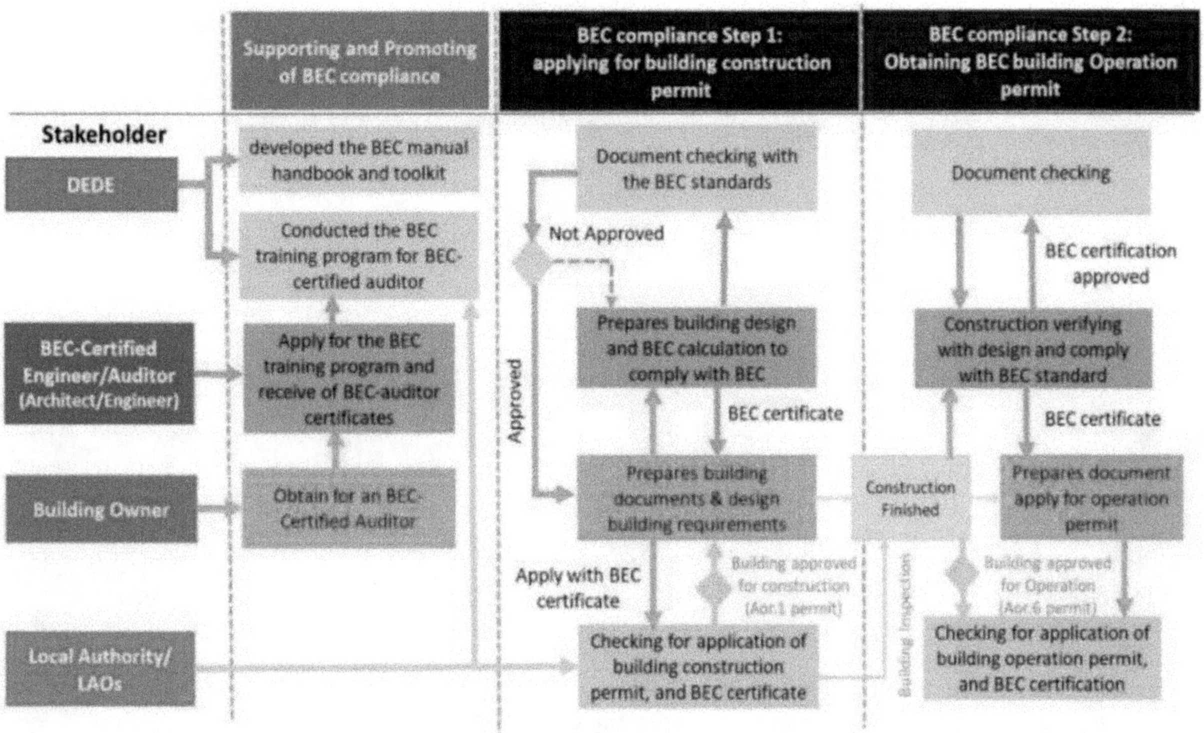


Source: Ananwattanaporn et al (2021[1]), Retrofitted Existing Residential Building Design in Energy and Economic Aspect According to Thailand Building Energy Code, 10.3390/app11041398

## References


Ananwattanaporn, S. et al. (2021), “Retrofitted Existing Residential Building Design in Energy and Economic Aspect According to Thailand Building Energy Code”, *Applied Sciences*, Vol. 11/4, p. 1398, https://doi.org/10.3390/app11041398. [1]

DEDE (2018), *Building Energy Code (BEC)*, https://seforallateccj.org/wpdata/wp-content/uploads/ecap17-thailand.pdf. [3]

Ministry of Energy (2022), *Building Energy Code*, https://bec.dede.go.th/wp-content/uploads/2022/05/ebook.pdf. [2]

www.ingramcontent.com/pod-product-compliance
Lightning Source LLC
Chambersburg PA
CBHW061213240926
51846CB00006B/1210
* 9 7 8 9 2 6 4 6 6 4 3 0 2 *